PRAISE FOR YKI COACHING AND A COACH FOR CHRIST

"Having a life coach is found in the Bible—Jesus is our LIFE COACH. La Vonne Earl skillfully makes that point in her well-researched book *A Coach for Christ*! You will learn keys to succeeding in life, in relationships, and heart-level communication when you read this book! I've not found anything more clear on the subject, and I can promise you it will move you forward in your influential ministry of blessing others. Read it as a manual, apply it as living truth, and pass it on as a Christ-centered model to those whom you want help in their journey."

Brian Simmons
The Passion Translation Project

"LaVonne Earl has immersed herself in the art of life coaching for several years. Her new book, *A Coach for Christ*, is the most comprehensive guide I have ever come across. Complete with power-filled words, mind shifting questions for the client, and Bible references. Whether you're new to life coaching or an experienced Life Coach, this book will help you for years to come. It seems that there is no end to the answers this book provides! 5 Stars!"

Annette Biggers, Filmmaker,
CEO of A Creative Change

"In this book, La Vonne is passionate in leading others to see themselves as God attended them to be—to experience God's more excellent way of living. She personally lives this foundational truth of a Christ-centered life. Her true desire is to see all people come into a relationship with Jesus Christ and experience true freedom! La Vonne's Christ-centered coaching method brings wholeness through biblical based tools to transform our body, mind and spirit through the Holy Spirit. Through these practices our true godly identity is revealed. She will help you to experience a healthy and blessed LIFE through coming to know Jesus our number one LIFE COACH!"

Rev. Julie Stott
Founder of South Pacific
Women Empowered Ministry

"*A Coach for Christ* is a fabulous book! La Vonne Earl has written a clear, well-organized guide to assist in gaining confidence as a life coach, or for anyone wanting to speak truth into their own lives or the lives of others.

This book explains how to establish clear goals to achieve with clients, offers practical advice for guiding client sessions, incorporates Biblically-based and sound psychological principles, and offers guidance in measuring client progress. Full of examples and step-by-step guidance, specific Bible verses, questions to ask, and even appropriate words to use in difficult situations.

This resource has helped me to feel more confident in my coaching skills. Written without technical "jargon", *A Coach for Christ* educates in sound psychological and Biblical principles in an easy to understand way. No magic gimmicks, no "tricks" of the trade are promised, just honest, practical, do-able principles for applying these truths in my own life and in the lives of my clients. As I read, I found myself soaking up the information like a sponge and growing even more excited to use these principles to help others. Don't let the title fool you; this book is not just for coaches by profession, but a go-to resource for anyone wanting a better life!"

Ginger Lehr,
Certified Professional Coach

"La Vonne Earl's new book *A Coach for Christ* is a great tool for counselors, pastors, and others who assist people in healing and offers great insight into your own personal growth. Combining her professional expertise and personal experience, La Vonne's book guides us and our clients through ways to become more balanced, joy filled followers of Christ. La Vonne's organization, YKI - Your Kingdom Inheritance, has been bringing hope and healing to people for over a decade. *A Coach for Christ* instructs counselors on how to help their clients discover solutions to life's difficult personal and relational challenges including:

- How the mind works.
- Reprogramming the mind with the truth of God's Word.
- Finding balance in life
- Putting it all into action to help clients heal and move forward.

This book identifies patterns that sabotage success and lays out clear concrete steps that can help your client overcome them. Each chapter offers strategies for overcoming self-defeating life patterns and offers tools to recognize and replace unhealthy thoughts by reprogramming the mind In order to move forward in a healthy and productive way based on God Word and God's grace.

Reading this book will not only make you a better counselor, you'll also learn about things within yourself that may be jeopardizing your having healthy relationships with God and others. You'll find out how to have a balanced life and how to develop a balanced approach to relationships.

With a winning combination of spiritual wisdom and concrete strategies, *A Coach for Christ* will put your heart and mind, and your client's, in the right place with God."

Karen Schadrack
Marriage, Family Therapist

"LaVonne Earl has given us a toolbox for coaches, leaders, parents and pastors! The coaching tools and techniques she presents here are practical and well practiced. More than mere theory, this book is the product of years of experience. By curating insights from psychology, wisdom and scripture over the years of her coaching and training, LaVonne has given us a valuable gift. You don't need all the answers to be able to help others toward success, but this book will help you ask the right questions."

Rev. Todd Rodarmel
Lead Pastor, Mountain View Church

A Coach for Christ

Becoming the Disciple You Were Meant to Be

LA VONNE EARL

NASHVILLE

NEW YORK • LONDON • MELBOURNE • VANCOUVER

A Coach for Christ

Becoming the Disciple You Were Meant to Be

Published in New York, New York, by Morgan James Publishing. Morgan James is a trademark of Morgan James, LLC. www.MorganJamesPublishing.com

ISBN 9781631954719 paperback
ISBN 9781631954733 hardcover
ISBN 9781631954726 eBook
Library of Congress Control Number: 2020924663

Cover Design by:
Christian Ophus

Interior Design by:
Christopher Kirk
www.GFSstudio.com

Cover Photo:
Heather Paris-Ybarra,
A Single Shot Photography

Morgan James is a proud partner of Habitat for Humanity Peninsula and Greater Williamsburg. Partners in building since 2006.

Get involved today! Visit
MorganJamesPublishing.com/giving-back

CONTENTS

DEDICATION

I dedicate this book to my family, friends,
and all those I may never meet.

May God continue to draw you near and equip you
even further as you follow His command in Matthew 28:19-20
to go and make disciples of all nations and baptize them
in the name of the Father and the Son and the Holy Spirit,
teaching them to obey everything He has commanded you.
He is always with you to the very end of the age
as you dedicate yourself to becoming
A Coach for Christ.

-La Vonne

ACKNOWLEDGMENTS

This book would not have come to completion in such a polished way without the awesome team that supported and helped me. I am so very grateful to you!

I would like to first thank Michele Chiappetta for taking my video training with all the enormous amount of material and helping me to compile it in a skillfully crafted way, making it enjoyable to read while also providing a great resource for Christians. This was a complex project and you were always so patient and willing to do the hard work. I greatly appreciate you!

I would like to thank my sweet husband, Michael, for supporting me and sacrificing much of our time together. I am grateful for his encouragement and his belief alongside me in the importance of equipping Christians to coach for Christ. You lighten my load tremendously and I love you!

And to all of the rest of you who know who you are, for encouraging me, reading transcripts, offering feedback, and writing reviews: thank you!

FOREWORD

by Reverend Houston R. Johnson, Jr.

LaVonne Earl has written an excellent *manual,* nearly equally divided in to three parts:

- Theory
- Application
- Resources

This format makes for a readable overview of what Ms Earl hopes to accomplish (Theory); how to use what we are learning (Application), and ample *resources* to substantiate her work and guide us to further study.

LaVonne's model has a title with dual purpose. She calls the model **YKI** *for Your Kingdom Inheritance,* and also meaning, *You Know* It. She says, "The YKI Method believes that Your Kingdom Inheritance is waiting for you...The acronym YKI also stands for You Know It, as we believe that each individual can hear from God."

"...the YKI coaching method utilizes both biblical principles and secular information that is in agreement with biblical truths, so that we can draw on the tools provided by both in order to assist our clients…Great Christian coaches are NOT counselors, advisors, expert consultants, or therapists. Instead we are motivators and encouragers."

There is such strong presence of biblical references to support LaVonne's thesis' that it is obvious this is A Coach For Christ. Nonetheless, she finds sound biblical evidence for her use of relaxation techniques, visualization and meditation. I appreciate the work Ms Earl has done to defend her inclusion of secular skill-sets that have proved helpful to hurting people.

My initial impression of <u>A Coach For Christ</u>, was that it might be similar to Jay E. Adams, <u>Competent to Counsel</u>, (1970). While there are some common premises, such as the answers are in the Scriptures and we are definitely, "…convinced, my brothers, that you yourselves are full of goodness, complete in knowledge, and competent to instruct one another. (Romans 15:14 NIV). Earl's method includes a broad scope of secular models and unpacks them well.

I like the way Earl approaches *rapport* . It reminds me of Gerad Egan's emphasis on '*relationships*' in *The Skilled Helper* (1975). Egan says there is no way to help unless a relationship is established between client and helper. Earl spends time wisely to explain her method of developing, building rapport, maintaining rapport, and the essential value of rapport. She says, "*Developing a good rapport with our clients is absolutely the most important skill we can learn as a coach*". (emphasis mine, because I strongly agree).

Earl says there are three (3) elemental coaching fundementals: Developing Rapport, Listening Effectively, and Easily Communicating. She covers each of these necessities well. Her explanation of Listening and Communicating remind me of the work of Robert Carkhuff's <u>Helping and Human Relations</u>. Her definition of *intimacy* is worth underlining in red, quite good.

I only mention LaVonne's peers as examples. Her work may remind me of different trainers and therapists, but her work is highly original in many ways. Her balanced presentation of secular and spiritual is unique.

Only four (4) lines into the Introduction, LaVonne firmly states the case for being 'A Coach For Christ'. She quotes John Baker, "I frequently talk with people who are still carrying hurts from thirty or forty years ago. The truth is, time often makes things worse. Wounds that are left untended fester and spread infection throughout your entire body. Time only extends the pain if the problem isn't dealt with". (Celebrate Recovery 1991).

Dan Allender would concur. (The Wounded Heart 1980).

LaVonne Earl's Appendices are a valuable addition and much like Neil Andersen's, "Who I Am In Christ", could stand alone (<u>Victory Over Darkness</u>). Earl quotes Andersen in her Appendix. Her Appendix is a virtual concordance of biblical support for the book.

Conclusion: I read a lot of books, two a week is normal. I read <u>A Coach For Christ</u> three times; *it was richer with each reading.* It impressed me with Ms Earl's challenging, albeit successful, marriage of biblical principals and secular skill-set. This is not an easy task; to be clearly Christ focused, present secular models with integrity and abstain from giving advise. And, her acronym YKI reinforces her belief system and is also a 'catchy' communication tool for both coach and client, Brilliant! (and Biblical).

Thank You for the privilege to preview your book.

Houston R. Johnson, Jr. M.Div., CPE

INTRODUCTION

Time heals all wounds." Perhaps you've heard this popular expression. Unfortunately, it isn't exactly true. John Baker, a Celebrate Recovery pastor I know, says this: "I frequently talk with people who are still carrying hurts from thirty or forty years ago. The truth is time often makes things worse. Wounds that are left untended fester and spread infection throughout your entire body. Time only extends the pain if the problem isn't dealt with."

I know this all too well.

Eleven years ago, I found myself depressed, hopeless, and suicidal. I was going through a very difficult time as I was in the middle of a divorce from my husband of twenty-three years. I never expected to find out that he was unfaithful. I didn't know if I could live through such a painful experience.

Thankfully, I reached out to Ron Konkin, a lay leader referred to me by Saddleback Church as someone with vast knowledge, some of it personal, in the area of marriage, infidelity, divorce, and reconciliation. He and his wife were hosting a marriage bootcamp the following weekend. During that weekend, I learned life-changing skills, and my husband and I began reconciling. Ron made himself vulnerable and shared what caused him to become unfaithful to his wife.

I began listening to more life stories and learning the unhealthy patterns people develop when they are unaware of what causes them to do what they do and are driven without intention.

I also began desiring to hear more life stories from others. I still had so much work to do on myself. Though I was a Christian, I was still having difficulty renewing my mind like Scripture talks about. I wanted more! I wanted complete wholeness with no emotional pain.

Seeking answers, I went to a Christian therapist, as well as a hypnotherapist, looking for relief and solutions that would bring lasting results. Though both were helpful, I wished that the Christian therapist offered guided meditation, as I had experienced success in renewing my mind during hypnotherapy. But I could not find a Christian hypnotherapist, so the experience was greatly lacking for me.

Because I saw that there was a need for Christian meditation in the therapy world, I then went through training myself to become a certified hypnotherapist through the Association of Integrative Psychology, knowing that as a Christian I could bring so much more power into my sessions through the help of the Holy Spirit. I began to practice Christian meditation myself. Through the same institution, I became certified in neuro-linguistic programming, often referred to as NLP. I became trained in Sozo healing through Bethel Academy and trained in inner healing through the International Association of Healing Rooms. Becoming a certified life coach was my next step. I then followed this with counseling training through Saddleback Church.

The entire time that I studied various secular techniques and theories, I also stayed in God's Word. I wanted everything I did to be theologically correct and honoring to my Lord Jesus Christ.

As I dove into these various secular trainings, I found that many were actually quite biblically sound. I realized that God had originally created many of these methods, but the people using them had removed Him from the concepts. As I continued to experience such great success through using my five senses and mental vision, learned through NLP, in addition to applying these concepts to Scripture, I became convinced that these teachings could be very helpful to others. I wanted others to experience this godly meditation. I found that it is in experiencing God's love through this godly meditation practice that one truly heals and transforms. Often, when people are hurting and vulnerable, they need someone to help them get their godly vision and identity back, to restore their hope, and to help them paint a word picture that will give them that vision. Pulling these concepts together formed the method I began using as I started my coaching journey.

Over the next several months, I began helping many people through guided godly meditations instead of secular hypnotherapy. This type of meditation includes relaxation, music, and word pictures that help clients visualize their godly goals so they can achieve them. Through coaching, I began teaching these same healing principles to others so they, too, could use these concepts alone with God, experience His love and healing, and help others do the same.

Through my many trainings, I understood that my previous *knowledge* of God's Word, which was quite substantial, was not going to heal me. Even though I *knew* God loved me, I needed to experience it. I also needed a new narrator to speak to me throughout the day, constantly helping me and encouraging me. For some people, this comes more naturally if they have had a healthy upbringing. But for someone like me, who had endured quite a dysfunctional childhood, I realized I would need the very tools I had developed through this process.

Since many others were receiving help and becoming healed through this new narration process and these powerful methods, I decided to write a program and train other coaches to do what I was doing. It has been ten years now, and the results have been life-changing. At YKI coaching, which stands for Your Kingdom Inheritance and also You Know It, we have trained many coaches through our Christ Centered Coaching Program and have helped many clients and coaches through the process too.

So, just what is Christ-centered coaching? To begin, Christ-centered coaching is biblically based and in line with the teachings of Jesus Christ. Because of this, the power to transform lives is available and noticeable. Christ-centered coaching is also forward focused. We certainly confront and deal with problems affecting our current lives, even if they stem from the past, but we do not stay in the past. We move ourselves and our clients forward. We give our clients the tools necessary to transform their minds, moving them out of victimhood and into victory through godly vision and empowerment.

None of us can control our past circumstances, but we can use our self-control and respond in a way that brings healing and wholeness to our lives. At YKI, we utilize several key tools, including the Five Keys to Success, Godly Anchoring, the I AM Tool, Godly Meditation, and so much more. The YKI method points to Jesus, our ultimate life coach. He will help us transform our body, mind, and spirit through His Holy Spirit.

At YKI coaching, we desire to equip and empower the body of Christ to become the disciples they were meant to be. We believe that everyone can help someone. We all need someone in our lives to hold us accountable and help us focus on that which is good. We can all embrace our future by using godly vision and meditation, which will help us to renew ourselves by changing our minds so we can change our lives!

At church, people are often encouraged to get into small groups and share their stories with each other. Though these groups have their place and can be helpful, they can also provide their own challenges. For many people, we have found that true healing comes best in safe, one-on-one sessions with a healthy, skilled, godly coach. When a client becomes the sole focus of the coach, the client not only feels important but also heard and understood. Clients have a much greater chance of resolving their personal issues and achieving success when a skilled personal coach offers them their undivided attention.

I can attest to the power of this one-on-one coaching approach firsthand. When I began looking into healing methods, I realized I needed someone to help me break down wrong thoughts and help me get back on track. Though I was part of a Bible study group and had many supportive, healthy friends, I found it advantageous and motivating to have my own coach encouraging me and helping me stay focused while giving me a great vision for my future.

Perhaps you have your own festering wounds or pain you still carry from decades ago. Perhaps your relationships are in tatters, your marriage at the end of its rope. No matter what you are going through, I can assure you that your pain matters to God. It also matters to me and our YKI coaches. We cannot compare pain. Negative things in this life, no matter how small or large, affect people differently. Nevertheless, emotional pain can be healed.

God wants to heal you just as He healed me. I am now celebrating thirty-three years of marriage! Since reconciling with my husband, our marriage is stronger than ever. My husband has gone through our coach training, as have my children. I have even used this godly meditation on my son to help him stay focused on Jesus and heal during a life-threatening condition. My own life is a testimony of the transforming power of Jesus that we use in our Christ Centered Coaching methods at YKI.

What to Expect from This Book

This book is going to help you discover so many important aspects about yourself that will equip you to be more effective in your personal life, in helping you bring others to Jesus, and in your coaching career. As you study the truths and techniques in this book, you will learn to communicate productively. You'll understand how to retrain your mind to think in ways that are healthy and beneficial to you. Your awareness is going to increase as you learn many new tools. What you learn will bring you peace.

What you learn will help you improve your own life and also train and equip you to help others. I find this so exciting because you and I were designed to help others! In fact, we experience our greatest joy when we help others—both as coaches and simply as human beings.

It is my dream to raise up coaches who will be trained and certified to find the lost and to help the hurting, the confused, and the broken experience God's blessings so they can change their minds in order to change their lives. My goal is to equip you with the most professional tools, methodologies, techniques, and systems available, so that you will be able to better relate to all people in order to lead them to Jesus Christ, who is their ultimate life coach.

Certified Christian professional coaches have the privilege and responsibility of discipling others in order to draw them into a close relationship with Jesus Christ. Through you, God will offer them hope, empower them, encourage them, and motivate them to set godly goals in order to live a blessed, fulfilled, and balanced life.

The methods you'll find here work. This book includes all the materials and methods we teach in our program. Plus, we have included so much more! The

YKI method believes that Your Kingdom Inheritance is waiting for you. God desires for His will to be done on earth as it is in Heaven, and He says so right in His Word: "*Your kingdom come, / your will be done, / on earth as it is in Heaven*" (Matthew 6:10 ESV). There is a good and blessed life waiting here on earth for you, and God wants to help you live it!

The acronym YKI also stands for You Know It, as we believe that each individual can hear from God. The Bible reminds us over and over that if we seek wisdom from God, He will give us the answers:

Proverbs 20:5 (NLT)
Though good advice lies deep within the heart, / a person with understanding will draw it out.

Romans 1:20 (NLT)
For ever since the world was created, people have seen the earth and sky. Through everything God made, they can clearly see his invisible qualities—his eternal power and divine nature. So they have no excuse for not knowing God.

John 16:13 (NLT)
"When the Spirit of truth comes, he will guide you into all truth. He will not speak on his own but will tell you what he has heard. He will tell you about the future."

Our coaches at YKI are here to equip and empower you to gain the answers from within. You truly do know the answers! Are you ready to become empowered to find those answers for yourself? Are you ready to improve your life and become equipped to help others? Then turn the page, and let's get started!

Chapter 1

A MORE EXCELLENT WAY

Therefore go and make disciples of all nations, baptizing them in the name of the Father and of the Son and of the Holy Spirit.
~Matthew 28:19 NIV~

Have you ever wondered how to make your life better? Perhaps you have asked yourself how to bring about a life filled with blessings. Maybe you are well acquainted with God's Word, yet you can't seem to consistently receive His promises in your life. Is there a more excellent way to do things that you (and the clients you want to coach) have been missing out on?

I can relate to those feelings. My life was a mess before I asked God to come in and be the Lord of my life at 19 years of age. My life certainly improved through knowing Jesus, but even as a Christian at that time, I didn't understand the principles I now know and share with my clients. I also didn't have an easy format to use like the YKI method, which is what this book is about. Nevertheless,

God took my broken, sinful life and began to transform it little by little as I began to understand His love and teachings. I was certainly able, by the grace of God, to turn things around from a sinful, immoral life to one of stability, love, and organization.

My growth wasn't an overnight miracle. It took consistent effort, and I had many questions along the way about how to be more free and more like Christ. I knew there had to be a more excellent way for me—and for all of us. I needed God's help and the help of others who could point me along the way and help me identify practical techniques to apply God's Word and guidance to my life.

As I have come to learn about and follow God's way of doing things, the more excellent way He has for us all, I have come to know Him better and gained more trust in Him. He has kept my family together, restored my marriage, healed my son, brought a godly woman into my older son's life, brought a godly man into my daughter's life, helped me know what to do in parenting, given me wisdom with difficult relationships, and helped me to heal from the relationships that couldn't be reconciled at this time. He has given me so many answered prayers that I could go on forever talking about them.

The most important thing of all is that God has saved me and given me peace. This joy-filled, balanced life full of blessings is what we all long for. And I believe it is something we all can have. How did I get there? And how can you and those you coach and connect with get there too?

We have a tendency to look at others who are being blessed and ask, "Why not me? What is it that they are doing that I am not?" Simply put, it all is rooted in obeying the principles set forth in God's Word.

When our prayers are answered, it is because we are praying the prayers God would want answered. It is much like a child asking a parent, "Can you help me with my homework?" The parent blesses the child because their request is in harmony with the parent's desire for the child to do well in school. By comparison, when we do things selfishly, of our own will, we'll often be in conflict with God's will, and we won't receive His blessings.

As we think about God's desires and pursue them according to His principles, this is the more excellent way He has for us. When we seek to do His will and line it up in every area of life, that's when we are blessed.

With the techniques I'll share in this book, we can give ourselves, our friends, our family members, and our clients godly tools to defeat the devil and resist his attempts to fill their minds with his poisonous thoughts. These techniques help people actually live out the more excellent path of living that God has ordained for us.

Do these techniques really work? Yes! I can personally testify that I was once a young girl who felt worthless, without a formal education, who came from a family that didn't really care. I didn't have purpose or direction. Now I have the most fulfilling life that I could have ever dreamed of because God is so good and I seek to do His will.

Because I have been so blessed, I seek to bless others through serving weekly at the Orange County Rescue Mission, teaching life skills to many who come to know Jesus through the mission and sharing these principles to help them transform their lives. I see the difference this approach to life coaching makes in their lives.

This is why I am a life coach—to make a difference by helping people come to know the Lord and live their life to the fullest. And this is no doubt why you are reading this book right now. You want to live your live fully, and you want to help others to do the same. Being a life coach is a valuable way to help others come to know their true identity and be all that they are meant to be. Doing life God's way is the more excellent way to achieve results that change people's lives for good.

Jesus: The Ultimate Life Coach

In recent years, the idea of using a life coach has become more popular and gained more attention. But truthfully, coaching is nothing new. This powerful practice for producing life transformations goes back to the most ancient of times, ever since humans began to realize we needed to find better ways to relate to ourselves and others. Our need to change our thinking has been around constantly since Adam and Eve blamed each other for their fall and Cain and Abel quarreled over how to properly worship God.

In the Bible, we see that Moses mentored Joshua. Elijah trained Elisha. Among other cultures, Plato mentored Aristotle, who later coached Alexander the Great. You probably have had people in your life who have made a positive impact upon you, such as a teacher, a sports coach, or a pastor. And there are so many other examples like this: it would be too time-consuming to mention them all here. The bottom line is that we all have power to influence each other for good. This is what coaching is meant to accomplish.

But throughout all of history, one man stands above all others in His ability to influence others. He is the most famous of people and the most famous of coaches. He is the model for how to live a fulfilled, fruitful, blessed life.

Yes, I'm talking about Jesus Christ! He is the ultimate life coach. Read through the Gospels, and you will see Him living out this great purpose of leading others into a better life every day that He walked the earth. Can you imagine being in His presence and not feeling understood, loved, and encouraged? I can't either.

Like any great coach, Jesus gave hope to those He connected with. He listened, encouraged, and asked great questions. He taught truth and identified with people where they were at. He gave them purpose and direction.

Today, He still does this for us. Jesus is relatable. He sees and understands. Jesus has something to say about each area of our lives. He wants to heal us completely and bring great success to our lives. He lays out the plan for successful living through His Word and holds each of us accountable for our actions. He doesn't leave us hanging in our pain. He moves us into new perspectives and helps us to find our solution. This is why He came—so we may have life and have it to the full (John 10:10 NIV).

From the very beginning of my business, even when it was just me coaching a few clients on my own, I have spoken of *our* purpose in coaching (rather than *my* purpose) because, truthfully, I was never alone in the work I was doing. I always had Jesus Christ and the Holy Spirit living within me, equipping me to accomplish my role as a coach, and God's Word was always available to help guide me as I worked with my clients.

Throughout those early years, I learned how to coach effectively and in line with God's wisdom. I trusted and relied on the Holy Spirit to bring me understanding and empathy toward my clients, so I could lead them to Jesus Christ.

With Jesus as our ultimate life coach, we cannot help but become successful. He wants to bless every one of us. His desire is to strengthen each individual's talents and to use them to build the kingdom of God. This truth is the basis of all we do in our coaching work. It's the foundation for the approach in this book and the YKI program as a whole.

As Christ-centered coaches, we must become like Jesus and see others the way He sees them—viewing them with compassion and picturing them walking fully in their true identity. By seeing them this way, we can help them move into their purpose and enjoy the spiritual, emotional, and mental freedom God created us all to have.

The Value of Christ-Centered Coaching

There are many approaches to coaching. In fact, this book will cover several of them, because it is essential for a good life coach to have the tools they need to help others. Having a full toolkit is wise. But as Christians, we know that the ultimate source of all truth that sets people free is found in God. And God shares His wisdom with us through the Bible. So, the Bible must be our first and greatest tool for helping people change their minds so they can change their lives.

Various human coaching and therapy methods can provide tools that work in some situations or prove useful in addressing some areas of our lives. But the Bible is complete; it addresses *all* our needs. In it, God has given us everything we need to know in order to live a fully abundant and blessed life.

So, in this book, we will be looking at life coaching principles taken from God's Word and also considering effective secular approaches to coaching that have roots in God's Word, even if those who practice them don't know it.

Remember, godly principles work because God has established them. If methods used by the world have their roots in principles God has designed, then they will work, even if people have removed God's name from them. It is my goal to teach you these godly principles that have been taught secularly, principles that work, and give the glory back to whom it belongs, our ultimate life coach, Jesus Christ!

This life certainly presents trials; there is no denying that. In fact, it's one reason why people need coaches. We've all struggled with difficult situations that life has thrown our way. This is a broken world and bad things do happen, but God has overcome the world and He desires to help us overcome it too. We simply need to know it and live it out.

But how exactly do we live it out? How do we tap into the power and truth of God to transform our lives? This is where Christ-centered coaching becomes so valuable as a tool to help people take what is true and apply it to their lives so they can be free of their hurts and hang-ups. We know Jesus is the one who overcomes all the trials of life. Because of this, we can encourage our clients to be overcomers. We can help them move past their darkest days into a truly healthy and productive future.

The impact that Christ-centered coaching can have to transform our clients is amazing. In essence, it's miraculous! This is the reason that Jesus came. It is God's will for us to prosper and be in health, even as our soul prospers. And as coaches for Him, we can help people accomplish this wonderful goal. We point people to the Bible and to Christ, so that through Him, they can have success, even when we are no longer coaching them.

Leading People to Christ for Solutions

We all want to be encouraged, understood, and to have someone to help us process what we are going through. Coaches provide that assistance and instruction, but we are not to replace God. We are to point to Him. We consult, but we don't advise. It is God's job to give direction to people's lives; we simply provide the tools for them to recognize and follow His direction more easily.

As a coach for Christ, you are a disciple of Jesus, and you are one who makes disciples. To be a disciple means to follow someone's path in order to go where they have been. To disciple others is to mentor them and lead them properly along a good path. In a sense, the word *disciple* is really just another word for coaching.

Certified Christian professional coaches have the privilege and responsibility of discipling others in order to draw them into a close relationship with Jesus Christ. Through you, God will offer others hope, empower them, encourage them, and motivate them to set godly goals in order to live a blessed, fulfilled, and balanced life.

This means we point clients to the Bible because the Word of God is the only thing that brings sustainable results. His Word protects us and gives great wisdom for living life successfully.

Remember also that every client is a unique individual. And there are many biblical principles we can use as we transform our lives. We can have several different Christians giving us input on our situation, and they will each give different solutions. What they say may be solid, sound biblical advice. But only God can tell us which piece of biblical advice is right to follow at a given time. He knows what we should do. This is why it is so critical to point clients to Jesus for their solutions, rather than trying to provide the solutions ourselves.

As Christians, we share a desire to bring others to a saving knowledge of Jesus Christ. We know that He will not only save them, but He will transform their lives. Fortunately, the program contained in this book will equip you with the professional tools necessary in order to lead your client to Christ and His teachings. You'll learn how to achieve the most effective and successful Christian coaching experience for every client you serve.

You are not responsible for your clients' choices, but you can certainly coach or guide them into godly ways that will bless their lives. And even if our client is not a Christian, we can bring them to good, which will bring them to God because everything good comes from God.

Good Coaching Starts with the Coach

From our Christian standpoint, we understand there is a right way to do things, a way that brings blessings. There is a way to live and act and be that brings us all we need—inner healing, peace, contentment, trust, innocence, wisdom, direction, health, eternal joy, security, purpose, true identity, right thoughts, freedom, true success, and more.

When people seek out a life coach, they do so because they are aware that something in their lives is not working as it should. They're aware that something feels off-kilter or out of balance. Maybe they have areas of their lives where they seem to be out of control. Perhaps they simply don't feel joyful or peaceful, and they want to enjoy their lives better, but they don't know how. They may be struggling with something terrible that has happened to them, and they don't know how to recover.

Simply put, the way they have been doing things has not been bringing the blessings they long for. And they know it. So, now they are seeking another way to go. Our role is to help point them to the way that will work to change their lives for the better.

As coaches, we will not be able to help those in need and show them the right way to go if we do not understand the right way to go ourselves. If we don't know or adhere to godly principles and follow God's more excellent way of doing things, we will be like the blind leading the blind. Christ-centered coaching means our coaching will be biblically based. Therefore, it is imperative that you, as a Christian, uphold the same standards that you are coaching your client on.

No one is perfect, and we all have areas where we can grow. But if there is an area of your life that needs addressing, it is important that you take care of that area first before trying to coach others. You must be as mentally, emotionally, spiritually, and morally healthy as you can be so that you are equipped spiritually to lead others.

When we are connected to Jesus, our life coach and savior, we can practice the greatest principles of all, which are loving God and loving others. When we become like a clear vessel where Jesus Christ speaks into our life, healing us and helping us in every single area, we then become filled and equipped to extend that out to others. It is like the cross. Our relationship is first vertical, between us and Jesus Christ. Then it extends outward and pours out horizontally to others.

For this reason, it is important that you yourself have a personal relationship with the Lord and that you spend time in His Word every day. Every disciple of Jesus Christ must begin with personal faith in Him. There is no substitute or secondary path. Everything begins here. This is a lifelong process.

Jesus will help you to make decisions about every area, bringing you the abundant life that He intended and called good. Allowing Jesus Christ to be your ultimate life coach and the Lord of your life helps you in every single area of your life, including your coaching.

Knowing the Ultimate Life Coach

Who is this Jesus? He is the creator. He is our Lord and Savior. He is everything good. He is all-knowing, full of wisdom, love, comfort, peace, and more. Jesus is the ultimate life coach! Choosing Jesus as Lord is the most important decision you will make in this life.

If you are someone who has not yet heard the gospel of Jesus Christ and would like to learn more, let's talk. You see, God has great plans for you. His desire is to see you live a healthy and balanced life. And He will guide and direct you into living your greatest life. He offers us a more excellent way of living because He is the only way to salvation. You have nothing to lose and everything to gain by accepting Him into your life as Lord and Savior. Give your life to Him and experience the greatest love and the greatest life you could ever imagine!

Let Him heal your life and give you the greatest purpose you have ever had: the purpose of loving and serving Jesus your Lord and bringing others the good news of Him as Lord in their life!

This Approach Can Work for Every Relationship You Have

Throughout this book, I will be referring to "your client." It's important to note that the word *client* also refers to each relationship in your life. In other words, the techniques we use to help our clients we can also use to improve our relationships with our spouses, our children, parents, and everyone else we are connected with.

As you read this book, you may realize you have a particular relationship in your life that needs more attention and would benefit from the techniques discussed here. If so, I recommend you keep a file on this relationship, just as you would a client, and put your energy into the productive methods we cover in this book to help create the change you are seeking in that relationship. Throughout this book, you will learn how to communicate in a way that will empower you with love so that even the most difficult of relationships will become easier for you. Remember that your most important client will be yourself and your most important work will be on yourself, which will in turn improve all your relationships!

ᴠe Keys to Success

Certified Christian professional coaches have the privilege and responsibility of helping their clients to take five steps to transformation and life change:

1. Identify the truth in every given situation.
2. Establish their personal goals and purpose.
3. Develop plans for success.
4. Take action and practice continued accountability.
5. Achieve success.

The first thing that our client needs to do is learn the truth. They have often believed lies for long periods of time about who they are and the world around them. These are their limiting beliefs. They will need to discover their true identity and the truth in every given situation in order to realize what their goals and purposes are. As a coach, we will discover with our client the necessary steps and action plans in order for them to achieve their desired success. Weekly meetings with our client will help to hold them accountable. Celebrating success with them and teaching them how to give back from the area in which they have achieved success will further perpetuate their success.

The ultimate goal is to help our client develop a saving relationship with Jesus Christ, so they can live according to His will, which will in turn bless their lives. Remember what Romans 8:28 (NIV) says: *"And we know that in all things God works for the good of those who love him, who have been called according to his purpose."* Although our clients might experience trials in life, through us they will gain encouragement and a hope to know that God will work all things out for their good because of their love for Him.

Scripture references for each of these five keys are provided in the appendix section of this book. I encourage you to study them, use them, and add to them as you work with clients. We will see these steps at work in more detail later in the book.

The YKI Method

The acronym I use for my business and this coaching method, YKI, stands for two foundational beliefs that are important for us to build upon as Christ-centered coaches:

1. Your Kingdom Inheritance—We believe that each individual can become a part of God's kingdom if they accept Jesus. When they do so, they are promised an inheritance they can enjoy while here on earth and also look forward to their inheritance in heaven. ***"Thy kingdom come, thy will be done in earth, as it is in heaven"*** (Matthew 6:10 KJV).

2. You Know It—We also believe that each individual, Christian or not, has the ability to be directed by the Lord. Innately, they know the truth. We help them by giving them biblical principles so they can walk in God's will. Yes, hearts are deceptive as the Bible tells us. This is why we are there as coaches, to teach and instruct in the ways of the Lord without Christianizing what we say to non-believers. We can trust and pray that they will recognize the truth. ***"Even Gentiles, who do not have God's written law, show that they know his law when they instinctively obey it, even without having heard it. They demonstrate that God's law is written in their hearts, for their own conscience and thoughts either accuse them or tell them they are doing right"*** (Romans 2:14-15 NLT).

Because of these two essential foundational principles, when we speak to our clients, we speak to them as though they are already believers in Christ. We trust that they know what is good and right, and we trust the Holy Spirit to work in their lives as we continue to pray for them to come to a full knowledge of Christ.

As we coach our clients, we are trusting God to work in every area of their lives. Let's take a look at that process in our next chapter, which focuses on how we evaluate the different areas of our life—what I refer to as the Circle.

Chapter 2

THE CIRCLE

Search me, God, and know my heart; test me and know my anxious thoughts.
See if there is any offensive way in me, and lead me in the way everlasting.
~Psalm 139:23–24 NIV~

Proverbs 20:5 (NLT) tells us, "*Though good advice lies deep within the heart, / a person with understanding will draw it out.*" This, in a nutshell, is our role as life coaches. Great coaches bring out the truth within their clients. When we know the truth and are honest with ourselves, we can understand what's really going on so we can take the necessary steps to bring about the desired change into our lives.

To bring the truth to the forefront in our clients' lives (and in our own lives too), we use the Circle of Personal Perspective (the Circle).

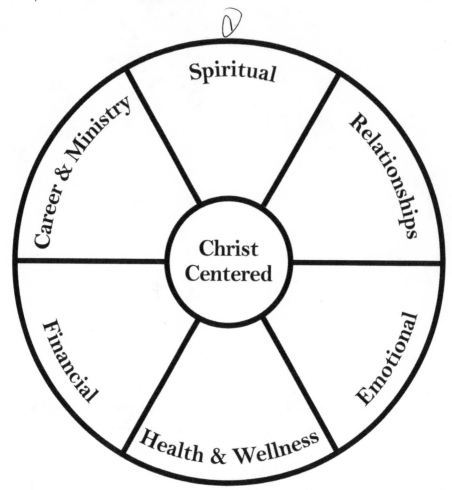

We use this Circle for many reasons. It is the foundation for so much of what we do, providing a wonderful framework for communication, self-evaluation, and leading ourselves and others into truth. It gives clarity to the key areas of life, showing us what needs attention and helps us to gain balance. We can then align ourselves better with God's will and that which is good in our lives, which equips us to make good decisions, enjoy better balance, and live life as God intends.

Using the Circle, you personally will be able to improve upon each area as you learn more about yourself. And you'll be able to lead your clients into doing the same.

This easy format and the other tools you'll learn in this book will help you to stay organized as a coach and will help you to measure the growth in your clients as you help them to succeed. You will continue to learn more things in each given area of the Circle, as there are many aspects about each one. We are all constantly growing and changing in our lives, and we need to continually evaluate where we are at and where we wish to be.

Evaluate Yourself

Now, the initial work on yourself begins. Remember, you are your most important client, and the most important work you will ever do will be on yourself! In the appendix, you have been given a list of questions for each area as prompts to help you explore where you are now, get an idea of where you are going, and make plans on how to get there.

I use the Circle to evaluate my life and establish goals at the start of every new year. I go through each area and ask God and myself how I am doing. What would God have me do in the new year? What relationships do I need to remove or improve on? I take an in-depth look at each area in this way. I keep this record on myself in both a file and in my journal. In this way, I am able to measure my growth, and because of that, I have achieved many of the goals that I have set for myself. This way of evaluating my life has been incredibly useful and has helped me to accomplish so much!

As you use the Circle on yourself, I recommend that you use it in this way too. Create a file on yourself, just as you would do for clients. Keep a journal and record notes, insights, goals, and results, so you can see how you grow over time.

During your self-evaluation with God, ask Him about each area of the Circle as it applies to your own life. Using Psalm 139:23-24, ask God to search your heart and see if there is anything that needs attention or work in your life. Start with spirituality and work your way through the entire Circle. Trust the Holy Spirit to reveal to you where you are at.

Do not rush through the process. You might not get through this entire Circle the first time you evaluate yourself. Spending time with God and resting in His love as you search yourself is the most important thing you can do. If you simply discover one thing in your time alone with God, you will have gained so much!

You will go through this process for each area many times throughout your lifetime. As you learn to improve your own life through doing a self-evaluation with the Circle, you will be better able to use this format with your clients as well.

As we go through this book, we will take a look at the areas of the Circle in more detail. As we do, I encourage you to apply what is shared here in your own life so you will gain more opportunities for growth and achieve greater balance and even more blessings. You may also desire to practice these principles on a trusted friend who is willing to go through an evaluation with you so you can improve your skills in using the Circle while helping them to improve their own life.

The Circle's Center: The Christ-Centered Life

Seek the Kingdom of God above all else, and live righteously, and he will give you everything you need.

~Matthew 6:33 NLT~

When people understand their solid foundation in Jesus Christ and His teachings, they will begin to live a balanced and blessed life. We can see this principle at work in the life of our Lord, because Jesus Christ lived His life according to everything His Father told Him to do. He said, *"For I did not speak on my own, but the Father who sent me commanded me to say all that I have spoken"* (John 12:49 NIV).

As our ultimate life coach, Jesus is our example of how to live. Like Him, we should be led by our Father God. As Christians, we set our center on Christ, making Him the Lord of our lives. As we do so, we can trust Him, knowing He works in every area of our lives.

Remember, we only have twenty-four hours in each day, and how we choose to structure and use our time will either bless our lives or curse it. There is to be no idolatry. We must put Christ first in all that we do. Christ is perfect. *"As for God, his way is perfect. / The Lord's word is flawless; / he shields all who take refuge in him"* (2 Samuel 22:31 NIV). When we have accepted Him, we become perfected. Where we lack in a particular area, Christ makes up for it because He is the one who perfects us; it is not that we are perfect, but that He is perfect.

This removes the fear of rejection and invites us to trust Him and what He has already accomplished. We can then press on in peace, as Paul did. *"Not that I have already obtained all this, or have already arrived at my goal, but I press on to take hold of that for which Christ Jesus took hold of me"* (Philippians 3:12 NIV).

This is an essential foundational principle for what we do as coaches for Christ. We point our clients to Jesus, and help them to walk by faith, because it is our faith in Him that perfects us. *"For it is by grace you have been saved, through faith—and this is not from yourselves, it is the gift of God—not by works, so that no one can boast"* (Ephesians 2:8-9 NIV).

Of course, many people do not base their centers on Christ. Sometimes, our clients know the Lord, yet they are not applying His principles to their lives, which creates imbalance. At other times, we may find ourselves working with those who do not know the Lord. If our clients have not yet received Christ into their lives, we can help them base their center on that which is good. It is important to relate to them by meeting them where they are at, creating and keeping a rapport with them. Listen to them and learn about their lives. As we have opportunities, we can share with them godly principles without "Christianizing" everything we say.

Our goal is to relate to clients in such a way that we can win them to Christ. If we can stand on common ground with our friends and clients, we can lead them to good, which will ultimately lead them to God, because everything that is good comes from God. By focusing on pursuing what is good, we are standing in unity with our clients, no matter their current spiritual beliefs. Even an atheist will want what is good in their life.

We do not need to fear eliminating the words "God" or "Jesus" when we are working with an atheist, an agnostic, or any other religion than Christianity. We also do not need to fear going slowly, being interested in the person as they are right now, seeing them and their needs so we can help them. As we relate to our clients in a positive, encouraging way, we can help them define and achieve appropriate good goals. The more they begin to reap good things in their lives, the more they will trust us and listen to what we have to say.

Once a client receives Christ and the anointing of His Holy Spirit, we will be able to help them learn to live by the direction of the Holy Spirit. It will then be easier to point them to their ultimate life coach, Jesus Christ, to gain direction.

This is why we believe in the acronym YKI—we believe You Know It! We trust that our clients also can hear from God and truly know the answers to what they need to do to be whole. As we coach our clients to live according to the Holy Spirit, their lives will be filled to overflowing. First John 2:27 (NIV) says, "*As for you, the anointing you received from him remains in you, and you do not need anyone to teach you. But as his anointing teaches you about all things and as that anointing is real, not counterfeit—just as it has taught you, remain in him.*"

As Christians, we are better equipped because of our access to and knowledge of God's Word. When we as Christians dive deeply into His Word and allow the Holy Spirit to speak to us, we will know how God is guiding us. We will recognize His voice and follow His direction and guidance, and we will be able to help others learn how to trust that they, too, can hear from God.

As we gain a deeper understanding of the Circle and keep God at the center, we will be able to help others to center on God, or to focus on good if they are non-Christian, so we can bring them to Jesus. Our clients will begin achieving that which is good in their lives and thus desire more and more of God in their lives. We will have the privilege of bringing many to Jesus because of it.

Recognizing Balance

The Circle is particularly handy in helping clients recognize where they are out of balance and what they need to change. People are searching for balance in their lives. Most are stressed, overworked, and underpaid. They are struggling in some way. Often, they know things are out of balance, or at least they sense it. But they may have no idea how to address it.

The Christ-centered life creates balance. As we lead people to good and ultimately to God, we are assisting them in arriving at a life that is centered on Christ and balanced properly in all six areas of the Circle. Balance is key—and it looks different for everyone.

Here is another way to look at it. Having balance is having a joy-filled life. When we are walking in balance, we have God's joy and peace operating in our lives. Someone who is on the mission field living in a tent could very well be living a balanced life, just the same as someone living in a nice home could be very much out of balance. Luxury is not necessarily wrong, but it doesn't equal balance or joy. What determines our level of balance is whether we are following the will of God, which will fill us with joy regardless of our outer circumstances.

Each individual has their own work to do with the Lord. As coaches, we simply encourage our clients to seek God to determine what they should do. There are, of course, sound suggestions we can make through asking them about their lives. We can help a client to make sure that they truly feel called to what they are doing. And there is also the Word of God available to us, which helps us to stay grounded in truth.

We must be careful not to make comparisons. Rather, when we seek God's will for our life, He will direct our path and bring balance into each area.

Listening to Our Clients

As we develop our skills with this Circle, we'll come to know all six areas very well. Using it as a tool will flow more naturally for us, making it easy for us to gain rapport with clients, friends, and family. Using the Circle will not feel like an evaluation but instead like we are very interested in the person we are speaking to. They will see us as someone with great communication skills because we know the key areas of life that concern people and how to build a conversation around them. You will be amazed how much people begin to like you because you have shown an interest in many different areas of their lives.

Remember, people do not care how much we know until they know how much we care! The Circle equips us to show that concern and interest in a tangible way.

Encouraging Life to the Fullest

Once we have become believers in Christ, He wants to bless us in every area of our lives so we can live the abundant life as promised.

Jesus said, *"The thief comes only to steal and kill and destroy; I have come that they may have life, and have it to the full"* (John 10:10 NIV). And Matthew 6:10 (NIV) makes it clear that God desires His kingdom to be lived on earth as it is in heaven: *"Your kingdom come, / your will be done, / on earth as it is in heaven."*

So, how is it that we don't always see our lives lining up perfectly with His kingdom, when it is His desire to bless us? To answer this question, we must realize that three things cause us to live outside of God's blessings:

1. We live in a broken world, where misfortunes can happen to all of us.
2. We have an enemy (the devil) who seeks to destroy us.
3. We are the cause of many of our own problems. We self-sabotage by making poor decisions and failing to follow God's will for our lives.

Self-sabotage is primarily the biggest cause of not living life to its fullest. It is easy to go astray in this broken world, believe lies from the enemy, and sabotage our lives. The role of a coach for Christ is to help people recognize and avoid self-sabotage, so they are better positioned to stand up against the enemy and overcome the world. We are here to help them set godly goals and achieve them through the principles that God has given to us through His Word.

As we get to know our clients and work with them, we will take them through the Circle and use it as a way to evaluate where they are balanced, where they are not in balance, where they appear to be lacking, and where they may be sabotaging themselves. Keeping a record of what we have learned and the improvements we have made is what helps us and our clients to move forward and maintain progress. Hebrews 2:1 (MSG) says, *"It's crucial that we keep a firm grip on what we've heard so that we don't drift off."* This illustrates the importance of making this evaluation and keeping a record of it. It shows the growth a person experiences, which motivates more growth.

As we listen to our clients, it is useful to reflect back to them what we are hearing them tell us. Be sure they know corrections are welcome if we have misunderstood anything, they have shared with us. For example, we might say, "Correct me if I am wrong. What I am hearing you tell me is …" In this way, we can ensure we are on the same page with our clients.

Leading the Client through the Circle

While working with a client, we use this Circle in the same way as our self-evaluation. This will help us get to know our clients better, help them to get to know themselves better, and establish the truth of where they are at and where they wish to be—in other words, their goals!

When we are ready to lead a client through the Circle to see where they are in their life and determine where they need more balance, it is important to ask questions without judgment. We must be careful not to create the impression that they are failures. Rather, focus on creating understanding and rapport, which is the foundation for helping a client improve their life.

We might say something like this to begin the process of self-evaluation with a client: "I would like to take some time to take you through a client self-evaluation. This will allow me to gain a little more information about you, and it will help you get the balance back in your life along with helping you with your goals. Is this okay with you? As we talk through these questions, I would like to ask you to rate yourself on a scale from one to ten, with ten being when you feel the best."

You may use some or all of the questions listed in the appendix to help a client arrive at a self-rating in all the areas in the Circle. Feel free to add or change questions as appropriate for the particular individual you are working with.

When using the Circle format, our communication should be done naturally and fluidly. It should serve as a guide to conversation. As we become more skilled as coaches, we might not even mention an evaluation and instead just begin writing it as our client is speaking. The conversation with our client should feel natural while we keep a rapport with them.

Another thing to consider is that each area overlaps. If a person is not doing well in one area, it will affect the other areas. For example, when we are not doing well relationally, it will affect us emotionally. When we are not doing well physically, it can affect our relationships and even our spirituality. Financial difficulties affect relationships, spirituality, emotions, and so on.

Ask the client to rate each area for themselves. Ask them to rate each area on the whole. Trust the Holy Spirit to reveal to them what they feel each area is. If something stands out to them as you go through the evaluation with them, allow them to talk. Do not rush the process. You might not get through this entire Circle the first time you meet with your client, and this is okay. Remember, the most important thing you can do with your client is establish rapport and help them feel safe and cared for.

Throughout the process, continually listen to what your client is saying. Notice their hurts and their fears. Gather as much information as possible and simply listen. Write down as much information as possible for future reference. Think of everything good that they desire to achieve and think of every encouraging word to write down. For many years, they might have been believing lies about themselves, but with God's Word, we have the opportunity to bring them the truth.

As a side note, spirituality is the only area in which I will allow a client to rate themselves as a zero. They are allowed to be an atheist and have no spirituality at all. For the other areas of the Circle, if they give a zero, I like to encourage them to find some areas of gratitude. For example, if I have an extremely depressed client, I will give thanks that they are there speaking to me and that I am grateful that they reached out. I will then ask their permission to give that area at least a 2 or 3 and let them know that the number will increase very quickly as we work together. This creates a sense of hope that things are going to get better.

Evaluating the six key areas of our life is invaluable because many of the issues we are currently facing could have roots in past events that we have not properly dealt with. The patterns of poor decision making, mistaken beliefs, and confused thinking are continuing in the present because we don't yet realize areas that need to be dealt with and healed.

For example, if we are having difficulty in a relationship now, the conflict may be rooted in past events such as abuse. Financially, if we are not able to manage our money well, it may be because we are spending too much money, not tithing, and in other ways failing to follow God's instructions about how to handle our finances. This might be due to the fact that we were raised in a home with a pattern of mishandling finances. There may be false beliefs instilled in us about finances. Finding the roots of these issues and dealing with them according to God's Word is essential, and the first step on the path to doing so is evaluating where we are right now.

At the center of the Circle is Christ. In teaching others life skills, we as coaches should keep in mind that God has something to say about every area of our lives. He has a part to play, which He has done through Christ and through the principles of walking in His blessings that are contained in the Bible. We also have a part to play, which is to obey Him. When we obey Him and line up our lives with biblical principles, we are blessed. As we learn to obey God and apply these principles, it makes our lives better.

God seeks to bless us and desires us to line ourselves up with His will so that He can bless us. This is how we receive the blessings we are seeking in our lives. As we learn to coach others, we will want to learn and know these six areas and be able to apply them in coaching sessions. This Circle will work as a foundation to be used with the other skills and methods taught later in this book.

Chapter 3
COACHING FUNDAMENTALS

*God is not unjust; he will not forget your work and the love you have shown
him as you have helped his people and continue to help them.*
~Hebrews 6:10 NIV~

Having a servant's mentality—the way that Jesus served us and the way
the Bible encourages us to act toward one another—is essential in
dealing with our clients. To have a servant's mentality is to think first
of the other person, their needs, and what makes them comfortable. By acting
as a servant, we are taking on the position of being more interested in the well-
being of others than ourselves. It means being willing to do the hard work, not
just the easy work.

Coaches who take on the servant's mentality have empathy, awareness,
intention, and purpose. They believe in their client. They are persuasive, show
foresight, and are interested in growth. They can imagine the greater good and

31

are inspired by a good vision of life. In fact, good coaches for Christ are able to visualize a bright future, and they are resourceful about how to get there. They have great understanding. They must be able to think without being told what to do.

As coaches for Christ, we will need to accomplish three things if we're going to help our clients. We will need to:

1. Develop rapport
2. Listen effectively
3. Easily communicate

These three elements are coaching fundamentals that will either make or break our relationship with our clients. So, let's take a look at how to develop these skills and use them to strengthen our connection with our clients.

The Importance of Rapport

Developing a good rapport with our clients is absolutely the most important skill we can learn as a coach. In fact, the most important thing we can establish in any relationship—whether it is friendships, business connections, marriage, or a client we're coaching—is rapport. Why? Because without rapport, there is no relationship.

Simply put, rapport is the act of meeting someone where they are currently at. It is connecting with them, showing we are interested in them and that we understand them. Rapport is the ability to relate to another, to make them feel valued so we can establish a strong common bond. It is a process of engaging with others in the way that they are comfortable being, which is gained through our ability to empathize, to feel what they are feeling, and demonstrate this through common actions such as body language, tone of voice, words, and mood.

When someone says they have a good rapport with someone, what they are really saying is, "I like that person." They like us because they feel we are similar to them and can relate to them. How do we get people to like us? How do we gain rapport? We become like them in order to win them over. God is our great example in this. He desired rapport with us because He values us, so He became human like us so we could relate to Him. Through that relationship, we are drawn to Him and can change for the better through His leadership. It is the same process between a coach and the client.

Another example of establishing rapport is the apostle Paul and how he related to others in order to win them to Christ. Paul was the greatest diplomat in the Scriptures. And it is easy to see why. He chose to mirror others so he could connect with them, saying, *"To the Jews I became like a Jew, to win the Jews. To those under the law I became like one under the law (though I myself am not under the law), so as to win those under the law. To those not having the law I became like one not having the law (though I am not free from God's law but am under Christ's law), so as to win those not having the law. To the weak I became weak, to win the weak. I have become all things to all people so that by all possible means I might save some. I do all this for the sake of the gospel, that I may share in its blessings"* (1 Corinthians 9:20–23 NIV).

We can do so much that is good and godly to demonstrate commonality with those we coach. As Romans 12:15 (NIV) says, we are to *"rejoice with those who rejoice; mourn with those who mourn."* By connecting with others, we are signaling to them that we care and understand them. Rapport is what will hold the relationship together like glue. It will hold you together even when there is conflict in important things like religion and/or politics.

The most important purpose of rapport is to lead and persuade people to take good actions that improve their lives. This is the key purpose of rapport—it serves to build trust so that we can lead our client to their goals, and ultimately to Jesus Christ!

Mirroring and Matching

Establishing rapport with a client begins from the moment we first connect with them. This may be when we first talk with them over the phone, but often it begins even sooner, when we are first meeting someone who we know nothing about. In these early moments, finding ways to mirror them and to match what they present to us can help. Creating rapport doesn't depend merely on words. Often, it begins with body language and nonverbal signals we send.

The art of mirroring and matching is the key to helping our client to be comfortable with us as a coach. Remember, we always want to meet people where they are at. There are so many ways to do so! We can mirror and match the client's mood, tone of voice, pace, and body language. We can learn their skills, hobbies, speech patterns, and semantics. We can take our cues from how they present themselves and even what they say.

For example, if they frequently say, "I see," and they also work hard to make eye contact and look at anything we refer to in our coaching session, we can guess that they are probably a visual learner (something we discuss further in chapter 7). As we establish rapport and seek to help them in ways that are relevant to them, we might use a visual style of interaction. Perhaps we sketch out something we're talking about or encourage the client to create a simple diagram that depicts a concept we want them to remember. If the client appears to be an auditory learner, we might accentuate our words. If they seem to be kinesthetic learners, we might encourage them to jot down notes.

In these ways, we match their approach to life, making it easier for us to first connect with them and, ultimately, to lead them. We all like people who are at least similar to us. When someone has the same likes and interests, possibly the same style of dress or culture, we tend to gravitate toward them. This is an extremely important skill to use for the purpose of leading. Through matching and reflecting who they are, we are better positioned to make a strong, healthy connection that can lead to the client's personal and spiritual growth.

Avoid Unhealthy Mirroring

Rapport is based in understanding and empathy, but to develop it, we don't need to make the same mistakes as someone else. We don't need to participate in their unwise behavior. We don't sin to win someone over or to have them like us. We can remain ourselves and walk in integrity with the Lord while also finding ways to relate to others.

As coaches, the purpose for rapport and for all we do is to lead. Therefore, we do not need or want to stay in an unhealthy mirroring position. Unhealthy mirroring doesn't lead. We must be intentional as coaches. We wouldn't want to encourage our client to stay in a position that is not good for them.

For example, someone who is suffering from depression typically moves and speaks slowly. This is because they are low on energy. Our goal in mirroring them would be to start off our conversation in an easy manner, using a soft tone, not going too fast. We would be gentle so that they would not find engaging with us too exhausting or overwhelming. Still, our goal is to connect and then to lead them into a better place. We don't want to mirror so much that we encourage the depression! We want to move them out of it as gently as possible.

We do not want to leave our client in an unhealthy position. We simply meet them where they are at and then slowly help them into a healthier position. The key word is *slowly*. Do not move too fast. The goal is to lead our client, and this must be done with patience and care.

Ways to Mirror and Match

There are many tools we can employ to be like our clients and communicate in ways they understand. This is what it means to mirror and match them. We adapt to others as much as possible. We reflect back to them what they present to us, so we can better establish rapport. Look for ways to mirror and match the client in their:

- Posture
- Gestures
- Body language
- Mood
- Words
- Speech (speed, tone, and rhythm)
- Breathing
- Clothing

If our client walks in feeling a little down, for example, we can match our posture and tone to theirs, which may mean being subdued and low-key. We wouldn't want to start off too excited and energetic, as they wouldn't feel as if we had compassion or understood their needs. On the phone, we can gain rapport by listening to the client's speech patterns, using their words, rhythms and tone as we communicate with them.

It is often natural to mirror and match in our body language, especially as we remain conscious of doing so, which helps us to build a stronger connection with our clients. How do we match and mirror body language? When someone is leaning in a direction, we as the coach mirror that leaning. Perhaps lean in as they lean in and lean back as they lean back. With eye contact, if a client often looks away, the coach could then look away also, perhaps in the same direction. We might mirror a client's facial expression.

Intentionally mirroring another person's body language promotes rapport. Mirroring is a skill and must be done without drawing attention or coming across as obnoxious or mocking. It must be practiced so we can do it naturally.

Mirroring can even be used to help encourage more openness from our client. As an example, a good coach would mirror the client's arm-crossing. Ultimately, though, if someone is crossing their arms, we would first imitate their posture, but then uncross our arms to invite relaxation and openness. If we have already developed rapport with the person, they too will uncross their arms in a mirroring of our behavior, without even realizing what they are doing. This act of following the client, then gently leading them, removes the barrier and helps improve their receptivity.

Avoid Breaking Rapport

In the same way that we mirror a client to build rapport, we also want to avoid actions that can break rapport. Maintaining rapport takes work. It can even be tiring because it requires a lot of energy and engagement. We may break rapport inadvertently as a result unless we are mindful not to do so.

What breaks rapport? Actions such as turning our body away from someone can signal we are no longer interested with them. We can unintentionally break rapport by interrupting when someone is speaking. We can allow our eyes to wander, check our phones, or otherwise show we are distracted or disengaged. Such behaviors break the often-delicate rapport we have with our clients. So, even when we need to end a session with a client, we must seek to do so in a way that is gentle, so that rapport is maintained.

Remember that in the beginning of the coaching relationship, we may find that mirroring and matching feels a lot like the client is leading us in how to be. This is normal, as it is the way to establish rapport. But as we connect with them and come to better understand where they are at and where they want to go, we can begin to lead them.

Going Outside the Comfort Zone

Mirroring and matching is also a skill we can share with clients as they seek to accomplish their goals. It can be used whether they are meeting someone for the first time, applying for a job, or doing anything else that requires them to form a connection with someone. Rapport is definitely a skill that requires intention and practice, as it often stretches all of us beyond where we are normally comfortable.

As an example, I had one client who was in the military, and she wanted a smoother working relationship with her superior officer, whom she felt she did not have a strong rapport with. She would often say to me, "I don't feel adequate around him." Now, adequate is not a word I normally use in my own daily conversation style. But it was meaningful to her, so I used it in our coaching sessions. It was a way for us to connect while she was growing in that area of her life.

After discussing the situation with my client, we came up with a plan for her to match her superior officer's approach to doing things, which was to move quickly and be to the point. This was not immediately comfortable for her. In fact, she had to learn how to operate outside of her comfort zone as she is a kinesthetic, more slowly moving type of person. She had to learn to speak and move quickly. We worked on getting her to get to the point quickly in her interactions with her superior officer. She met him where he was at. And it was so effective that she not only developed a stronger working relationship with him, she got promoted.

Listening Skills

When we take the position as servant or coach for our client, we will truly listen to them. Remember, their coaching session is their time, and it needs to be all about them. James 1:19 (NIV) tells us, *"My dear brothers and sisters, take note of this: Everyone should be quick to listen, slow to speak and slow to become angry."* There's a saying that God gave us two ears and one mouth because He wants us to listen more than we speak. And it's important for a coach to do so, because as we listen to our clients, we will learn about them. Listening both develops rapport and allows us to see how we can help our clients find balance in their lives.

Isaiah 50:4 (NIV) says, "*The Sovereign Lord has given me a well-instructed tongue, / to know the word that sustains the weary. / He wakens me morning by morning, / wakens my ears to listen like one being instructed.*" A well-instructed tongue is one that shows great restraint and listens so that we can know the right word to speak to our client at the right time.

To be a great listener is one of the greatest skills one can possess. When we are listening, we are looking for so much information from our client. As we listen, consider these questions: What is our client trying to tell us? Where have they been hurt or wounded by life? What distortions in their thinking and view of the world have developed as a result of their experiences? What are their unspoken dreams? Have they been suppressed for far too long? Do they have a learning disability? What lies are they believing? Possibly that they are unloved? Not good enough? Fearful?

Keep in mind that listening involves so much more than hearing words. We must also listen for and recognize the patterns (both good and bad) that our clients have established in their life, the lies they have believed, their fears, their buttons or triggers (in other words, what upsets them), and their deletions, distortions, and generalizations. (These are known as meta models, which will be discussed in more detail in chapter 7).

While we are listening, we should remember to write as much as we can about what our client is saying. These notes will go in the client's file. And they will serve several purposes, from helping the client pinpoint goals they want to achieve to seeing progress and growth over time.

Common Obstacles to Listening

To become a better listener, it helps to recognize the ways we can inhibit our listening skills. All of the following positions and behaviors can impede our ability to accurately hear what our client is trying to share with us. Learn these obstacles and avoid them!

- Being Judgmental: This is listening only to confirm our judgment. It involves labeling the client, which blocks our ability to see the client's true identity, and thus prevents us from helping them become all they were created to be.

- Rehearsing: This is the act of creating an answer in our mind while the client is speaking. When we are planning what we will say, we will miss much of what we are being told. What we say can end up being irrelevant to what the client is actually saying, which breaks rapport.

- Mind Reading: This is the act of assuming what a client is thinking or intending to say. Assumptions are often incorrect. It is better to ask the client to tell us more, so we can find out what they are thinking.

- Advising: This is the act of giving advice. Instead of just listening, we are advising. Often, we do this when we wish to make ourselves feel needed or to fix things. Our role is not to advise, but rather to lead a client to finding the right answers for themselves, which are already within them.

- Pleasing: This means we fail to ask questions or raise issues because we desire to maintain peace. Pleasing is often based in fear. But it can also be a lazy approach to interacting since it takes effort to ask a question in order to gain clarity.

- Filtering: When we filter, we are hearing some things the speaker says, but not everything.

- Deflecting: This is changing the subject or telling a joke when the topic a client is discussing is uncomfortable for us.

Guidelines for Good Listening

As we learn to listen more effectively, we will find ourselves building greater rapport with clients and coming to understand better where they are at. Here are some basic principles for listening well.

- Always make the client feel important.
- Allow the client to complete their thought before asking questions.
- Eliminate distractions.
- Maintain eye contact as much as possible while writing notes.
- Show interest.
- Keep the rapport by mirroring and matching the client.
- Give verbal and nonverbal responses to what the speaker is saying.

Communication Follows Listening

After listening, the next step is to communicate. This can involve putting our client's words back out there, matching their tone and pace. It also means sharing both verbal and nonverbal communications that are empathetic.

When we as coaches are in tune with the Holy Spirit, He will guide us in this process just like He did for the believers in Acts 2:4 (NIV). That verse tells us, "*All of them were filled with the Holy Spirit and began to speak in other tongues as the Spirit enabled them.*" They were empowered by God to speak in a tongue that was not even their own language.

Acts 2:6-8 (NIV) goes on to show the reason for what the Holy Spirit did: "*When they heard this sound, a crowd came together in bewilderment, because each one heard their own language being spoken. Utterly amazed, they asked: 'Aren't all these who are speaking Galileans? Then how is it that each of us hears them in our native language?'*" Through these verses, we can see that the Holy Spirit enabled the believers to speak in ways that others could understand, even in tongues they themselves didn't know—all to benefit the crowds who came and heard and were therefore led to Christ.

When it comes to coaching, communication happens through asking great questions so we can continue to gain information and understand our client. Through this technique, we can then speak in a "tongue" that they can understand, furthering our opportunity to bring them to the Lord. Let's talk now about how to keep the conversation going through great questions.

Chapter 4

IT'S ALL ABOUT THE QUESTIONS

Ask and it will be given to you; seek and you will find; knock and the door will be opened to you.

~Matthew 7:7 NIV~

One of the most essential things we ask from our clients as a coach is information. We cannot get the information to aid them in achieving their goals if we do not ask. The details we gain from our clients as we interact with them is what gives us the ability to lead them in the right direction so they can come to good and to God! We gain this information through asking questions—not just any question, but great questions that will give our clients self-realization and empowerment.

Entire conversations can be built around questions—if the questions are the right ones! And learning to ask great questions is a powerful tool that you'll make use of over and over as a great communicator and a coach. This skill has the ability to open up paths to growth for anyone we interact with.

Imagine, for example, a parent who needs to teach a child to make good decisions. This is no simple process, but it can be made easier or harder, depending on the approach the parent takes. If the parent learns to ask great questions that encourage the child to think critically about what they are doing, it is more likely to lead the child to finding the right answer. Gentle, reasoned questions are less likely to offend the child than telling the child what to do or shaming them. The goal is to teach them to recognize what is good and true, so that their own thinking empowers them to make the right choices.

Coaching is much the same way. Developing and mastering our skills as a coach is what gives success to each client we serve. We do this in large part by learning to ask questions that are relatable and empowering, effectively phrased, thoughtful, kind, and inviting. Great questions give our clients freedom within the conversation and within their lives. Good questions can help a client think through a future decision, but they also help with assessing the past.

A client who is anxious, for example, can be asked a great question that enables them to talk about how past experiences (like how they were raised) can tie into what they're experiencing now. This opens up ways of seeing the situation in a new light, which opens up new possibilities for how to respond. This pinpoints a truth that will help them to set a goal to achieve the peace and freedom they desire.

Remember that even the best therapists and coaches will never know all the ins and outs of a client's life. Only the client and God will know all the details. In fact, God knows even more about it than the client does because He is the one who sees clearly and knows all things. Rather than pretending we know it all, we can, as coaches for Christ, simply learn to ask great questions and bring forth the information that our clients already know.

As coaches for Christ, we are to help our clients arrive at the answers for themselves. And this happens as we are careful to listen to them; we must not do all the talking. There is a balance we must achieve between listening and asking questions. As we ask the questions that will inform us to help our clients, it is also important that we listen with great skill so that we are able to continue the conversation with more great questions.

Listening helps us to learn about another individual. It also validates them and empowers them. The challenge is that we can't truly listen to someone unless we get the conversation started. And questions do that—they open doors of communication.

The basic premise of the YKI style of Christian coaching is that our clients have all the answers within them. Our job as coaches is to help them to discover those answers within. Therefore, our job is to ask great questions, because great questions empower our clients to discover the truth needed to make decisions and changes that lead them to good, which will lead them to God.

Remember, to be a great coach, we do not need the answers. We only need the questions! The client will provide the answers as you help them to discover the answers within themselves through your thoughtful questions.

Therefore, it is important to understand the different types of questions we can use as we work with clients and learn more about their lives, their needs, and their goals. Asking great questions will help make communication more natural and productive with our clients, especially since they often do not know where to begin to share what is needed to change their lives. Master the art of great questioning, and you will be able to easily communicate with others.

As with the Circle, I encourage you to take some time to use what you learn in this chapter to ask questions of yourself. Remember, we use questions to get ourselves and our clients to think and process what is going on in our lives. By asking questions, we often discover that our thinking is off in some way, which invites us to process what might really be happening and examine ways to improve our lives.

Asking Great Questions is from God

Let's look at who truly originated this questioning model—God Himself! Jesus asked many questions throughout Scripture—307, to be exact. He is our example in all things, and I will refer to many of His questions here and in the appendix because they are so useful with our clients. Jesus, of course, learned this technique from Father God, who is the ultimate source of this powerful form of communication.

The first recorded act of asking a question of someone in need of aid is seen in the garden of Eden. Father God was looking to connect with Adam and Eve, but they were in hiding after they ate of the tree of the knowledge of good and evil. Father God was gentle as He asked them, "Where are you?" (See Genesis 3:9.)

Of course, God knows all things, so He already knew where they were located physically. What He really wanted to know was their state of mind. What was the purpose of knowing that? There are two reasons.

First, Father God desired intimacy with Adam and Eve. He desired for Adam and Eve to allow themselves to be known by Him. The word *intimacy* means "into me see" (or "see into me"). Questions bring us closer to others, bringing about deeper intimacy and connection as we learn to see into another person's point of view.

Second, God loves to empower us. He wanted Adam and Eve to know their own state of mind and where they were at for themselves. With this self-knowledge, they could then be empowered to take action. God always gives us respect, freedom, and choice. Through His gentle questioning, He was able to take Adam and Eve out of their shame and into their freedom. Once they discovered where they were at—meaning what they had done to be in the state of shame they were in—they could then learn that Father God was not going to be harsh and judge them, but instead would offer them a way to get the connection back that they desired. God restores our lives!

As coaches, it is our job to help restore our clients' lives by helping them to discover what happened to throw them out of balance or cause the issues that have led them to seek coaching. Discovering truth is the first key to success. Great questions help in that discovery. As we ask great questions, we can empower our clients to understand what brought them to the place they are in now. This enables them to discover how to avoid the things that brought them to where they are. It also positions them to learn how to get to where they want to be—restored back to the joy-filled, balanced life that they were intended to have, a life filled with self-control, passion, and purpose.

The Socratic Questioning Technique

Since our society likes to name other individuals instead of God for the creation of things, someone gave Socrates the credit for this technique and named it

Socratic Questioning. I will refer to it this way here because you are likely to see this technique mentioned in other learning materials you may come across.

Named for Socrates (ca. 470-399 B.C.), the early Greek philosopher/teacher, a Socratic approach to teaching and mentoring is based on the practice of disciplined, rigorously thoughtful dialogue. The instructor professes ignorance of the topic being discussed in order to elicit engaged dialogue with students. Socrates was convinced that the disciplined practice of thoughtful questioning helped the scholar/student to examine ideas logically, which then allowed them to come to their own conclusion about the validity of those ideas. Also known as the dialectical approach, this type of questioning can correct a client's misconceptions and lead to the more reliable building of ideas based on accurate information.

Although Socratic questioning appears simple, it is in fact an approach that requires great focus and self-control to execute. It requires the coach to simply ask, without offering advice or providing answers. As described in the writings of Plato, a student of Socrates, the teacher must pretend to be ignorant about a given subject in order to allow the other person the opportunity to express their full knowledge of the topic.

What is the reason we simply ask questions, rather than offering advice or answers? We must allow others to be empowered and come to their own solutions. This is the purpose of coaching for Christ! We empower others with critical thinking so they can begin to search for the truth and discover answers.

We all have the capacity to recognize truth. "*Even Gentiles, who do not have God's written law, show that they know his law when they instinctively obey it, even without having heard it. They demonstrate that God's law is written in their hearts, for their own conscience and thoughts either accuse them or tell them they are doing right*" (Romans 2:14-15 NLT). The Socratic questioning method assumes that incomplete or inaccurate ideas will be corrected during the process of disciplined questioning. Hence, if we trust the process, it leads to progressively greater truth and accuracy for our clients.

We are to learn to dive deeper within ourselves and trust the Lord to give us the answers. As coaches for Christ, we are here to help others do the same. We desire to help others learn to think for themselves. As we (and our clients) learn to critically assess the facts and think things through from every angle, applying Scriptures to the situation as well, we will learn more about ourselves. As coaches, we are equipping our clients to recognize what is causing them to have certain beliefs that block their success and remove their peace.

Remember, to be a great coach we do not need the answers; we only need the questions. God will supply the answers to us and to our clients.

Questioning with Restraint

Long before Socrates came along, Father God taught us through His Word the concept of restraint and listening as we ask questions of others. Proverbs 17:27-28 (NIV) says, "*The one who has knowledge uses words with restraint, / and whoever has understanding is even-tempered. / Even fools are thought wise if they keep silent, / and discerning if they hold their tongues.*"

Remember that when we are talking, we are not listening and learning. So, it is up to us as coaches to ask questions and then to attentively listen to our clients. In this way, we can allow them to examine their thinking and come up with their own solutions. We believe the answers are within them, and we allow those answers to spring forth over time, as our clients learn to ask questions of themselves, critically think about their lives, and identify the more excellent way God has for them.

Through questioning with restraint, we can help our clients dive deeper in each area of their lives and discover more about themselves. They can then come up with their own goals in each area, making the goal more achievable since it will be coming from them.

Never Advise

Though it is tempting for us as coaches to offer advice, we must restrain ourselves from doing so. For what reason? Because we are human, and we do not always know the correct answers. If we advise others instead of allowing them to come up with their own solutions, we could possibly regret our advice later on, as it may turn out to be wrong. Only God truly knows the answers, and God will reveal those answers to our clients as we help guide them through questions.

Let me offer an off-topic analogy of this concept to broaden your understanding. Suppose a client would like to attend a theater that we have told them about. If we give our client specific directions instead of giving them the address of the theater, we will have removed their ability to critically think and to move with the flow of traffic. It would be impossible for us to know if there is going to be an accident along the way. Thus, our client will need critical thinking skills so they can go in another direction if needed and arrive safely.

Similarly, there may be changes in our clients' lives. From week to week, my clients' lives often change, thus often changing the goal and plan. It's tempting to offer solutions for our clients that we might imagine for them, solutions that are biblically sound and may seem perfectly appropriate. Yet those solutions might not be right for them.

For example, let's say your client is confused as to whether or not they should get married. One of their Christian friends may tell them they should marry. Another friend might say they shouldn't get married at all because the apostle Paul said it is better to be single if possible, so we can concentrate on doing God's work. If both of these answers are based on the Scriptures, then who is right? The only correct route for a client to take, the only solution that is right for them, is the specific solution that God Himself is guiding them to.

Here is another example, one from my coaching sessions. I had a client one time who wanted to quit her corporate job and become a makeup artist. She felt trapped in her corporate job. I could have advised her by saying that if she felt trapped, then it must mean she would never feel fulfilled unless she quit and pursued a different career. But how could I ever know if that was the right advice for her at that time? What if she ended up without health insurance, income, or other important needs met because I advised her to do something that was not the right path for her to take?

On the other hand, I could have advised her to keep her corporate job because it was safer, or because trying to work as a makeup artist would be hard, or because makeup work might seem frivolous to other people. But suppose God had a plan for her? Perhaps He wanted her to become a makeup artist. How could I know this?

I was able to help her realize what the right decision was for her by asking her questions like, "Is becoming a makeup artist going to bring in the income that you need at this time? Will you have health insurance? Are you able to gradually move into the makeup business, or should you save enough money first so you can get your makeup business going without the financial stress?" Asking these questions and more gave her the opportunity to explore what was right for her. Ultimately, only my client could know what she felt in her heart was God's will for her at that time. I simply coached her with important questions in each area of her life, allowing her to make the right decision for herself.

The clients who come to us are in a vulnerable position. It is tempting in such situations to want to offer advice. But it is better to encourage the client to think about their choice from all angles and come to a decision they are comfortable with, one they can live with, and one that feels right.

Only God knows what is best for that particular person at that particular time. And He wants to lead that person into the right decision for them. Ultimately, only God and our client truly know the answer of what is best. Even if our clients are non-Christians, we can help guide them to discover for themselves a healthy and good solution that is right for them.

So, instead of offering advice, we step back and ask questions about the details of what the client is sharing. All decisions have consequences, good and bad, and our clients need to weigh those things out. Great questions help our clients do that and arrive at a decision on their own. Remember, we must demonstrate through the questions we ask that we trust our client to know what is best. We exercise restraint and allow the client to arrive at their own solution.

Questions Can Improve Critical Thinking Skills

When clients first come to us seeking our help as a coach, it is usually because something in their lives is unbalanced, causing them to struggle or feel unhappy. And often, at the root of their issue, there is a misconception or a lack of awareness that is leading them to decisions that are not working well for them. Their focus may have narrowed down so much that they cannot see the truth. They may be giving too much weight to one fact, while downplaying something else that is very important. It is so human to do this!

To move forward, we must correct our misconceptions, become more aware of what is true, and widen our focus to encompass the whole picture, including what God would say about it. In other words, we need to draw upon critical thinking skills that can help us see things as they are so we can make good choices.

Questions are a way of helping our clients to see the bigger picture, understanding what is going on within themselves, and recognizing where changes can be made that would benefit them. Asking the right questions will help our clients to gain clarity and increase their thinking ability.

Remember, too, that the word *client* refers to every relationship, including ourselves. Think about who we will begin to empower through asking great questions. Possibly our spouse or our children? Perhaps our friends or coworkers? Asking good questions in a gentle, open way can help all those we care about begin to recognize wrong thoughts and find what is good in their lives.

As coaches, we get better at forming good questions with practice and experience. As I was gaining my skills as a coach, I would search for and find many questions on the web. I came up with several categories of questions to help guide me to meet clients where they are at, such as:

1. Probe the client's reasoning and evidence for what they say, do, and believe—Questions such as "What makes you say that?" allow us to delve deeper into something a client says. The idea behind these types of questions is to get our client to explore their beliefs, the reasons behind events, and patterns that have developed in their lives.

2. Considering alternative viewpoints and perspectives—We can help our clients to recognize new or different ways of thinking by asking questions such as, "What alternative ways are there to look at this?"

3. Goal-setting and empowerment—We can help clients to envision their options and identify what goals they would like to achieve with questions such as, "What do you want out of life? What legacy would you like to leave behind?"

4. Gaining clarity—At times, a client may state something we want to clarify. Or they may want to ask us something. Questions like, "Could you explain to me the purpose of your question?" can draw forth valuable information so we and they can discuss what the real concern is.

5. Probing the implications and consequences of choices—These questions help our clients to discover their fears or what is holding

them back. Many times, people are living in fear. Questions such as, "What makes this important?" and "What would happen next if …?" are effective at aiding clients to think about the results of action.

6. Approaching difficult situations—A client may be facing extremely difficult circumstances. Questions such as, "Do you believe God wants the best for your life?" can help the client to address the mistaken belief that God wants them to suffer.

Not all questions need to be complex. In fact, sometimes the greatest questions of all are quite simple. The key in questioning is to pause as a coach and think about what you would like your client to discover. Their empowerment? Their skills? Perhaps their distorted viewpoint? When you have a clear purpose for your question, and that purpose is to empower your client in some form, you will deliver the question that is just right for them.

One of the greatest results I have seen from a series of questions I asked came when I was working with a client named Zoey who was under great stress and experiencing a lot of anxiety due to not having her first-born daughter in her custody. The child was with the client's ex-husband, and she wanted her child with her. I simply asked her if she had faith that her daughter would know that she loved her. I asked her what she could do to help her daughter know that she loved her. And I asked her what she could think about that would bring her peace.

This series of questions may *seem* very simple, but they empowered my client. They gave her back her sense of control because she realized there were several things she could do to help her daughter feel loved. She realized she could begin to walk in more faith toward the outcome she desired, thus empowering her to experience more peace as well. This was exactly what she needed. Zoey ended up getting full custody of her daughter and is living a very fulfilled life with her daughter. She now also serves on our board of directors for YKI coaching.

As you can see, asking great, purposeful questions will help us to gain more information about our client, what they have been thinking about, and what ideas are foremost in their mind. Learning these details will not only help us as a coach, it will also help the client to sort out misconceptions in their life and find the solution inside themselves that God has provided for them.

When we show interest in another individual's life and they solve their own problems through questions we asked, they will think we are a genius. But in essence, what we have really done is guided them into finding the answer they already know to be right within themselves. Often, they simply don't see the answer until questioning causes them to dig deeper and bring the truth to the surface. And knowing the truth can then begin to set them free.

I have compiled a list of questions and categorized them for you in the appendix section, so you can reference them and use them in your coaching sessions. Build your knowledge by studying them. Asking great questions will become more natural to you the more you do it.

What to Avoid When Asking Questions

As we ask questions of our clients, we want to do all we can to maintain rapport. Remember, when we maintain rapport with our clients, we remain in a position to be able to help them toward good and toward God. There are several things we can do to break rapport that we must be aware of so that we can avoid them. These include:

1. "Why" questions

Asking a question using the word "why" can often break rapport with our client. Here is an example. Consider the difference between these two questions:

- Why did you have an affair?

    vs.

- What do you think caused you to have an affair?

Notice that the first question carries an accusatory tone, while the second one is more open and exploratory.

Here is another example:

- Why do you continue to over-drink?

    vs.

- What do you think is causing you to over-drink?

You can see how the first question might make a client defensive, while the other will encourage them to reflect. The question why tends to feel as if an accusation or a judgment is being made. This can cause a client to feel defensive, pull away, or disconnect from the coaching session.

At YKI coaching, we avoid using the word why to ask a question; instead, we use the word why as a way to explain a concept. For example, we might say, "This is the reason why we use the word what instead of why." As an informational statement, why can create explanations and be informative.

2. Words like *seem, assume, and assumption*

Avoid using the word assume or assumption when asking questions. Seem can also be a problem word. Here's why:

Phrases such as "you are assuming ..." or "you seem to be ..." can lead us to make an incorrect statement. Listen to the difference:

- You are assuming that your boss does not like your performance.
  vs.
- Could you tell me more about what causes you to think your boss doesn't like your performance?

Making wrong statements or appearing to make assumptions about the client can create distance between us and the client.

Instead of using assume, assumption, or seem, we can ask probing questions in ways that allow us to gain more information in an open, inquisitive manner. Here are some examples:

- Could you tell me more about that?
- How can you verify or disprove that information?
- What would happen if you did this?
- Do you agree or disagree with this?

3. Negative or judgmental tone and body language

It is important to keep in mind that the way we ask questions, including tone of voice, body language, and even the words we choose to use, will often make or break our rapport with the client. Tone of voice is especially important. Our hearts will reveal what we feel through the words and tone we use, so if we have a judgmental heart toward someone, this often comes across in how we speak. Maintain an open, kind, patient manner as you work with the client.

4. "I" statements

When working with a client, the conversation should be focused on them, not us. So, we must be careful to remove "I" statements when we communicate.

Instead of saying, "I want you to tell me more," empower them by making them the subject of the sentence, and ask them, "Could you tell me more about that?" Rather than saying, "I need to know what happened in the past to cause you to say that," ask them questions such as, "What causes you to say that? Is that true for you now?"

Remember to act and speak as if you don't know the answers. Never assume anything. It halts the conversation and risks offending the client, breaking rapport, and stopping us from helping the client. If we as coaches begin assuming things about our client, we set them up for offense. The minute we begin to act as if we know the answers or begin advising is when the information stops. The conversation then becomes about how much we know instead of empowering our client.

We can, of course, offer suggestions and ask if this feels right for our client. But remember to keep the focus completely on the client, not yourself.

5. "Poison" questions

Our approach to asking great questions at YKI coaching also helps us to avoid what I refer to as "poison questions." Poison questions assume and/or plant negative seeds that are not productive for helping the client. Satan asked a poison question in the garden and planted a seed of doubt when he asked, "Did God really say …?" We want to avoid questions like this!

Here are some examples:

- Do you think your husband doesn't love you?
- Do you have a learning disability?
- Did you cheat on your spouse?

Notice that these types of questions can create poisonous thoughts. Yet our goal is to lead our client to clear, useful thinking that brings about good. Let the client reveal their thoughts on these difficult subjects, rather than suggesting thoughts to them. Simply ask them if they can tell you more, with questions like these:

- Could you tell me more about that?
- How are things going with your spouse?

Additional Tips for Asking Great Questions

Now that we have considered what to avoid, let's consider how to ask questions in ways that maintain and strengthen our rapport with our client. Questioning in the right way, without assumption or judgment, models for the client the right way to gain information and gives them the opportunity to get out of assuming, judging, poisonous thoughts, and other wrong thinking. This is beneficial to their long-term growth. So, trust that the client knows the answer. Remember, YKI (you know it), and so does our client! We simply ask the questions and let others draw the answer out of their own hearts.

Great questions accomplish many goals. They invite our clients to consider their perspectives, open up their thinking to new viewpoints, prioritize and clearly articulate their desires, stay accountable to their goals, and find new solutions for the concerns they have. Great questions help to reveal a client's rationale or reasons for doing what they are doing. It allows the client to consider the evidence behind the events in their life. The idea is to get our client to explore their beliefs.

Many times, through these questions, the client will discover patterns of thinking and behaviors that have developed in their lives, many of which they may not have realized until we ask them. This can help them to clarify why something is happening. It can even cause them to realize that the situations they are imagining in their mind are not actually happening at all, but instead are based on a lie they believed. Allow them to come to the conclusion for themselves.

When the client gives a rationale for their arguments, dig into that reasoning rather than assuming it is a given. Often, our clients haven't completely thought through their arguments or beliefs. Most conflicts are caused because of a certain position or viewpoint one holds. So, invite the client to explore the position. Invite them to think of alternative ways to look at their situation, evaluate the strengths and weaknesses of their position, and identify common ground. This helps them to see that there are other, equally valid viewpoints.

As we ask these types of questions, we must be careful about our tone. Make sure the client knows that you are on their team and that you are helping your client gather facts and evidence. There is no need to make them feel like they have it all wrong. As clients explore their viewpoints, they will gain their own internal "aha" moment. Trust the process.

Remember, too, that we want our clients to discover their fears or what is holding them back. Many times, people are living in fear of outcomes that will never happen. Even if those events did happen, clients need to see that they can handle the outcome, thus eliminating the fear to move forward. We can invite clients to consider what the consequences are for the decisions they might make and to imagine what might happen next.

Questions for Difficult Situations

As a coach, we will sometimes find ourselves helping clients who are facing difficult situations. For example, the client might be experiencing abuse at the hands of a family member, and they may feel there is no way out. They may even feel that God wants them to suffer. Or perhaps they have believed lies about themselves and don't understand that there are different approaches to the situation. They might be unaware of the resources available to them or their own ability to make a change that is better for them than their current situation.

In situations such as these, gentle questions are invaluable! We can come in as coaches with kind, open questions that help our clients explore other possible options beyond where they currently find themselves. (Of course, if they are being harmed or going to harm themselves or someone else, as coaches, we must report that.)

Perhaps they themselves are abusive in their actions and communication, and it is impeding their relationships. The questions we ask can help them explore the truth about what is happening and the consequences of their actions, as well as help them define what might be causing them to be abusive in language and action.

In any case, if the client believes in God, then it can be useful to invite God into the conversation, considering Scriptures and how God's approach to life would affect the client's situation. If the client is not a believer, we can still focus on their morality and values as ways to determine what is the right course of action for them to take.

The Greatest Question of All

As we consider ways to invite God into our coaching and into our clients' lives, it's worth remembering that there is one question that rises above all others in importance. It's the greatest question that any of us will ever be given the opportunity to ask:

"Would you like to accept Jesus Christ as Lord of your life?"

Let us not forget that everything we do as coaches for Christ is to bring our clients to good, which ultimately comes from Father God. Whether we ever have the opportunity to directly invite a client to accept the Lord ... or whether we invite them to see God's work in their lives ... or whether we encourage them to move toward what is good without mentioning God (if they are not Christians), we can always be mindful of God's presence in our coaching sessions.

Our role in asking great questions and in avoiding questions that break rapport is ultimately to serve as a servant of God. In this role, we are opening up the way for Him to help our clients know the answers that will change their lives. Ultimately, Jesus is the source of all that is life-transforming and good. Therefore, as we lead our clients to good, keep in mind that we are leading them to the One who is good—our great and mighty God.

In the appendix, there is a model or sample prayer for accepting Jesus Christ as Lord that you can use as a reference for yourself or any client who wishes to accept Him. I encourage you to refer to it so you can be ready at a moment's notice to pray with those who need it.

Being ready to lead someone to Christ is one of the many ways we help others. Let's look in more detail in the next chapter at what makes us a great coach for Christ.

Chapter 5

WHAT MAKES A GREAT COACH FOR CHRIST?

Keep a close watch on how you live and on your teaching. Stay true to what is right for the sake of your own salvation and the salvation of those who hear you.

~1 Timothy 4:16 NLT~

L et's review some characteristics that make someone an effective and impactful coach for Christ. These traits will attract friends and clients to us. They open the door for us to lead others to what is good and godly, to decisions and actions and changes that truly transform their lives for the better.

Before we delve deeper into the details, let's step back and consider from a big picture view what it looks like when we are an effective coach for Christ.

57

And this first means asking: what do our clients want? What are they hoping to receive when they walk in the door or call us on the phone to start coaching?

What People Really Want

This may seem like an enormous question, because at first glance, people want all sorts of things. There are as many individual goals as there are individual people. But when we boil everything down and distill what people say they want, especially when it comes to the clients we serve, then we eventually arrive at one thing. At the root, people are looking for purpose and direction in their lives. We all want a sense of meaning for our lives.

Even when people do not know what their purpose is, and even when they don't know what direction to take, they usually have a general sense that there is "more" to their lives than what they are currently experiencing. This longing for more is often what drives them to seek a life coach to begin with.

As a result of their desire for meaning, purpose, and direction, they long for someone who will speak truth into their lives. They are looking for a coach who can help them set good goals, as well as to discover the purpose behind the goals they are longing to accomplish. They want someone to hold them accountable so that they will not just talk about change but actually take the steps needed to get where they want to go.

Ultimately, our clients want to accomplish things that are lasting and meaningful, things that make their lives better. They are longing for long-term success in order to live the abundant life that God intended for them to have. And as clients, they want the unwavering support of a Christian coach who will help them to become grounded in something that is eternal.

Our secular clients might not know that this is what they need. They might not be able to put words to this longing. But the desire for meaning and purpose is something that is God-given. We all have that desire within us. So even our secular clients long for that eternal purpose. Because of their true nature and design as creations of God, when we as Christians begin to speak of their true identity in a way that they can understand, they will long to be near us and to learn more. They will be drawn to what is godly and biblical. And this is a good thing!

Pointing Clients to True Success

Success is a term that is largely misunderstood. For example, there are very wealthy people who are not successful, nor are they living the "abundant" life. They may have beautiful homes. They may have fame. They may have the ability to travel the world. Yet they may also still feel empty, longing to be filled by purpose or joy. When they begin to place Christ at the center of their lives, that is when they will reap the success that they long for.

Do you recall the rich young ruler that Jesus spoke with (Mark 10:17-31)? He fell on his knees before Jesus and asked what to do to inherit eternal life. Jesus told him to give what he had to the poor and follow Him, but the rich young man couldn't do it. He went away sad. Imagine the happiness, peace, and God-given success that he could have experienced if he had followed what Jesus said.

The woman caught in adultery was also looking for a sense of fulfillment (John 8). She wanted to be loved. But the way she tried to obtain love was not something that would lead to the true success she longed for. Jesus knew that, which is why He both forgave her and instructed her to "sin no more." Without God at the center of our lives, the pleasure we seek after ends up being temporary and hollow. What we seek, including relationships, only fulfills us when the presence of God is within us. We are not to let sin get in the way of achieving our goals in a way that is godly and blessed.

Remember, true success in God's definition is peace, fulfillment, and joy. It comes when the Holy Spirit is present and filling us so that we are content. As coaches for Christ, we have the great privilege of helping others recognize the pathway that will lead them to the success they truly desire. Ecclesiastes 12:10 (NIV) says, "*The Teacher searched to find just the right words, and what he wrote was upright and true.*" We follow that approach. As coaches, we show restraint, pause and listen, and say what is helpful to give truth, purpose, to help them plan, take action, and reap success.

What Makes a Great Christian Coach?

A great coach for Christ is, of course, Christ-like in all they do. Remember, Jesus is the ultimate life coach, and He is our example. Think of all the ways in which He helped others to grow during His ministry on earth.

Like Jesus Himself, a great coach for Christ has a heart to serve others and is a great listener. A great coach is one who is compassionate, caring, and able to ask contemplative questions that invite the client to grow. A great coach is someone who is nurturing and able to motivate and inspire others. A great coach has high ethical standards and behavior.

And of course, as a Christian coach, it is essential that we have a personal relationship with Jesus Christ and have a good understanding of His Word, the Bible, and how to apply it to our lives and our clients' lives. After all, the Bible is the basis of all we do—and it is where the truths that change all of our lives for the better ultimately come from.

As a great coach, we take the steps needed to show our clients that we are truly on their side. After all, we *are* on their side! We are rooting for them to reach their goals. We want them to come to a good place in life, one that is rich in all that God has to offer them. Therefore, our clients should see evidence of empathy in our interactions with them. As we work with them, we show genuine interest in their lives. As a great coach, we are able to mirror and match our clients through tone and mood, continuing the rapport that we have established with them.

By committing to be a great coach for Christ, we are also committing to clearly understanding what it means to live a Christ-centered life. As we live such a life ourselves, we not only grow more like Him and more free and content in our own lives, but we also come into a position to help others. By knowing how to live a Christ-centered life, we are ready and able to help identify and guide our clients as they define and refine their vision, needs, and goals.

Not only do we help clients identify the big picture goals of their lives, but we also help them develop plans to achieve their goals. At each step, we aid and encourage them to be in alignment with God's Word so that they can be truly blessed and prosperous in all they do. We provide the support needed to ensure our clients are nurtured and motivated to achieve their goals from start to finish. We hold them accountable and show measurable results that encourage them to continue moving toward what is good and godly.

Most importantly, as great coaches for Christ, we help lead our clients to a closer relationship with Jesus as we celebrate the success of each and every one of their goals. Through us, our client will always be growing more like Christ! What a tremendous privilege this is!

What is the Goal of a Christian Coach?

Like our clients, we as coaches also want purpose and direction. We also have goals to set for our lives. And we should definitely have goals that relate to our coaching.

Our overall goal as a Christian life coach is to help our clients develop their purpose according to God's Word. This is where understanding what it means to live a Christ-centered life is so essential. Knowing what the Bible says is what allows us to guide our clients into identifying and pursuing goals that are godly and productive and healthy. After all, God promises to bless us as we keep His Word. So, when our goals are in alignment with what He desires for us, we are on our way to success.

While we will discuss the roadblocks that get in the way of a client's godly goals later in this book, for now, let's just clarify why it matters to choose goals that align with God's Word.

Often, a client will come to us with a goal that is simply not in line with biblical teachings. Many times, the client's true goal is off course because of who or what they are choosing to focus on and what they *think* they want, rather than what they would truly want if they were to explore within themselves the outcomes. For example, a client could have a goal to marry a certain individual, yet that person happens to be already married. (This happens more often than you might think!) In a situation such as this, the goal is not in line with God's Word and therefore the outcome will produce bad results. It is also leading the client away from God because of sin rather than toward Him.

This is where you, as a Christian coach, have the opportunity to help steer the client in the right direction according to God's Word. Their heart's desire needs to be explored with great questions. What do they truly desire? Maybe it's love and connection. Maybe it is lust getting in the way. Many times, the client may think they desire something that they actually do not want. They simply haven't clearly thought through all of the consequences of their choice. Through coaching, we can help explore some of the possible outcomes that would be contrary to their true desire and design. Through coaching, we can help them to have a different perspective and other options that would truly bless their life, helping them to live the abundant life God promises.

Our ultimate goal as a Christian coach is to bring our client into a saving relationship with Jesus so they can reap the success that comes from following Him and His teachings. This is why it is imperative that we as coaches understand what God's teachings are.

What Christian Coaching is All About

It is critical for us to understand what a Christian coach is because many times our clients initially think that they want someone to give them all the answers and "make their life easier." We as people have this in common. In general, people want things to be effortless. It would be so simple, we think, to have a checklist of the things we should do to mark off. And if someone else gives us that checklist, even better! But the truth is, telling someone else what to do does not solve the problem, as the true answer can only be found within the client.

At its heart, successful Christian coaching connects the methods we use to help clients accomplish their good goals with the purpose of leading them to God and the good life that He has prepared for them. With this in mind, Christian coaching is unique. It focuses on asking the right questions so that we can assist our clients in discerning for themselves where they currently are at, what their good goals and purposes are, and how they can achieve them in a way that upholds God's standards, even if they are not a Christian.

As a Christian coach, we listen and understand the client in order to help them to prioritize their life and goals. We help them to clearly articulate their desires and stay accountable to biblical, good objectives. We help them to develop strategies to overcome roadblocks to their success. In this process, we identify and eliminate negative or limiting beliefs. We hold them accountable to their dreams and help them step outside of their comfort zones so they can achieve their goals.

Notice the Five Keys to Success (mentioned in chapter one and in the appendix) in this process? These five keys will help you in all that you do in life, along with helping you to become a great coach.

Most importantly, Christian coaching is about pointing our clients to Jesus and His Word. We help clients draw close to the Lord and look to Him for *His* answers to the concerns they have.

Roles and Responsibilities of a Great Coach for Christ

It is important to understand what our role in being a coach is—and what it isn't. Great Christian coaches are *not* counselors, advisors, expert consultants, or therapists. Instead, we are motivators and encouragers. We are objective in our guidance. We're discerning and we ask great questions that make it easier for clients to draw out the answers from deep within. We properly use Scriptures and point to Jesus in all we do. And we are passionate about seeing our clients succeed!

As Christian coaches, we are very forward focused, and we trust that our clients know the answers. We help them explore what those answers are and the plans that are right for them in order to achieve their success. For all of us, our thoughts create the feelings that we experience. Helping our clients focus on the thoughts that bring about the success they desire is something we can do.

Of course, sometimes clients will have mental blocks that are keeping them from achieving their goals. Perhaps they haven't forgiven someone. Maybe they have had a traumatic experience in their life. There are many reasons they may have a mental block that is stopping them from moving forward. Our goal is to help them identify the block and find solutions that allow them to move toward success, toward good, and toward God.

As discussed in the previous chapter, we can help our client by asking the right questions without assuming or advising. As a great coach for Christ, we can listen and then direct the client to their goal by helping them find solutions in order to achieve it.

For example, if a client's goal is peace of mind, but their thoughts keep getting in the way, our role and responsibility as a coach is to ask them questions such as, "What could you think about that would help bring peace into your life?" Never tell, advise, direct, or counsel the client! Allow them to come up with their own solutions. If needed, we can offer them several different suggestions to see what fits right for them.

One of my clients I was working with had a past filled with trauma. Those experiences were entwining with her current life with her husband and daily tasks. As a busy mom with much to do, she found herself distracted by the thoughts from the past. Even with her husband, these thoughts were getting in the way.

I began by asking her questions on what she would like to think about, what she would like to get done, what characteristics and abilities she would like to have, and what kind of a relationship with her husband she desired. Through these questions, I was able to help her develop a new narration that would give her thoughts that were pleasant, thoughts about her ability to focus and be productive, even thoughts about her love and connection with her husband. I then offered her a godly meditation using her new narration and taught her godly anchoring (a technique we will discuss in chapter 10), which fully transformed her into the godly person she desired to become!

When she first came to me, this client did not fully understand what her true identity looked like. It was through the questioning process that she began to realize her true identity and who she wanted to become.

In summary, a coach for Christ takes on these roles and responsibilities: We help our clients to clearly identify and articulate their goals and desires. We help them to develop strategies to overcome roadblocks to their success, identify and eliminate negative or limiting beliefs, be accountable to their dreams, and step outside of their comfort zones to achieve their goals.

A Coach's Code of Ethics

In serving others who come to us vulnerable and seeking our help, it is essential for us as coaches to uphold a high standard of ethics. Without a commitment to treating our clients as Christ would treat them, we cannot truly be a great coach for Christ.

At YKI coaching, we have established a set of ethics for our professional, certified coaches. Ethics and morality have endless areas to expand on. I encourage you to continue to seek God in all that you do and uphold the highest standard of care for your client. Our coaches pledge to:

1. Maintain a professional relationship with our clients at all times.
2. Always keep our clients' interests above those of our own.

3. Guard and guarantee our clients' confidentiality.
4. Not advise or counsel any client.
5. Never do harm to any client.
6. Use our experiences, energy, and focus to help every client we serve.
7. Expect success from every client we serve, and not be limited in our expectations by our clients' past performances.
8. Encourage our clients to believe in themselves, set realistic goals, take appropriate actions, and celebrate success.
9. Provide our clients with a safe and nurturing coaching experience that will allow them to be themselves without fear of judgment, criticism, or failure.
10. Remain committed to professional excellence in all we do and all we provide.

In addition to establishing a set of ethics to be led by, it may be useful to review this list of activities that we engage in as coaches. I encourage you to review this list because doing these things will equip you to be the great coach for Christ that you desire to be. In your role as a coach for Christ, you will:

➢ Listen
➢ Ask questions
➢ Help the client gain clarity
➢ Help the client identify the truth of where they are at
➢ Help them identify their goals and purposes
➢ Help them to set an action plan
➢ Hold the client accountable
➢ Help the client to articulate and build on their strengths
➢ Reframe their experiences in ways that align with truth
➢ Point to Jesus in all you do
➢ Share Scriptures
➢ Coach biblically
➢ See the potential of an individual as God does
➢ Pray for clients
➢ Encourage clients
➢ Offer hope

➤ Celebrate success

➤ Report any suspected abuse of a minor

➤ Report any life-threatening situations

What will we *not* do as a Christian coach? We'll avoid anything that is not Christ-like. We will also do all we can to maintain rapport with our client so that we can continue to help them.

In practice, this means that we will make it our goal not to act like we are better than the client or convey a sense that we are judging them. We do not place an emphasis on our own life above that of our client. Sometimes coaches will begin talking so much about a situation they have faced that may be similar to their client, and in the process, the client becomes the listener as the coach is telling their story. Avoid this. Our client is the center of attention. We avoid thinking (or worse, telling them) that our story is more relevant or the same as theirs. We will refrain from telling a client what they should do or offer advice. Do not argue theological differences.

A Note about Mental Illness

The role of a coach for Christ is much different from the role of a licensed clinical psychologist or psychiatrist. It is essential to keep in mind that we are not to diagnose or treat someone's mental illness. That is a skill that requires a trained professional.

As coaches, we work with capable people only—meaning people who are able to set goals, make decisions, and follow through. If at any time you suspect that a client has a mental illness, do not try to diagnose them. Do not even state to them or others what you think would be a diagnosis.

Instead, in a diplomatic and polite way, direct the conversation to their physical health and ask them how they are and if they have seen a doctor lately. Then steer the conversation toward asking if they have ever seen another counselor or mental health professional. Delicately suggest that they might consider getting an evaluation.

Great Coaches Make a Difference

Now that you know what coaching is and isn't, and what makes a great coach, I am going to help you understand the excellent tools and techniques that we use as coaches to help our clients move toward the abundant life God has for them. The tools we use and the knowledge we gain as we work with our clients in their sessions will ultimately help our clients grow and obtain the good things God has for them.

To help our clients in this process, we will need to help them change their thinking for the better. To do this, we first need to understand how the mind develops and forms thought patterns. In the next chapter, we look more closely at the theory of the mind and how to help our clients change their mind so they can change their lives!

Chapter 6
HOW THE MIND WORKS

Don't copy the behavior and customs of this world, but let God transform
you into a new person by changing the way you think. Then you will learn
to know God's will for you, which is good and pleasing and perfect.
~Romans 12:2 NLT~

A s time goes by, science provides more and more evidence that our brain is malleable, meaning it can and does change. In fact, the mind is continually changing in response to our lifestyle, physiology, and environment. This concept is known as neuroplasticity, or brain plasticity. Because of it, we are literally reforming our brain with each passing day.

Since our brains can and do change based on our habits, we can offer our clients hope for positive change. The information we will be covering in this chapter and the following ones will explain how the mind develops and how we can help our clients improve their lives with the tools we offer to help change their thoughts, which in turn will change their brain for their good.

As we go on to discuss theories of the mind, remember that the human mind lacks some of the mechanisms that other parts of our bodies have to keep us safe. The mind is not like the stomach, which recognizes when we feed it poison and reacts by throwing it up. The mind will take in garbage and start thinking about it, creating unhealthy thought patterns. To free ourselves of this poison, we have to take conscious action to identify and get rid of those thought patterns and replace them with healthy ones.

The YKI coaching method covered in this book is designed to help clients recognize their unhealthy thought patterns and form healthy, godly patterns instead so that they can enjoy a more productive, successful, joyful life as God intends for them to have. Therefore, the YKI coaching method utilizes both biblical principles and secular information that is in agreement with biblical truths so that we can draw on the tools provided by both in order to assist our clients. Not every method in the secular world is completely true, but they do hold some truths that are useful to us as coaches. We can and should learn from secular methods that are consistent with the Bible so that we can better relate to others and help them as well as better understand ourselves and even the Bible.

As I share different theories from different doctors in the next few chapters, keep in mind that what psychologists and scientists "know" are all just theories—ideas, opinions, and hypotheses that they are testing out. God, of course, does not have theories, but truth—which He gives to us in His Word. By knowing His Word and bringing it alongside the theories of the mind we'll be discussing in this book, we can learn from these theories while holding true to biblical facts, giving us the best of both worlds.

Changing Our Minds for Our Good

Helping our clients to succeed requires that we first understand the way the mind works, why we like to stay the same and what it takes to make changes that bring about good. The first concept we'll consider is what is commonly called the comfort zone, specifically the work in visualization done by Dr. John G. Kappas (1925–2002). His concepts will help us gain an understanding of how people develop comfort zones and how they can move beyond those zones into new ways of thinking and acting.

You've probably heard the term *comfort zone* many times. The comfort zone is often described and thought about as a negative phenomenon, but it isn't always so. There can be good comfort zones too. In essence, when we are in our comfort zone, it simply means we are in a psychological state that feels familiar to us, that feels manageable, and gives us a sense of control over our environment. A good comfort zone is one in which we are doing well, enjoying life in a healthy way, and experiencing calm rather than stress.

The problem that can arise with comfort zones, and something we are likely to see with our clients, is that people can become complacent. As humans, we often want to remain in situations that feel familiar and comfortable, even though they are not good for us. Even a satisfactory comfort zone can cause us to stagnate if we remain there too long. As Christians, we are not meant to stay in one spot, never changing. Rather, God desires for us to grow and become more like Him day by day.

Positive growth and change are good. But the process of change can be stressful—which is why it is so tempting to avoid it. As coaches, we help our clients recognize the thought patterns that are keeping them in situations that are not good for them. We help them move into healthier comfort zones by identifying where they are currently complacent and help provide pathways to change. This means that we, as coaches, are helping our clients to change their minds so they can change their lives.

Renewing the Mind

The Bible tells us in Romans 12:2 that we are to transform ourselves through the process of "renewing our minds." In essence, God is sharing with us that the way we change our lives and become more like Him is a process that involves changing how we think. We are to adopt His way of seeing ourselves, others, the world, and our purpose in life. This is how we will change our lives for our good.

Yet how do we actually do this? How do we change our minds so that our thought patterns truly align with His Word? Many Christians know they should do this, but they don't know how. What they are doing is not working, and they are not sure why. The answer lies in how we think, how our thought patterns develop, our tendency to remain in our comfort zone, and what it takes to move beyond our comfort zone.

As we look at various theories of the mind, how it is developed, and how our thinking is formed, you may notice that secular theorists may mention ideas such as meditation, relaxation, visualization, and even hypnosis as tools to move past our comfort zones. In fact, one of the questions I occasionally receive from new clients at YKI coaching is whether the work we do with changing their minds includes hypnosis. As a coach, you may have clients ask you a similar question.

It is understandable that questions like this may arise because our clients are often apprehensive about what to expect from coaching sessions, especially when they first inquire about how we can help them. We can assure them that everything we do aligns with the principles found in God's Word. We do not use brainwashing. We do not force anyone to do anything against their will.

As Christians, we can be discerning in how we make use of what secular theories tell us about the mind. As coaches for Christ, we can learn to recognize when secular techniques are effective and make use of them in ways that align with God's Word. For example, though I am a certified hypnotherapist (C.Ht.), I do not actually hypnotize anyone. Instead, I offer relaxation and visualization as tools to help clients to achieve their goals in a biblical and godly way. I use godly meditation as a tool to help bring the client closer to the Lord.

I believe it will be useful here to explain a few facts that are often misunderstood. First, all hypnosis is self-hypnosis in the sense that the person being hypnotized must agree to the process. It doesn't work to force someone into hypnosis. The individual must decide how "suggestible" or willing they will be. Second, hypnosis using secular methods is very different from godly meditation, but they share one thing in common—they begin with our thoughts. But they can have very different outcomes because godly meditation is rooted in God's Word and the truth about who we are in Him, while secular hypnosis can be based on all manner of beliefs.

As with anything, it is important that the person you are allowing to speak into your life agrees with your point of view. One would not go to a pastor who directed them to disobey God. In the same way, a Christian would not seek a coach or therapist who has views that conflict with God's Word. Because a coach's beliefs and intentions can inform the results of a client session, it is extremely important for the client to make sure they are working with someone who adheres to biblical principles and is committed to speaking those biblical principles into their life.

For this reason, here at YKI coaching we do not hypnotize anyone! When we use godly meditation, we invite the client to decide that their goals are going to be offered to them in a therapeutic way with word pictures. But unlike hypnosis, we do not offer an induction that would cause someone to go into an altered state. Our godly meditation practice uses music and relaxation techniques as a way to prepare the mind, in much the same way that one would quiet oneself for prayer. We then offer a guided visualization, using the Bible and painting word pictures for the good goals our clients would like to achieve. In this way, we help our clients learn how to actively practice techniques that enable them to truly transform their minds for positive change.

Because our coaches are dedicated to following this very important approach of adhering to godly principles and beliefs, it makes for a very safe and relaxed way to reprogram your mind toward all that is good and of God. We help our clients achieve their goals in a biblical and godly way. We are using godly meditation as a way to not only achieve their goals but also help bring them closer to the Lord.

As coaches for Christ, we encourage our clients to use godly meditation daily to help them develop positive thinking, so they can produce the changes they desire in their lives. We use wisdom and discernment based on God's Word, the Bible. Ultimately, each client is responsible for the choices they make. We are called as Christians to be self-controlled, and we teach this godly principle in our practice. This godly meditation helps to affirm the client's positive choices and can help them adhere to following God's Word by choosing to continually think on what He has said. By using tools such as music for relaxation, words from the client's godly goals, and Scripture, clients can make use of this meditation practice to create a new inner voice, causing positive thinking patterns based on who God says they are. This good inner narration speaks the words that the Lord would say to them and to others—words of love, kindness, and positive affirmations that are in agreement with His Holy Word.

As Christians, we know that true transformation comes when we accept Jesus Christ as our savior and allow His Holy Spirit to transform us. This is a truth we must continue to guard as we work with our clients. We must be discerning to recognize what parts of a theory align with God's Word and which do not (2 John 7-9).

That said, we can and should learn from others in order to gain an understanding of all people. Remember, we can respect others without accepting every belief they espouse. When used properly, tools such as meditation can be used by our clients to take charge of their own thinking. As coaches for Christ, we can continually remind those we work with that changing is their choice. They must be willing to allow themselves to be transformed by the renewing of their minds with God's Word.

Therefore, in this book, I am filtering these theories of the mind through God's Word, so that they agree biblically and are productive and focused on what is godly. Read on with that in mind.

Thought Patterns are Formed Over Time

Remember that the mind does not discern between healthy and unhealthy thinking. Instead, it takes in all things, including that which is not good or true, and starts thinking about them. This is how unhealthy thought patterns evolve. If we want to see change, we have to consciously get rid of negative thought patterns and replace them with healthy ones.

This process begins with understanding how we develop our thought patterns as we go through life. In this respect, let's consider a common theory of mental development that can be useful to us as we work with our clients.

In this theory, there are three main stages of mental development that coaches can be aware of. This knowledge is valuable in helping our clients because so much of what we think and do is automatic. It occurs in our subconscious, and we are so used to it that we barely notice it is happening. This subconscious way of thinking develops from the moment we are born. So, understanding how our mind develops over time can be useful as we work with clients to examine their thinking and learn new, godly patterns of thought that benefit them.

Let's look more deeply into how our minds develop over time so that we can see how comfort zones come into existence and how we can more easily move out of them using our coaching methods.

Development of the Mind: Stage 1

According to Dr. Kappas and others, the first stage of the mind's development encompasses our lives from birth until eight years of age. At this youngest part of our lives, our minds are still very new and thus very susceptible to the information we are learning. We draw in new information quickly, but we do not yet have the knowledge or skills to evaluate it.

During this earliest period of mental development, we begin to create and build our own mental library of associations and the things which we identify with. We are experiencing so many things for the first time, and we tend to accept everything that happens to us and around us as normal. We do not know anything different.

For example, small children may feel that it is normal to eat fried foods and desserts at every meal, as this has been their daily routine as a young child. It is only as we grow older and learn more that we can evaluate whether this is a healthy habit for us or not. Another example we may see as coaches is with clients who, as children, didn't have their emotional needs effectively attended to. Some were taught as children not to express their emotions, therefore establishing a pattern of not communicating well. In our current day, many children spend way too much time on computer devices and have not interacted with the world around them and so develop a pattern of isolation.

These are just a few ways that cause children under age eight to develop certain unhealthy comfort zones. Biblically, this is known as the patterns that we develop and conform to. And according to the Bible, we are to transform our minds so that we gain godly patterns that are better for us.

Development of the Mind: Stage 2

The second stage of mental development occurs during the ages of eight to thirteen years. During this second stage, we are still young, but we are more equipped to consider whether what is happening to and around us is "normal" or not. This is when we begin to grow in our reasoning skills. We begin developing a young version of a critical conscious mind.

Because of our life experiences and the concepts we have learned from birth, we develop a certain set of beliefs about the world, ourselves, other people, and God—both negative and positive. In other words, we are beginning to assign *meaning* to our experiences at a whole new level at this stage of our mental development, based on what we have been taught and experienced. These life events create patterns and triggers, both positive and negative, toward certain things.

For example, in the United States, we have developed a specific meaning for the color red. When we see red, we know to stop because it is the signal for stopping in all our street signs and traffic lights. It is the color that is usually used to draw a "no" sign through something, indicating that we are to stop or not do something. This understanding of how red is used is so ingrained into us when we are young that by the time we are adults, we don't even think about it.

Other belief systems in our lives develop on a larger scale. For example, what does an "authority figure" mean for you? For some of us, authority figures might invoke fear, while for others they create comfort. Our reaction to an idea or experience depends on the meaning we have given to the patterns we have experienced and the things we have learned. If we have learned the belief that "authority figures hurt us," we'll be afraid or resistant to them. But if our experience with authority figures is that they protect and provide, we'll trust them.

In other words, we begin to evaluate people, events, experiences, and ideas through the lens of whether they are positive or negative. And our beliefs are grounded in those evaluations and meanings we are making.

Development of the Mind: Stage 3

The third and ongoing stage of our mental development extends from the age of thirteen and up, for the remainder of our lives. We retain and increase our ability to evaluate and weigh the things we are exposed to. Our critical conscious mind becomes even more refined. We establish our mindset and tend to protect and persist in it.

During this life phase, the patterns and beliefs we have developed keep us in our comfort zone, and our drive to remain there, without changing, is strong.

We are driven not just mentally and emotionally, but even physiologically, to remain there—often when it is not even good for us. The fear of the unknown becomes greater than the current state or comfort zone that has been established in our lives.

We can certainly learn how to move out of our fear and past our human comfort zone to our true comfort zone, which we find in Jesus. And we can help our clients do the same. As Christians, we understand that God goes before us and works all things out for us when we love Him. We can renew our mind in Christ and become a new creation as God intended with the right beliefs and patterns. "*And we know that God causes everything to work together for the good of those who love God and are called according to his purpose for them*" (Romans 8:28 NLT).

We can also help our friends and loved ones move toward their true source of comfort, God, and His blessings through the rapport we maintain with them and through our leadership. And for those clients who are not Christian, we can certainly use the words that God would use in order to gain rapport, thus leading them to their true source for comfort, contentment, and blessings.

Moving Beyond Our Comfort Zone

Choosing not to conform to the natural patterns we developed as children takes effort, especially as we age. The older we get, the harder these mental patterns are to break and change. Yet it is not impossible. Jesus told us in Mark 10:27 (NIV) that, "*With man this is impossible, but not with God; all things are possible with God.*" This is why it is important to bring biblical principles into the work we do with our clients. He empowers us to change for the good.

Let's now gain an even better understanding of the physiology and the state of homeostasis—which is another way of referring to the comfort zone.

Homeostasis is the subconscious, physiological process of maintaining a stable physical state of equilibrium, regardless of varying external conditions. It is the ability and tendency of our bodies to regulate internal conditions, such as the chemical composition of body fluids, so as to maintain health and functioning. Homeostasis drives us to return to the state of wellness and balance when conditions deviate from their optimal state.

The maintenance of a steady body temperature is an example of homeostasis. In human beings, the homeostatic regulation of body temperature involves such mechanisms as sweating to cool one off when the internal temperature becomes excessive and the generation of heat through the metabolic processes of shivering when the internal body temperature falls too low.

In other words, our body will maintain its internal conditions such as relaxed breathing, sweat, and nerves when we are in the state of homeostasis, or our normal comfort zone. This comfort zone happens at a subconscious level. We don't have to realize it is happening for it to be occurring. All we know is that we are either comfortable or we are not.

Homeostasis is as natural as breathing. It happens even when we are unaware. We don't consciously take each breath, nor do we consciously realize that we are being pulled back into our comfort zones and old mindsets. This process happens at a survival level, just like breathing. It's subtle and is much like an instinct—totally unconscious, yet powerful in its ability to affect us.

The good news is, just as we can become aware of our breathing and control it when needed, we can also become conscious of and exert control over our thinking patterns and comfort zones and determine when we need to make a change.

Let's look at an example of this unconscious process and how it can be brought under our conscious control.

Imagine that you are about to step onto a stage to give a speech. This is one of the top three most stressful things we can do; people tend to be fearful about this experience. Because of the stress that occurs at the mere thought of giving a speech, we may notice physical changes occurring in our bodies. We might experience a rapid heart rate, quickened breathing, sweating palms, dry mouth, and butterflies in the stomach. These symptoms are signs that our body is preparing for the fight or flight response to the stress of public speaking.

Now, since public speaking is something that is not going to hurt us physically, we can train our body and mind to prepare for this good stress by premeditating on all that public speaking entails. We can imagine it happening and learn to visualize good outcomes, thus training our body to respond more easily to the moment. Through this practice, we can then become very familiar and "experienced" in public speaking, making it much less stressful.

Taking Control of the Stress Response

Most of us, our clients included, consciously realize that we want to make a change and achieve our goals. Yet subconsciously, our minds pull us back to our comfort zone. Just like we are subconsciously programmed to sweat so that our bodies don't overheat, we are subconsciously programmed to eliminate stress to protect our physical bodies and our mind.

We instinctively see our comfort zone as safe and comfortable. It is a place that seems less stressful to us, even though it may not be what is best for us. This is one reason why we might resist change, even though we know logically that it would be good for us. As a client reaches for an unfamiliar goal, they can't help but be pulled back into the comfort zone. When we as coaches help them reprogram their level of comfort to fit the new end result they are aiming for, they will no longer experience the self-sabotage that so frequently stifles change.

How, then, do we help our clients to change?

We need to help our clients to eliminate the subconscious stress associated with change. It's useful to note here that both positive and negative stresses afflict the body and mind. We will feel the effects of the change, even when it is ultimately for our good. So, we must mentally and physically prepare for making the changes that will help us reach our goals.

Another way to say this is that even positive change is hard for us to adapt to. Good changes that can initially stress our clients include new living conditions, new relationships, and a new job. And of course, changes that are perceived as negative are especially stressful and difficult to adapt to, such as being suddenly unemployed, losing a loved one, divorce, illness, or injury. All of these things, positive and negative, push us out of our normal mode of being. And it is uncomfortable!

Within the comfort zone, our anxiety and stress are lessened because we know what to expect. There is no fear of the known. As a result, people tend to remain in a space that is not best for them simply because they don't want to face what they perceive to be the fear of changing. When we get out of our comfort zone, we often begin to experience an unconscious level of stress and anxiety. We feel "out of control." What brings back a healthy sense of control and confidence? A new healthy comfort zone. Success!

Success happens when a new godly goal is set, the mind and habits are changed, and a new homeostasis is developed. As a new comfort zone is developed, the client begins to feel at home in their new way of being and living. Our clients can learn how to be back in control by learning to adapt to change. The more we adapt to change, the better our mental and physical health will be. You will then have established a new comfort zone and experience contentment and joy in this new area of growth and change.

The key is in knowing how to adapt. Adapt to change and you will master life, as we are constantly changing! Change is the inevitable in life. This is why we must hold onto our Rock who never changes.

Remember that as Christians, we are constantly growing and changing into the likeness of Christ. If we are not reaching our godly potential, then complacency and our comfort zone have become our normal, and it is time to get moving and open ourselves up to further growth in Him.

Taking Charge of Our Mind's World

Happiness and success are habits that can be learned, the same way that failure and misery are learned. Fortunately for us and our clients, negative thoughts and habits can be changed to create success. The mind creates a world of illusion that can drive us, dominate us, or benefit us. By changing our thoughts, we change the illusion and thus experience a different reality.

Let's talk more about the conscious mind and the subconscious mind. The conscious mind is what we are aware of, while our subconscious thinking happens automatically. The subconscious deals with what already has been learned. Earlier, we covered the different stages of mental growth and the patterns and beliefs that have been developed in our lives over time. These patterns and beliefs happen on a subconscious level. Therefore, they will continue to drive our behavior unless we take action to change those patterns and beliefs.

We also have thought processes that take place regardless of whether an incident is real or whether we are simply picturing it. Did you know that even when you imagine something, the subconscious takes it in as real? The mind does not know the difference. It experiences both reality and imagination the same way.

The five senses make us aware of the real world around us. Seeing the solidity of the objects around us and feeling their impact on our five senses is something that is obvious and tangible to us. Both the conscious and the subconscious mind are attached to the five senses and accept everything as real without questioning. When we bump into a table or a wall, and we feel pain, we cannot say that we are imagining it. When we see with our eyes, hear sounds, smell, or when we feel heat or coldness, we understand that these things are real. Our subconscious mind uses word pictures or thoughts to understand what is real. We can therefore create an environment to help the subconscious mind imagine what is desired to be real.

As Christians, we know that there is much that cannot be seen or felt by our physical senses, and yet it is very much real. This is why it is so very important that we make the choice of what we will believe.

Tapping into Our Imagination to Create Change

Because of the connection between our sensory perception and our mind's creation of what we believe, we can actually use our five senses as a tool to create our mental reality. Our imagination was created for this purpose. We are to imagine the promises of God. We paint them with word pictures, using all the senses to really see them in our mind's eye and believe them in our hearts, until they come into being. We can take the godly goals that we have and paint very vivid pictures for ourselves so that they come into existence.

Word pictures cause us to imagine and then feel something. We can see examples of this technique in the Bible! Consider, for example, what the prophet Isaiah says about God's redemption in Isaiah 1:18 (TPT): "*Though your sins stain you like scarlet, / I will whiten them like bright, new-fallen snow! / Even though they are deep red like crimson, / they will be made white like wool.*"

Through this word picture, we can envision the red stains of sin, and then, like a supernatural experience, these sins are gone! Suddenly, through God's forgiveness, we can be made white, clean, and fresh—just like new snow or freshly knit wool. Simply picturing in our mind's eye this powerful image of change can help us feel whole and clean and forgiven! This is how we can use our imagination and visualize the truth in God's Word, through meditation, for God's glory and our good.

You see, our imagination allows the subconscious mind a way to experience things, whether they have actually happened or not. Imagination allows the mind to learn so that the intended patterns and beliefs we want to build and strengthen become automatic to us. Change occurs because our desire has been captured in our mind.

Remember, experiencing something in real life is the same to the subconscious mind as imagining it. The subconscious mind does not know the difference between real and unreal. It accepts what we feed it. So, the use of deliberate, strategic imagery in times of meditation will give our subconscious mind a way to experience what we want our patterns and beliefs to be.

By the way, isn't it interesting that doctors and psychologists are leaning toward integrated approaches such as this? These days, they are recommending meditation, relaxation, and visualization to help patients in addition to physical treatments and medications. The reason for this is that they cannot establish real change to a person's mind. The individual must choose to do that! With their integrated approaches, they are getting closer to working with patients in ways that aim to renew the mind.

What is even more powerful than all of these secular approaches is filling people with the truth found in God's Word. Now, we can certainly use these techniques God's way through trust and reliance on Him.

A great example of this meditative practice in action is seen in the ministry of Jesus, who used parables to help people relate to what He was teaching, giving them ways to experience new concepts through the mind and thus learn them. *"And He said, 'How shall we picture the kingdom of God, or by what parable shall we present it? It is like a mustard seed, which, when sown upon the soil, though it is smaller than all the seeds that are upon the soil, yet when it is sown, it grows up and becomes larger than all the garden plants and forms large branches; so that THE BIRDS OF THE AIR CAN NEST UNDER ITS SHADE"* (Mark 4:30-32 NASB).

In this parable, Jesus was painting a word picture to demonstrate how even small faith can grow very big.

In another way, the image of a tree also can indicate something going on below the surface, like the formation and growth of roots. Just as a tree grows when it develops roots, our lives develop as we become rooted in what happens to us over time. Our patterns and beliefs are rooted in what we have experienced in our lives. Some roots need to be pulled out as new roots are established. The subconscious mind (which is where we develop and hold our thought patterns) is where we find these roots.

And since these roots, also known as our subconscious mind, are what drive us, we need to make sure that our roots are good. Good roots produce good results for us. They bring about success.

An Exercise in Guided Imagery

The body, mind, and spirit are all connected. What goes into the mind and spirit comes out in the body. To demonstrate this, let us use our imagination to create a vivid image. I am going to give you an example of what it is like to imagine something and thus experience it.

Take a moment to visualize yourself closing your eyes and take a deep breath. Inhale and exhale. As you inhale, relax your feet and your legs. Continue to breathe in deeply, relaxing each and every muscle in your body. Relax your shoulders and your neck. Relax your head, and allow it to sink deeply into relaxation. You are relaxed, safe, and peaceful.

As you breathe in deeply, you see a beautiful kitchen, perhaps your own kitchen. You see big windows looking out on a beautiful sunny day. You see the lovely granite countertops that feel smooth and cool to your touch.

You notice a bowl full of fresh, bright yellow lemons on the countertop. You pick a lemon up in your hand, and you feel the oil on the skin of the lemon. You feel the bumpy skin of the lemon, and you can smell its citrus scent. It smells so good. You find a knife and cut the lemon in half. Inside, it's full of juice, and it's just the juiciest lemon you've ever seen. You tilt your head back and squeeze this juicy lemon into your mouth.

It is so sour! It causes your mouth to salivate. Your teeth can even feel the sour, strong taste.

Now visualize yourself opening your eyes. Did you feel your body respond to the word pictures you gave it? How did you feel? Did your mouth water? Did you actually get a physical reaction? Remember, this was just a visualization, and yet your body responded.

This visualization demonstrates that we have a subconscious physical reaction to an imagined experience. We just can't help it. The same subconscious response that allows us to taste an imaginary lemon happens when we visualize the godly goals we desire. Our mind and body respond in order to bring the success we are visualizing!

We can use this fact to our advantage as we coach our clients to change their thinking and create new patterns of believing. "*Finally, brothers and sisters, whatever is true, whatever is noble, whatever is right, whatever is pure, whatever is lovely, whatever is admirable—if anything is excellent or praiseworthy—think about such things*" (Philippians 4:8 NIV).

The way we begin to help ourselves and our loved ones or clients toward success is through daily visualization and meditation. The more our mind and body are programmed to do that which we desire, the more familiar we will become with our goal, which sets a new comfort zone for our body and mind.

This is how we use meditation and visualizing in a godly way to create the life God intended for us to have. Not only will our own lives be blessed, but also, we will be able to have more compassion for others as we imagine what life is like for them. Our clients will be blessed by godly vision as they are guided with the imagery that God intended for them to use to reach the goals He has given them.

Real change comes by changing the mind and heart. Only God can change the heart, which is what makes Christian meditation that much more powerful than meditation that does not draw upon God's Word. As we meditate according to God's Word, His truth, and His plans for our lives, we will become congruent in our body, mind, and spirit.

This experience of achieving success is one of the things that helps people come to know the Lord. The reason is that they need to experience God through you! Many people have not yet experienced that which is good. Since everything good comes from God, if we bring people to that which is good, we can bring them to God.

Creating Better Imagery in Our Minds

Imagery means to use figurative language to create the word pictures, actions and ideas in such a way that it appeals to our physical senses: Hearing, Sight, Smell,

Touch, and Taste. Think of these examples, and you'll see how powerful they can be at creating imagery through the senses.

It was dark and dim in the forest. The words "dark" and "dim" are visual images.

The children were screaming and shouting in the fields. "Screaming" and "shouting" appeal to our sense of hearing or auditory sense.

He whiffed the aroma of brewed coffee. "Whiff" and "aroma" evoke our sense of smell or olfactory sense.

The girl ran her hands on a soft satin fabric. The idea of "soft" in this example appeals to our sense of touch or tactile sense.

The fresh and juicy orange is very cold and sweet. "Juicy" and "sweet" when associated with oranges have an effect on our sense of taste.

God gave us our five senses for our good. Yet they can work against us if we are not in control of them. It is important to be careful of what we allow into our senses and also into our minds through both reality and imagination. Just as earlier we experienced a physical sensation through an imagined lemon exercise, our five senses create feelings and emotions that cause us to experience just about anything, whether it is good or bad for us.

Another example of imagined or guided imagery that creates feelings and emotions are movies; they can cause us to feel scared, sad, lustful, or courageous and holy. The same is true for a book, which can cause you to experience the word pictures created by the author.

The subconscious records everything. It doesn't care what's being recorded. It doesn't analyze. It cannot differentiate what's "real" from what's "imagined." It simply records and accepts. This means that everything we think, hear, say, and feel has been and is being recorded. This information forms our belief system and *must* produce for us that which has been recorded—that which has been our focus—positive or negative.

The language of the subconscious is images, created through the five senses. These images produce feelings and emotions. The subconscious mind readily accepts the therapeutic, godly guided image suggestions that are used in our Christian meditation practice. True transformation begins to happen through this process because these images become a "learned experience," which becomes a new comfort zone and a new positive habit, transforming you into the likeness of Christ.

The Power of Godly Meditation

Through godly meditation, our clients can eliminate the fight or flight response that they have experienced when desiring to make a change in their lives. By eliminating the stress, we help them eliminate the drive to go back to their negative comfort zone. In fact, reprogramming the subconscious mind gives our client a new comfort zone. Imagine that! When they receive this vision of their godly goal through us, they will then be able to trust and experience through visualization and imagination what it feels like to have success in that particular goal.

Once we begin to experience for ourselves this godly transformation through guided and self-meditation, we can then begin to practice this method on our friends and clients, helping them experience their godly goals and moving them into a closer relationship with Jesus.

Pastors have been known to use this technique when preparing for their sermons. They visualize themselves speaking, what they will say, how they will look, and what the mood is going to be. Visualizing is actually from God, as long as what we are envisioning lines up with His Word. God wants us to be prepared to think about that which is lovely and of good report.

It is very biblical to use our mind, visions, and imaginations for God's glory. Unfortunately, there is so much misconception about how to use our imagination the right way. As a result, many Christians are missing out on a tool that is very effective at helping them receive God's blessings for their lives.

For example, I have clients who are afraid to be alone, and I encourage them to imagine that God is with them. I have one client who was concerned that it was wrong to imagine God holding her hand! How terribly sad that many Christians have become so legalistic in their approach to God that they cannot use their imagination for God's glory and simply imagine Him holding their hand and being present with them.

Remember, Jesus has given us a sound mind, and we are not to walk in fear. And we are not to feel ashamed of using tools that align with God's Word and produce positive, godly changes in our lives. Shame is not of God any more than fear is. Often, Christians can become so legalistic out of fear and shame, and much like the Pharisees, we can create a set of rules we expect others to adapt to, even though these rules are not in the Bible.

I personally love that Jesus did not adapt to the rule-oriented community, but instead went to His Father and the Word of God for direction. That's what we do as coaches for Christ as well. The methods of healing that I practice on myself, my family, my clients, and my community, and that we teach through YKI coaching, have been given to me by God and are in line with His Word. The wisdom of using meditation, contemplation, and visualization to renew our minds and adopt healthy thinking patterns is from God! He gave us our minds and told us to use them for His glory and our benefit.

We need to have visualization for good and God in our lives. When we focus on being loved, understood, and valued; and on our goals, our character, and other good things, these things grow in our minds and become our realities. Our lives becomes the good that God intended. The beautiful, good, and godly experiences in life are what our souls long for.

To not have vision is to be hopeless. (See Proverbs 29:18.) But God offers hope! He desires us to envision all that will be ours, based on the Bible's promises.

Here's just one example of how powerful it is to visualize ourselves accomplishing God's will for our lives. Imagine, if you will, that someone who has never spoken in front of an audience comes to you for coaching so they can successfully speak on the subject of helping parents lovingly raise their children. Since their goal is biblically and ethically in line with what is godly and good, you help them to create their own vision, a vision of them speaking comfortably in front of an audience. Going through every detail in their own personal words, you help them envision with all of their senses themselves speaking comfortably in front of an audience.

Through this godly meditation, no longer will this client experience the sweat, the butterflies, and the nausea that they used to feel at the thought of public speaking. Now, the client will be freed from their own self-sabotage of anxiety and stress because they have undergone a successful change in their beliefs, patterns, and comfort zone. What great news!

The same happens when we visualize the godly goals we desire. Our minds and bodies respond in order to bring the success we are visualizing. This is such great news for not only us, but also for our loved ones and clients! As we practice programming our mind for success daily, we begin transforming into the "learned" behavior through meditation, and our actions reflect the success we have been "practicing" through meditation. This is the basis for how we work with our clients. We help them move out of their unhealthy comfort zones toward the positive goals they want to achieve in their lives!

Let's look more closely at how we help our clients to renew their minds in practical, effective ways. That's the subject of the next chapter—Neuro Linguistics Programming!

Chapter 7

UNDERSTANDING CLIENTS THROUGH NLP TECHNIQUES

May the words of my mouth and the meditation of my heart be pleasing to you, O Lord, my rock and my redeemer.
                                        ~Psalm 19:14 NLT~

W e've taken a look at how our thought patterns develop and ways we can begin to shift them toward more godly thinking. Now, let's take a deeper look into the practicalities of renewing our minds by studying the concept of neuro-linguistic programming and how it makes a difference in the work we do with our clients.

Simply put, neuro-linguistic programming (NLP) is an approach to understanding how people think, process information, and make decisions. It is also very much about the thoughts we think and the words we speak—a very biblical principle. This theory of the mind was developed in the 1970s by John Grinder, a linguistics professor, and Richard Bandler, a psychologist. But make no mistake; NLP is nothing new. In fact, it is God who created it, and it can be found in the Bible.

Psalm 19:14 (NKJV) says, "*Let the words of my mouth and the meditation of my heart / Be acceptable in your sight, / O Lord, my strength and my Redeemer.*" And Ecclesiastes 12:10 (NLT) says, "*The Teacher sought to find just the right words to express truths clearly.*" The Cambridge commentary for this verse tells us, "The object of the teacher was to attract men by meeting, or seeming to meet, their inclinations, by falling in with the results of their own experience." In other words, the teacher was careful with the words he used so that it would meet the audience where they were at so they could hear more clearly from God.

In both of these verses, the emphasis is on using the right words that are acceptable to both God and man. In fact, when our words are pleasing to people, we are more able to draw them to God, and this pleases Him.

There are times when we as coaches will use words to relate to our clients that are not our preferred words, or maybe they make us feel uncomfortable. Semantics are important and can help our clients feel as though we understand them. We need not be afraid of words that will help others come to know God. Remember, our goal is to lead them to God. For example, I conversed with a coaching student who worked at her church in Wyoming. She was concerned with using the word "centered" in her coaching sessions, as there are many New Age people in Wyoming. She felt that she was acting like them by using that word. I told her, "I would totally use the word 'centered' as there is nothing wrong with it, and it is a great way to attract New Age people so you can bring them to the Lord!"

Our words are powerful in both expressing and shaping our thinking. This truth is the basis for the many Scriptures in the Bible that tell us to speak as God speaks, to avoid negative speech, and to use His Word in our conversations and in our prayers. As we use neuro-linguistic programming in God's way, it becomes a powerful coaching tool. We use God's words in a way that creates rapport with our clients, drawing them to Him. As they draw nearer to Him, they can begin to experience lasting change.

As we incorporate God's Word into our lives and shift our thinking toward more godly ways, and meditate upon and visualize His Word and His purposes for our lives, we become transformed into the likeness of Christ. NLP is a powerful coaching tool that utilizes the imagery we discussed in chapter 6 and implements God's words to help create the lasting change we desire for ourselves and our clients. The principles of NLP can be used to eliminate negative mental states, habits, or beliefs that are holding a client back. For our purposes, we will only discuss the most appropriate NLP strategies for coaching, for reprogramming the mind and helping our clients to achieve their goals according to God's Word!

Using NLP tools and techniques will help you to easily identify a client's learning method (or learning modality), which in turn will help you, as their coach, to appeal to them and help them learn and grow, providing them with a successful coaching experience.

Our Different Modes of Learning

Coaching is, at heart, a process of helping clients learn. We are helping them to discover things about themselves and teaching them ways to improve their lives. So, it makes sense to consider the learning process from our client's point of view. As we work to build rapport, we can discover how our clients prefer to learn, which helps us relate to them and helps them to gain all they can from their coaching sessions. This also helps us keep rapport with our clients so they can continue to learn and grow.

There are three different learning styles and sensory modalities that people are accustomed to using as we take in new information: visual (learning through what we see), auditory (learning through what we hear), and kinesthetic (learning through what we feel or do). Most of us use all three modalities to varying degrees, but there is usually a predominant mode that we prefer. Our modalities may also change depending on the context in which we find ourselves. For instance, someone may be visual at work, where learning is more focused on what they see, yet they may be more kinesthetic at home where they have more opportunities to do something involving touch.

Statistics show that 60% of people are visual learners, 25% auditory, and 15% kinesthetic. Let's take a look at how to identify each one so we can recognize it in our clients.

A visual learner will use words such as "I see. Let me observe. In my mind's eye. I imagine. Look at this. Show me." Their language indicates they are taking in information by sight. This is a great reason to listen to our clients carefully! Doing so allows us to identify their specific modality. Visual learners also speak at more of a staccato pace. They will often look up as if imagining something. Their breathing is generally shallow, high, and quick. They often point to things.

When working with visual learners, I often draw things for them to help emphasize a point. I may show them a picture of something online or allow them to show me pictures.

An auditory learner will use words such as "It sounds like. Does this ring a bell? Listen. Hear what she is saying? It is loud and clear." Auditory learners tend to speak more rhythmically. Their eyes appear to be looking left or right. Generally, this is because they are trying to listen. Their breathing happens more in the mid-chest area. They might touch their face or chin as they listen or speak.

For an auditory learner, we can suggest listening to podcasts or worship music to help them get closer to the Lord. Also, we can encourage them to speak out loud their affirmations and prayers, as well as singing.

A kinesthetic learner will use words such as "I feel. Grasp the wheel. Handle this carefully. Touch the fabric. Feel this. Hang in there." They speak slowly with pauses. Their eyes generally appear to be looking down. They breathe more deeply and slowly. They may rub their arm or leg frequently as they talk or listen.

As we work with our kinesthetic clients, we may find they benefit from sketching out ideas, writing down Scriptures and affirmations, and underlining in their readings.

How Learning Modalities Benefit Our Clients

As coaches, when we pinpoint our own preferred modality and that of our client, it will help us tremendously in being flexible, relatable, and connected with our client. It helps us maintain rapport as well as suggest options that will help our clients succeed.

Understanding how a client learns can help us as coaches in many ways. As an example, if we understand that a client is a visual learner, we will be aware that the physical world is important to them. We can use visuals in our examples and analogies as we coach them; this helps them to relate and hold onto new, healthy ideas.

Knowing the client's modality is also helpful to us during times of meditation, where we have the opportunity to create the atmosphere for their visualization of the godly goal they desire. For example, if they enjoy the beach and are visual learners, we might paint our word pictures by using as many visuals of the beach as possible. We can invite them to envision the sun glinting on the ocean waves and seagulls flying through the bright blue sky as they imagine what God's peace feels like. The specifics help a visual learner comprehend more deeply what God's peace can mean to them.

For a kinesthetic learner, by contrast, we would emphasize the way things feel, in a good and godly way. For example, if we are using the beach as an image, we might call the client's attention to imagining how the gentle breeze coming off the ocean feels comforting or the way that the soft sand feels warm and relaxing beneath their feet. This helps them realize they can "feel" the comfort of the Lord.

For someone who is an auditory learner, we would emphasize sounds. We might invite them to think about the rhythmic sound of the calm ocean waves hitting the sand, which reminds us of the Holy Spirit's presence or the power of God to handle any situation. We can suggest our client imagine the sound of the birds soaring above, so they can think about how these sounds bring them a sense of godly peace.

I have personally experienced how useful this information about different learning styles can be! It has worked wonders in my own life and in my family's life! When I was first studying the principles of NLP several years ago, I realized the concept of learning modalities could help me address the support my son Nicholas needed with his school studies. At the time, he was thirteen years old, and he was not doing well in his classes. I attempted to help him learn by pasting words all over the place so he could see them. This seemed like a logical approach to take, and I obviously was willing to take the time to help him. But it wasn't effective.

After I learned about the different learning styles, I thought about my son and realized that he is primarily an auditory learner, rather than a visual one. No wonder the cue cards hanging on the walls weren't helping him improve his grades. Instead, I worked with him to develop study skills that involved his natural, auditory style of learning. After teaching him to read out loud the instructions for his homework and talk himself through what he was studying, his grades improved significantly. In fact, he no longer needed a tutor. He instead understood how to help himself to learn. It was amazing!

During this same period, I also discovered I am a kinesthetic learner. For me, writing things down and underlining while I read helps me to remember tremendously. Knowing what works for me helps me to learn. And it is the same for our clients. As we teach them to know what works for them, they will find it easier to take in what we are sharing with them in their coaching sessions.

In essence, we are always teaching ourselves new things through our preferred way of taking in new information. So, the better we understand ourselves as students, the better we become at being our own teachers. Schools are now teaching these learning modalities to teachers and giving students quizzes to help identify their learning patterns, thus making the process of learning more impactful and effective for students. And we can do the same for ourselves as coaches and for our clients.

Mirroring Our Client's Mode

Do you remember our discussion about rapport in chapter 3 and how to establish it as a coach by mirroring and matching your client? Recognizing which learning modality our client prefers is essential for helping us to establish and maintain rapport with them. This is especially important because often the different learning styles don't mesh well. In fact, when two people with different learning modalities interact, they can end up inadvertently irritating or bothering each other because their differences in learning styles rub each other the wrong way.

For example, a visual learner typically thinks and speaks quickly, and they will often become annoyed with a kinesthetic learner, who normally processes thoughts and communicates at a slower pace. At the same time, a kinesthetic may feel nervous approaching a visual because the visual learner acts so much more quickly. Neither is better or smarter than the other; they are simply two different approaches to taking in information. But the difference can lead to friction.

I remember a time when I served in the Saddleback counseling ministry, and a fellow counselor would come into our supervisor's meeting, which all of us counselors were required to attend. This particular woman had a very high-pitched, staccato way of speaking. She was a visual personality, so she would speak quickly. Her voice and fast pace would literally raise my blood pressure, as I am a kinesthetic type of person. I like people to speak slowly and with softer voice tones. Our supervisor did not address the issue with this fellow counselor, and so it was never resolved. It certainly impeded my ability to feel a sense of rapport and connection with this fellow counselor.

As skilled coaches, it is our responsibility to adapt to our clients. We mirror their modality so that they are comfortable and able to receive from us. This is the heart of servanthood that a great Christian coach embodies.

Rapport is an ongoing necessity used in every relationship and in every interaction if we want them to be successful. To help our clients renew their minds, we must make sure the meditations, visualizations, and affirmations we craft with them are designed to fit their needs. What is our client seeking? Where do they lack? How would they like to grow? Remember, each individual is unique and must not be stereotyped or placed in a box. It is imperative that we get to know and understand our client so we can help address their needs.

Preparation for our client brings success. They will feel heard and understood. As we get to know our client better with each visit, we will also discover their "buttons." What upsets them? What specific characteristic could they fall under as far as feeling unloved or not good enough? Addressing these areas will help them grow in the Lord.

Language Patterns and Meta Models

Now, let's talk about NLP's meta models, also known as language patterns. A client's meta model is their way of seeing the world, their worldview. And their worldview becomes evident in how they speak. Through understanding our client's culture, characteristics, skills, hobbies, language patterns, fears, and learning modality, we can better understand how best to speak with them and communicate in ways they can receive.

For this reason, God instructs us to watch our words. Proverbs 13:3 (NIV) says, "*Those who guard their lips preserve their lives.*" Even God Himself created our world based on what He said. Our words shape our world! As we notice how our clients speak and see the world, we can begin to guide them to what God would say and how He would see things. This allows them to align their lives with His Word.

We do this through mirroring and matching our client's personal prose—their choice of language. Ephesians 4:29 (NLT) says, "*Let everything you say be good and helpful, so that your words will be an encouragement to those who hear them.*" What words can we use that are similar to the way they speak? What will connect best with our client? For example, if a client says to us, "I feel like a no-good loser," we can consider what they might say if they wanted to express a feeling or thought that was positive. Perhaps they might say, "I am a confident woman of God," or "I succeed in all I do." We can mirror their speech pattern in a positive way to help them envision what God sees in them in a way they can understand and be open to receiving.

There is more than one way to say positive things, so we adapt to our client's language and character. Semantics are important, so as our clients are discovering their true, godly identity we write down the positive words that God would say about them. This will help them to create a new narrator that is used in their godly meditation. As we mirror and match their patterns of speech in the meditative practices we are offering, the client is more likely to receive what we are saying. In this way, we help them by leading them to that which is good and filling their heart and mind with that which God would say to them.

Misleading Meta Models

There are some meta models—some ways of seeing the world and speaking about it—that can unconsciously prevent our clients from reaching their goals. For our purposes, we will concentrate on the three overall categories of misleading meta models—known as *deletions* (leaving out important ideas), *distortions* (misshaping important ideas), and *generalizations* (making assumptions that ignore variations and flexibility). You may have heard of these terms before. These models cover a variety of misleading language patterns that our clients may find themselves stuck in.

As an effective coach, it is our responsibility to understand and recognize these models when coaching our clients. There are underlying roots to each of these negative models of communication. Digging deeper through the questions we ask our client is the way to get at the root issue of these negative communication styles. As a coach, we are discovering the root causes for the statements our client makes.

As we listen carefully to our clients, we come to understand their worldview. Then, we can effectively, gently challenge the ways their worldview contradicts what God says is true. We ask great questions that challenge our client's assumptions and distortions so we can help empower them to choose to believe the best—so they can experience the best! This will help them change their views and their words so they can succeed in life as God intends.

Deletions

The first category of misleading meta models we are to be aware of as we coach our clients is known as deletions. What this refers to is our tendency as human beings to say only part of what we are thinking or what we know. Deletions often happen because people are in a hurry to tell us their story, so they leave out details that are important—such as who they are speaking about or what exactly they are feeling or expecting.

It is important to clarify the deletions that clients leave out so that we can effectively guide our clients to what is good and godly. God Himself is a God of clarity and truth. But Satan likes to confuse people and is a liar. Keep in mind that miscommunication happens because of a lack of clarity. If a client leaves out information, we as coaches could become confused.

We must be clear on the details of what our client is sharing with us so we can help them meet their goals. Therefore, it is imperative that we gain the needed information from our client through great questions. Here's an example from my coaching practice.

I had a male client recently who told me one of his goals was "independence." But independence is a big concept, and it can mean different things to different people. I needed clarity on what he was referring to, as well as what he was thinking and feeling. In other words, what was being deleted or unsaid. So, I proceeded to ask him, "What do you mean when you say your desire is for independence?"

He answered, "I wish to drive." But that did not tell me all I needed to know.

Since I still needed more clarity, I asked him what was the reason he was not driving. He told me he was in a car accident. I then needed to know what happened in the accident, so I asked about that. He revealed he was on medication while driving. This made the issue much clearer and opened up what we truly needed to work on for his life—issues such as what led to the need for medication, whether it was an illness or an addiction, and how he could make choices that would better position him to safely drive again, thus gaining his *independence.*

So much of the information we need as coaches must be gained through thoughtful questions that help elicit the full story behind what the client initially says. We do so in order to help clients see the bigger picture. Even when our clients truly know the answers, they are often not aware of how all the dots connect. It is our job as a coach to gain clarity about our client's situation, so we can help them connect the dots.

As we ask questions about deletions, it is a good idea to be careful with our tone. We want to make sure they know we are on their team. Be gentle while being direct. Keep the rapport while gently leading the client in a positive direction.

Distortions

Now, let's look more closely at the second category of misleading meta models—distortions, which has several subcategories. Common types of distortion that you may notice in a client's speech include making assumptions, mind-reading, faulty cause and effect, seeing a wrong vision for one's future, and making unfair judgments about circumstances. All of these language patterns reveal that our client is not seeing the world clearly and objectively. By forcing the world to fit into how they see things, the client can often miss opportunities for freedom that are right in front of them.

Often, the root of these distorted beliefs is poor programming from broken individuals in their life who didn't know how to love or speak to their true identity. It doesn't mean the individual didn't love them or doesn't love them. Our clients need to come to know their true identity apart from fallen people. When they do, they are more free to live life as they want to, based on who God says they are. Let's look further at the different subcategories of distortions we may come across as we coach.

Assumptions and Mind-Reading

When a client engages in mind-reading or making assumptions, they are often believing and acting on beliefs that are not true. We want to help our clients know and understand their true identity, apart from what others say and do. We want them to know how God sees them and to believe it.

Most often, clients are coming to us because their views are distorted, and they are assuming things that are not actually true. And because the Bible tells us that knowing the truth is what sets us free (John 8:32), it is important for our client to learn to recognize their untrue thinking. Our role as a coach in such cases is to ask questions that encourage the client to examine their assumption.

For example, a client may describe a relationship by telling us, "He doesn't understand me." In such situations, we would challenge the client with a question such as, "How do you know he doesn't understand you?" This invites the client to consider what underlies their assumption. Sometimes, they will feel it's true simply because they came to believe it is true for all their relationships as a result of things that happened earlier in their lives. By asking questions that challenge the assumption, we can help the client recognize untruths in their worldview.

If they give compelling evidence that the individual truly doesn't understand them, we might follow up with a question such as, "What could you do to help this individual understand you better?" or "Would you be able to live a victorious life regardless of whether or not this individual understands you?" With questions like these, we can help the client see that they have more freedom and control in the situation than they may have realized.

Clients may also assume they know another person's internal state or belief. If this is happening, they may use phrases such as, "He or she doesn't like me," or "They think I'm dumb." We would then ask, "How do you know that he or she feels that way?"

Assuming is generally an indicator that the client's inner narrator (that inner voice in which they speak to themselves) believes something negative or untrue about their life. Because this is a broken world and the enemy has crept in through dysfunction, the client has gained a belief system that is dysfunctional in some way, causing them problems. Gaining information will help your client to get a better perspective of where they are at, what information they have that might be wrong, and what steps they need to take in order to gain the results they desire.

a.   Faulty Cause and Effect

Another common distortion in our meta models is assumptions of cause and effect where no such relationship actually exists. A client may say something like, "They make me angry." The reality is how we feel is our choice; our feelings can be within our control. So, as a coach, we might ask our client to consider, "How specifically does what they are doing cause you to choose to feel angry?"

As coaches, we have the ability to help our client to see that they *can* be the "cause" in their life—meaning they can choose to have a different outcome in their circumstances. They have more control than they often realize. As we ask questions that invite clients to examine their assumptions and their views of their world, we can help bring to light the true roots of what they are saying and feeling, allowing the clients to discover for themselves their own empowerment.

b.   Wrong Vision of the Future

Another common distortion in our thinking is having a wrong vision for our future. This is when we assume that our future is already determined by something beyond our control.

A client might say something like, "I'll never be successful because I don't have a college degree." They are assuming their future is destined to have a lack of success because of a lack of a college degree, which is not necessarily true. In the book, *The Millionaire Next Door*, for example, the authors Thomas J. Stanley and William D. Danko report that the majority of millionaires do not have a higher education.

As a coach, we can bring to light that faulty assumption with questions such as, "How does having a college degree mean you will be successful? Do you know someone successful who does not have a college degree? What if you worked to be successful without a college degree?"

Again, as coaches, we are striving to discover the basis for our client's statements and asking for evidence of the validity of their statements. During this process, a client can begin to see their "evidence" isn't as true as they have previously believed it to be.

c.   Judgments on Circumstances

Another way a client's worldview can be distorted manifests itself in the judgments they are making about their circumstances. For example, a client might say, "It's bad to be divorced." This is a value judgment that the client has placed on themselves. To address the assumption, we can ask, "Who says it's bad? What causes you to feel it is bad?" Often, the client has made wrongful assumptions of what others are thinking about them. It is important for our client to realize that not everyone feels it is bad to be divorced. God certainly has love for them even if they are divorced, and they can still be victorious regardless.

Such distortions can cause a client to believe things that contribute to the struggles they are facing. The Bible, though, helps us to have clarity and remove our distortions, so we can be free.

d.   Judgments about Other People

One of the most common distortions we can have is the mistaken belief that our battle is with other people, with flesh and blood. The Bible clarifies for us that our battle is *not* with flesh and blood, but rather it is with forces of darkness and wickedness (Ephesians 6:12).

The only way our clients are going to get over their relational problems is to realize that the source of the issue is not the people around them, but Satan and his forces that are so strongly influencing people. Once a client gains this biblical perception, then they can stop fighting the people and properly respond by putting their spiritual armor on, according to Ephesians chapter 6. On the flip side, if we continue to think the problem is with people around us, we are never going to be able to find the Lord's joy and peace. We will be too preoccupied using man's sinful methods of getting back or overcoming them. We simply will not be loving them.

When our perception is off in this area, we tend to make wrong choices about our interactions with others. We find ourselves operating from a place of inaccuracy and fear, instead of truth, clarity, and power from the Holy Spirit. When our clients understand their real struggle and how they can eliminate that struggle, they will be filled with power and success. Our job as coaches is to help our clients gain the right perspectives so they can have the abundant life God intended.

Generalizations

The third misleading meta model is what is known as generalizing. A generalization is a blanket statement that is assumed to apply to all people and all situations, without acknowledging any exceptions to the rule. Generalizations essentially assume that there is only one way to view something, which then limits what we can believe and do about it. This kind of thinking inevitably leads to judgment, racism, and other false and even harmful worldviews.

Interestingly, God clearly points out how generalizations can be wrong in the Bible. Look at Noah. The book of Genesis tells us that the whole earth was wicked, yet there was Noah and his family whom the Lord saved.

Later, God has a conversation with Abraham about the fate of Sodom and Gomorrah. Most of the city has fallen into evil, but Abraham asks God, "What if there are fifty people there who are righteous? What if there are twenty? What if there are ten?" God says, "For the sake of those ten, I will not destroy it" (see Genesis 18:32).

These biblical events assure us that God does not generalize. He also sees the one. And we must too. We must be careful not to place people in generalized terms. It is our job as coaches to help our clients break out of this pattern as well. Let's look at common subcategories of generalizations that we may come across in our coaching.

a.   Black and White Thinking

Black and white thinking is a form of generalization in which it is assumed that there are only two choices available to us, such as that a thing or a person is "all good" or "all bad." It is limiting because we can't see the nuances of a situation or a person. Often, black and white thinking stirs up our dissatisfaction and heightens feelings of anger or despair. For some people, this dangerous style of thinking can lead them to think their only options are to harm themselves or others.

But when we can acknowledge that there are some grey areas, our feelings of upset can be defused. It is helpful and can even be life-saving to correct distorted generalizations for the good of our client and others.

A client's black and white thinking is evident when they use words such as *all, every, everyone, no one, never, all of them, all of the time,* and *everything.* For example, a client may say something like, "She's never happy with what I do." The word *never* is a blanket statement, meaning "this situation is always true, without exception." But there usually are exceptions we can make.

To help a client see that they are stuck in black and white thinking, we can follow up with great questions like, "Has she ever been happy with something you have done? Can you think of a time when she expressed some level of happiness with what you did? What would she do if she were happy with you?"

Another example is a client saying something like, "Everyone is in a relationship." We might say, "Everyone? Really? Can you think of anyone who isn't?" It is important to help them to realize that they can be loved and complete like others who are not in a relationship. This gives you an opportunity as a coach to explore what might be going on more deeply that is possibly causing them to feel that they cannot be loved or in a relationship in their future.

When people generalize, they remove the ability to see a victorious outcome for themselves and others. I once had a client who believed all teenagers were trouble. Because of that belief, when her daughter became a teenager, she was expecting poor behavior. Because she was expecting this behavior, her daughter began to act out more and give the mother trouble. The mother needed help with her worldview and her habit of generalizing so she could begin to speak life into her beautiful daughter and create the relationship that she truly desired with her.

You can see how a client who adheres to black and white thinking can find themselves in situations that are unhealthy for them and may not be able to see a way out. By addressing the distortions in their thinking, we can help them open up to new options that are God-ordained and good for them.

b.   Unreal Requirements or Expectations

Another form of generalization happens when we assume there are requirements or expectations we have no choice but to meet. These unrealistic, false assumptions manifest themselves in words such as *I should, I shouldn't, I must, I cannot, I have to, I need to.* Such thinking and language indicate that a client is believing they have no choice in the matter. But God wants us to be free to choose! And He desires us to have a good future, one filled with hope (Jeremiah 29:11). It is for freedom in the Lord that we have been set free by Jesus!

As we coach a client through this type of thinking, we can listen for statements in which a client indicates they feel a lack of options. The client might say something like, "I have to loan them money." We can challenge that distorted belief with questions such as, "What causes you to think that you have to? What would happen if you didn't?"

c. The Impossible

A third form of generalizing is statements of what is impossible. Remember, the Bible says, "*With God all things are possible*" (Matthew 19:26 NIV). And "*What is impossible with man is possible with God*" (Luke 18:27 NIV). It is our role as coaches to help clients see when they are limiting the possibilities in their lives.

Notice when clients are saying things such as, "I can't. I will always. I won't ever. I can never. It is impossible." Use great questions to challenge these thoughts and open up the client to seeing more of their options.

For example, when a client says something like, "I can't ever get ahead," we can ask questions like, "What is keeping you from getting ahead? What are some steps you could take to make a small difference?"

Practice These Skills Daily

How can we use this information in our coaching practice? Remember, we want to listen for patterns in how the client speaks, lies they believe, deletions, distortions, and generalizations.

A great way to practice listening carefully is to work on ourselves. Remember, your most important client is you! Take inventory of the patterns you have developed, the lies you have believed, and your own deletions, distortions, and generalizations as you speak. Discover your learning modality. Once you do, you will retain so much more of this skill set, and it will benefit your clients greatly.

After we have become more aware of ourselves, we can move into becoming more aware of language patterns, learning modalities, and misleading meta models in our day-to-day conversations with others.

It's even useful to find a friend who is willing to help us practice by playing the role of a client. First, establish rapport just through friendly conversation. Then ask a few questions and listen to them. See if you can identify patterns they might have established in their life, lies they have believed, distorted worldviews, generalized statements, and deletions in their conversation with you. Listen and look for their learning modality. Write down what you discover as you do this exercise.

Continue practicing these skills in your daily conversations. Begin to become more aware of others. There is so much going on in each individual's life. This exercise will help you to become so much less judgmental, as you will begin to notice that many people are going through their days unaware of their distortions and patterns. This positions you to become a light to others, helping them expand their worldview in a positive way. You will begin empowering others simply through awareness and questions while displaying for them the love of Christ.

Let me give you an example from my coaching practice to show the tremendous positive impact that can happen when we identify our client's learning modalities, language patterns, and distorted worldviews to help them achieve their goals.

A recent client of mine came to me feeling very suicidal. He was sad because he was a victim of childhood emotional neglect, an experience that leads people to feel deep guilt, shame, and anger about their feelings and needs. As a result of this neglect, the client felt very unloved, and even as a grown man of fifty years old, he was still hurting over the rejection of his parents.

I began to relate to him in his learning style, which was kinesthetic. He communicated more slowly with feeling. I spoke to him with the same kinesthetic approach. I had an understanding tone while I listened to his pain, mourning with him as the Bible tells us to. The simple approach helped us develop the rapport necessary for him to reveal even more of his story. I discovered he was raped as a young boy of five. His parents never knew. He had no one to tell. The mood was sober, somber, and quiet as I listened for a long period of time.

As the session progressed, I was able to clear up some of his distortion, which was that he wasn't loved. Through our sessions, he began to discover and *feel* that he was loved, that he would never be alone, that through God, things were going to get better. He needed what I offered, which was truth, clarity, and a better worldview filled with hope, love, comfort, peace, and understanding. As the session shifted to a place where now I was leading, I could then offer him a godly meditation, using the beautiful words he needed and longed to hear—that he was understood, that he was being transformed into the man God created him to be. I created a peaceful word picture using his learning style and painted a beautiful vision of him walking outdoors, as he felt the warmth of the sun and the love of God comforting Him.

Helping him to *feel* the presence of the Lord through godly meditation gave him something he could do also on his own. He began seeing himself progress in his mind as someone who was a strong man, with a kind spirit, and yet able to set healthy boundaries. He was able to see himself, in his mind, as someone who can also go to the gym and take care of his body, and to pray and meditate in order to feed his spirit and *feel* the love of God. As he read God's Word, he was now about to visualize and sense God's presence, further transforming his mind.

His transformation in just that one session of seeing himself as able to care for himself in spirit, soul, and body was incredible! He learned the tools necessary to continue his growth with the Lord, apart from me, and he was also encouraged to continue with his sessions until he felt solid in his godly identity. This is the positive change we are working toward with our clients.

Chapter 8

NLP Meta Programs

Instruct the wise and they will be wiser still; teach the righteous and they will add to their learning.

~Proverbs 9:9 NIV~

Now that we have looked at the general ways in which our clients learn, how they develop their thinking, how their worldviews can become dysfunctional, and ways that their worldview creeps into their language, we can move on to the next step in helping our clients to set goals and make decisions. In NLP, this is referred to as our preferred *meta program*. Meta means *key*, and so a meta program is simply the key way we are motivated to set and achieve goals. As we discover how our client prefers to be motivated, it will empower us as coaches to help them succeed!

One of the main approaches we take with our clients is helping them choose a new path that is right for them that will move them toward their good desires.

You've probably heard the saying, "Insanity is doing the same thing over and over yet expecting different results." Our role as a coach for Christ is to open our client's eyes to the repetitive patterns of thinking, speaking, and behaving that are continuing to yield results they don't want in their lives and helping them break those patterns.

Truth and clarity are the first step. The next phase is to decide how we as coaches approach our client to encourage them to move forward or discourage them because of a wrong approach. If we are unaware, we can either motivate them to push ahead or cause them to disengage. We must become aware so that we keep rapport with them during this critical phase of coaching. To do so, it is necessary that we understand our client's *meta program*, their preferred way in which they make their decisions, set their goals, and respond best to receiving our help.

It's worth noting that a client's meta program is not necessarily good or bad—it is simply a fact about how an individual engages with their decision-making. Each of us has our own way of establishing and achieving our goals. It's wonderful that God has made us all unique, and as coaches, we can honor and support what works best for our clients as we lead them toward what is best for them. As we learn our client's preferences, we can keep our rapport with them and act as an excellent influence as they move toward change. We can help our clients identify if there is perhaps a better meta program to identify with to help them move toward their goals.

Many of our clients will be unaware of their own meta program. They won't always realize how they are motivated, what works for them, and what doesn't. Often, therefore, your client may not know exactly how to ask you for help. This is the reason it is helpful for us as coaches to know about the concept of meta programs—so we can help them identify what their preferred encouragement will be to move them toward their success. You will then be able to give them the prompts that will influence them for their achievement.

The four meta programs that influence our behavior and motivation are:

- Toward vs. Away
- Internal vs. External
- Global vs. Specific
- Once vs. Several Times

Let's look at each in more detail so that we can learn ways to better lead our clients toward the goals they want to achieve.

The Toward vs. Away Meta Program

This meta program describes our tendency to desire to either move away from something or move toward it. This is easier to envision when you think of our relationship with food. Some of us want to move toward a healthy weight. Some of us want to move away from being heavier than we would like. How we see the situation can either encourage us to make changes or make it harder for us.

Whenever we are focused on an "away" concept, we are focusing on something that we think of as negative. This can become a challenge because we are human, and humans often end up doing the things we are trying to avoid doing. The more we tell ourselves not to eat a second piece of cake, the more we think about that cake—and guess what? We may end up eating it. This is simply a fact of our human nature, together with the fallen world we live in.

God's solution to this is to have us focus on what is good. Philippians 4:8 (NIV) says, "*Whatever is true, whatever is noble, whatever is right, whatever is pure, whatever is lovely, whatever is admirable—if anything is excellent or praiseworthy—think about such things.*" As we think about good, it is easier for us to move toward good.

As Christians, we move toward Christ; we do not focus on Satan. Therefore, we want to encourage our clients to focus on moving toward their good goals, rather than away from something they want to avoid. If the client is Christian, we encourage them to move toward Christ, not necessarily away from Satan.

Using Rapport to Focus a Client Toward a Goal

Using everything we know about maintaining rapport is essential to helping our client move toward a positive goal. First, realize that the way we identify a client's desire to move toward or away from something is to listen to them. As we speak with them and ask great questions, we can consider their words. Is our client using terminology that describes moving away from something?

If so, our first step is to use rapport with them by rephrasing what we hear them saying. This confirms we are hearing them properly. Once they agree that we understand them, we can then lead them to rephrasing their desires to focus on what is positive in their life so that they are moving toward their goals. This will put their good goal at the forefront of their mind instead of what is negative. We want them thinking about the goal—the reward.

For example, imagine the client wants to move away from feeling heavy. They may use that phrase, or they may say something else where the focus is on what is negative, such as, "I want to stop being so overweight. I don't want to feel like I weigh too much." We can begin by relating with him or her in their meta program language and then begin moving them toward their goal of being slim and healthy.

We might say something like, "I hear you. You want to move away from feeling heavy. That is an awesome goal! What would it look like for you to feel slim?" Let them answer, and begin writing those things down. Then, begin directing them with those words as if they have already achieved them.

For example, they may say, "If I felt slim, then I would feel happy. I would feel light and healthy." We would use those words and say to our client, "You look happy, light, and healthy. What might you do to look happy, light, and healthy? Is there a step you can take to look happy, light, and healthy?"

Here is another example. Suppose a client says, "I want to stop yelling at my kids." We would then say, "That is an excellent goal! How do you want to go about speaking more kindly to your children?" We would then begin to bless him or her with words like, "You are such a kind and patient person."

This is language we can use anytime we are discussing their goal, which is now phrased and visualized in a positive way, inviting them to move toward it.

The Internal vs. External Meta Program

The second meta program is internal versus external motivation. Our clients are either motivated by someone else's opinion or they are internally driven, or both.

We want to encourage our clients to be internally motivated because it is something we can control and choose for ourselves. Of course, some concern for what people think about us is not all bad. Our reputation is important, after all. We would be completely self-absorbed if we didn't care about what others think.

However, if our motivation is entirely focused on what others think, say, and do, then we end up making decisions based on what others want.

God has designed us to make decisions based on what we know to be true and good, and based on what is inside of us. Often, clients need help recognizing what they themselves know on the inside is a good and godly goal for them.

As coaches, we must use wisdom and help our clients to desire that which is good, which is what God has planned for them. When our client is in tune with God, they are in tune with what He has placed inside them, His purpose for their life. When the client is self-motivated, their goal is coming from within themselves. As we bring them to the Lord, their desire becomes to please God, which becomes both an external and internal motivator.

Coaching Our Client Toward Internal Motivation

Again, the key here is to listen to the client. When they describe a goal they have, ask them to describe the reasons they desire this particular goal. If they are initially focused on how others will see them or how others think this goal is important, we can acknowledge that we hear and understand. We meet them where they are at and validate them. Then we can help them to critically think and decide if this goal is right for them. If it is, they can then come to desire the goal for themselves.

For example, our client who has told us they want to stop feeling heavy might now say, "I want to lose weight because my husband is pressuring me to do so." They might say, "I want to lose weight because I want my husband to be happy." That is an external motivation, focused on someone else—the client's husband, not the client herself.

As coaches, we don't see that motivation as all bad, but we recognize that external motivation alone is not enough to help our client to make changes that bring about the best in their lives. So, we gently come in with a question that encourages them to consider their internal motivation too. For instance, we might ask, "Do you desire to lose weight? How would you feel if you lost weight and made both yourself and your husband happy? Do you want to please your husband in this way?"

Another example might be a client who says, "I want to go to college because my parents want me to." We could follow up with, "Do you want to go to college? Do you feel like if you went to college, you would resent your parents, or would it make you happy to go?"

As we have these discussions with our clients, we must be careful not to immediately think it is bad that someone is doing something for someone else. Maybe this will make them happy; maybe it won't. The client knows the answer. For this reason, we do not advise as a coach. We wouldn't tell our client whether they should lose the weight or go to college. Instead, we would ask great questions to help our client identify and then achieve the good goals they desire.

The Global vs. Specific Meta Program

The next meta model involves global versus specific learning styles—in other words, taking in the big picture versus focusing on every detail. Clients who see things from a global perspective are interested in the end results and usually don't want to waste time on the small details, while clients who are more specific in their focus may want to review every line in the contract.

Both the big picture and the details are important for our client to consider. But the method of approach we use with our client will be based on their learning style and state of mind as they share with us their dreams and goals. Remember, our goal is to establish and keep rapport, so we must first meet them where they are at.

For example, if the client begins sharing with us their big dreams, this is a sign we are dealing with someone who is thinking of the global, big picture. In such a case, we want to listen and allow them to speak. If we were to interrupt them and say, "Let's get to the details on that," we would break rapport with them—and the result would be that they would feel discouraged from sharing their dreams. The details might even overwhelm them at this stage, making it seem difficult or even impossible to achieve their dreams.

But as we allow them to completely share with us their big dream, we can encourage them along the way. We can let them know through rapport that we believe in them and their ability to achieve their goals. We will not only win favor with our client as their supporter, we will also be showing them that they can accomplish what they put their mind to doing. When they feel encouraged and ready to move toward their goal, we will have the opportunity to discuss the details and steps they will take to get there. As coaches, we can help them discover the specific steps they will take through asking great questions when the timing is right.

Now, on the other hand, if we have a client who is very detail-oriented, they may begin sharing with us a bunch of details. At times, we may not even see the big picture clearly because they started to discuss the little steps and finer points of things. When this occurs, we must take care to remember that we as coaches are the servants to our clients. We follow the practice of rapport, allowing our client to share all the details. This allows them to feel heard and validated. Then, when the timing is right, we can begin to ask questions to discover the big picture.

Again, both the big picture and the fine details are important. One is not better or worse than the other. Both are needed to reach our goals. We just meet our clients where they are at with their learning meta model. The first step is to see *their* picture in order to gain rapport. Then we can get to the specific details or the global big picture, and then we gently begin to lead them toward success.

The Once vs. Several Times Meta Program

The final learning style we will take a look at is how our clients like to be communicated with. Do they prefer to be told something once or several times?

Think of your own learning style. Do you need to be told something more than one time? Or do you prefer to mark your calendar and only have something mentioned once? Maybe it bothers you if someone is repeating something often to you. It may feel like nagging to you.

This is what we do not want to do with our clients. We want to hold them accountable and yet not nag. So, it is important to learn their preference. As we communicate with them in the way they respond to best, we are maintaining rapport and being supportive, leading them toward accomplishing what is good and godly in their lives. Accountability is a vital part of success, as it keeps us on track and focused.

To help us identify the communication style our client prefers, we simply ask. We might ask, "How often would you like me to remind you of that?" or "Shall I check in with you about this once a day, once a week, or once a month?" This form of respect is helpful in keeping rapport with our client. We are also modeling this respect for them, which helps them to understand how they might use this approach with others, such as their children or spouse.

When we understand how someone thinks and learns, we are able to communicate better with them and also help them to achieve their goals faster. As a coach, we may find it helpful to mark the dates on the calendar and establish the reminders with our client's agreement in order to not bother them and yet, at the same time, help them move toward their goal by creating accountability check-ins on a schedule that seems good to them.

Using the Meta Models to Help Clients

As we work with our clients, we will discover that these meta models may overlap or work together to help create results. We'll be able to recognize areas where the client is out of balance and lead them to greater balance and greater joy.

For example, I worked with a client who was dealing with strong depression. He was sleeping until four in the afternoon. When he shared with me his situation and his goals, he expressed that he wanted to move away from feeling depressed. But he was so focused on moving away that he couldn't see clearly what he wanted to move toward. So, I began to ask him questions to help lead him from moving away to moving toward. What were some passions he could dream about accomplishing or making time for?

I also asked if he thought it would be useful for me to make some suggestions, and if so, we could start small, such as setting a goal to get up at nine a.m. Focusing on a specific, small detail (getting up at an earlier time) rather than the global, big picture (getting over depression) helped him because, in his current depressed state, taking a global focus would have caused him to feel overwhelmed.

This client also had external motivation in the form of his wife, who was trying to help him by pushing him to take many steps to improve his situation. She would try to push him to get up earlier than he desired, for example. But he was not feeling a sense of internal motivation. To create that internal desire to make a change, I asked him how I could simply help him stay accountable. And we discussed what he preferred and what might work best—a single reminder or several. At this time in his life, he agreed that frequent reminders or check-ins could be helpful.

Of course, as the client's situation begins to change, some of these approaches might change as well. For example, he might not need to be reminded of things as frequently as his life becomes more balanced. Or he might begin to set reminders himself in the form of calendar notes or alarms, becoming more internally motivated to get up early out of his own desire to do so apart from his wife's desires. All this is good as our client begins to achieve his goals and become more balanced.

Once we have discovered how our client learns and communicates and their preferences for moving forward toward their goals, we can begin the deep and satisfying work of walking out the path of transformation—reprogramming the mind with God's Word, which is what we discuss in our next chapter.

Chapter 9

REPROGRAMMING THE MIND WITH GOD'S WORD

The words I have spoken to you—they are full of the Spirit and life.
~John 6:63 NIV~

S o far, we have covered a lot of concepts that are essential to becoming a successful coach for Christ. Now, let's dive into the material that really changes the lives of our clients—using God's blessings to reprogram (or "renew") the mind with God's Word. This is the most powerful tool you will use in your coaching practice. Master this skill, and you will create not only a great life for yourself, but you will become a partner with the Lord in helping people change their minds and change their lives as well.

What is God's Blessing?

The term "God's blessing" may sound deeply theological or something out of a sermon, but for the purpose of coaching our clients into a better life, it doesn't have to be complicated. In our daily practice, God's blessing can be as simple as a compliment or a word of encouragement. It may take on the form of a vision statement or a meditation we create for a client to use as they reshape how they think.

In essence, what we are doing for our client is offering a blessing to them in a time of need. We are offering up a godly means to help someone when they are facing something difficult. This is a valuable act because when a client is going through something challenging and feeling vulnerable, they are in need of genuine, godly support. When we are vulnerable, it is harder to bless ourselves.

Think about what happens when we are physically sick. Our bodies become tired, our minds become tired, and we may not have the energy or strength to pray for ourselves. In fact, James 5:16 encourages us to pray for one another for healing for this very reason. Likewise, when we are emotionally struggling or when we are having trouble in our relationships, we can become exhausted by our efforts to stay afloat and handle the stresses we're facing. At such times, we benefit from someone of faith coming alongside us to support us, pray with us, and offer God's blessings to us.

Of course, we can always pray for ourselves and ask God to give us His words of encouragement. But there are times when we need the help of others. The people who come to us for coaching are in a position where they recognize there is some need in their lives that would benefit from our help. By learning how to offer God's blessing to them in a way that is kind, loving, and in line with who God says they already are in His Word, we as coaches are offering our clients the tools they need to overcome what they have been struggling with and move toward what is good in their lives.

Blessings offer our clients hope for their future. It lets them know what God has already given to them and the great things in store for them as they practice godly principles. As we help our clients develop their good and godly goals, we help them to paint word pictures so they can achieve that which is good.

Replacing Lies with God's Truth

Proverbs 18:21 (NIV) says, "*The tongue has the power of life and death, / and those who love it will eat its fruit.*" So, the words we speak over ourselves and others are very important. We must seek to bless others—to speak life.

In biblical terms, to bless is to declare God's truth into someone's life. To bless is to proclaim our God as the good God He is—as the God who desires to bless His children in each area of their lives. Blessing someone means to impart something of value to someone else. When we bless ourselves and others with God's words, we are giving substance to our life and theirs, something we can count on as we move through life.

Offering blessings is something we do for others and also for ourselves. Remember, you are your most important client. Bless and satiate yourself with God's words daily and give yourself daily blessings in your words, thoughts, meditations, and prayers, so that your inner narrator (that inner voice which is talking to you about who you are and what you are experiencing) becomes what God would say to you. As coaches, we have to become healed so we can heal others.

Isaiah 50:4 (NIV) says, "*The Sovereign Lord has given me a well-instructed tongue, / to know the word that sustains the weary. / He wakens me morning by morning, / wakens my ear to listen like one being instructed.*" As Christian coaches, we belong to the Lord who has blessed us and desires to bless others, so we live for Him to bless others through us. As we allow Him to instruct us in what to say and do, we will be well equipped to help our clients.

The Power of Words of Blessing

Words are powerful. They don't just say something; they *make* something. God spoke the word, and the earth was formed. Psalm 33:9 (NIV) says, "*For he spoke, and it came to be; / he commanded, and it stood firm.*" Words create our reality, and they shape how we interact with the world around us.

Let me offer a quick theological note here. Knowing our words are powerful is *not* the same as practicing the "name it and claim it" kind of gospel. At YKI coaching, we walk in sound theology. Though our words matter, we are not little gods, nor will we ever be a god.

What I am speaking about in this chapter is blessing others with our words, speaking to them God's blessings. As coaches for Christ, we are speaking words that God would say to our clients because we are speaking to their true identity in Christ. We are addressing the person that God intended for our client to be. We are helping to give them a new inner narrator, so they can more effectively form their life for His glory. Keep in mind that this doesn't eliminate the need for truth. We have addressed that need in our Five Keys to Success. Once you have established the truth of where your client is at, where they wish to be, and have planned for their good goal, the next step is to offer them a mental picture of obtaining that goal.

Listening for the Blessing to Offer

When we are communicating with our client, we are listening for so much information that will help us identify the godly blessings they need at this moment in their life. This is why the listening skills we have already discussed are so vital. We are listening carefully and thoughtfully for indications of where they are broken, where they hurt, the lies they have believed, and the fears they are facing, along with their learning styles and the goals they wish to achieve—all so that we can be of service to them and help them to receive their purpose.

As we develop great listening skills, we will begin to automatically hear where our client is in need. We will easily learn their language and come to recognize the positive, godly words that are right for us to use when we speak to them.

Our ability to ask great questions also comes into play here. As we ask our clients great questions, we will elicit what they truly need and begin to identify the roots of their issues along with their aspirations. In doing so, we will be able to create for them a new godly narrator, the voice inside of them that can either make or break them. As coaches, we are helping our clients to shape that inner voice, adding beautiful words to their narration so they can achieve their godly destiny.

To help you develop the skill of finding and offering the godly blessing your client needs, I encourage you to use the questions given to you in the appendix for the Circle, which represents each individual's life, including yourself. What you are practicing is the skill of hearing the negative things your client believes, the lies they think, along with their goals and aspirations. As you replace these lies with the truth of who God says they are, along with their desires, you will be developing the blessing to be delivered.

Remember, the list of lies the enemy bids one to believe is endless. The enemy seeks to steal, kill, and destroy us, according to John 10:10. But the only power he has over us is in our mind. If we believe his lies, then he can destroy our life. However, with God's Word, we have the power to conquer any lie and to fill the lacks in our life with His truth! This is why God has said, "*You will know the truth, and the truth will set you free*" (John 8:32 NLT). Remember that truth can be found in every area of our life, not just spiritually. There is a truth to how people are believing and how they are acting. Often, they are acting from a place of hurt because they have believed a lie.

Building our knowledge of godly words will help us to know the true identity of our client—their identity in Christ, as children of God, fulfilling the destiny He has created for them. Just remember that God's words are positive. His words lift and encourage an individual. It is the exact opposite of the negative thoughts and lies that they believe. Here is a list of some of the most common lies our clients believe about themselves, and the corresponding truth from God's Word that replaces each individual lie.

Enemy's Lies	God's Truth
Abandoned	Cherished, cared for
Alone	Connected
Bitter	Forgiving
Failure	Success
Fearful	Faithful, trusting
Incapable	Capable, confident
Indecisive	Stable
Irresponsible	Responsible
Lonely	Loved, connected, accepted
Not good enough	Good enough

Not loved	Loved
Insecure	Secure
Stuck	Productive
Unfocused	Focused
Unsafe	Safe

Here's what this tool looks like when we use it in a coaching session. As we ask our client questions and listen well to their responses, we may hear them say that they feel abandoned. At that moment, we write down the words "cherished" and "cared for" because this is their God-given identity. God cherishes them. He cares for them. This is what is true. If our client is feeling alone, we would write down the word "connected." If they are feeling bitter, we would write down that they are "forgiving." If they mention failure, we write down "success."

As we listen to our client, we take a piece of paper and write down words that are the positive opposites of the client's negative words. Our role as a coach is to write down as many positive word pictures as we can to help our client form a new narration to achieve their goals. These positive words will become a part of their goals, words that encourage them, words that transform their mind according to Romans 12:1-2.

What we are writing down is their blessing. We will use these words of truth to bless our clients, for prayer, for encouragement and direction, for their vision statement, for anchoring, and to form the meditations that we lead our clients through.

Always remember, we must believe in our clients! As coaches, we are not only the hands and feet of Jesus, but also the mouth, speaking the words He would say. He believes in His creation. He believes in us! And with His words, He causes people to reach their greatest potential. Through godly meditation, we can help our clients learn to make God's words a part of who they are.

The Mind-Heart Connection

Knowing the truth is the first step we take to leaving the lies that hurt us behind. We then need to get that information from our mind into our heart, which is where all the issues of life flow forth (Proverbs 4:23). God's words may enter our client's mind and thoughts, but the goal is to get the words into our client's innermost being, their heart. This mind-heart connection is what will turn God's words into reality in their lives.

In the Common English Bible with Apocrypha, there is a verse that says, "*The key to change is the heart*" (Sirach 37:17). From the heart comes belief. This is why God says, "*For the mouth speaks what the heart is full of*" (Matthew 12:34 NIV).

Faith comes by what we hear. "*So faith comes from hearing, that is, hearing the Good News about Christ*" (Romans 10:17 NLT). The problem is many people have heard the wrong message most of their lives. Do you remember our discussion in chapter 6 about the theory of the mind and how beliefs are developed? Over time, many wrong beliefs have developed in our own lives and in our client's lives. To correct the wrong beliefs that have filtered into our hearts over the course of our lives, God says the heart must be circumcised (Deuteronomy 30:6; Romans 2:29). And He is the master surgeon who will do it!

This circumcision of the heart, the work of God in our deepest parts through His words, creates change! Our role as coaches for Christ is to partner with God in this process on behalf of our clients. This is where His Word comes in.

Hebrews 4:12 (NLT) says, "*For the word of God is alive and powerful. It is sharper than the sharpest two-edged sword, cutting between soul and spirit, between joint and marrow. It exposes our innermost thoughts and desires.*" His word will convict us and create within us a changed heart, but we must allow it. And we must hear it often! This is what is so helpful about a qualified Christian coach giving a guided, godly meditation.

I like to say that instead of "brainwashing" (as some people worry a coach will try to do), we as coaches for Christ are helping our clients experience the transforming power of God's Word washing our brain with His love. Through this infusion of His love into our clients' lives, they will not only feel loved, but they will love others as well because the hearing of God's Word has transformed them!

This is so important because so many people are yearning to be blessed! Many people have never heard anyone speak words of blessing that God would say to them. They've never been told positive truths such as, "You are loved. You are my treasure. You are safe and secure." These words are true even for our clients who are not Christian, and because they are true, they are freeing. We can bless our clients, Christian or not, with that which is good, which will in turn bring them to God, since everything that is good is from God.

As we are helping our client to gain a new narrator, it is important to understand that it is not necessary to know where the lies they believed first originated or the details about it. This is one way in which coaching for Christ differs from the work of a secular therapist or psychiatrist. Sometimes, our client will know the root of it and share it with us. Sometimes, they will not know or maybe they will not want to share. And we can respect that. It is not important for us to dig out that fact. It is only important to discover the lie and replace it with truth.

What matters is helping the client to gain a new narrator, a new way of viewing their life and speaking to themselves and about themselves, so that they begin to say and feel that they are cherished, loved, forgiven, forgiving, and every other good thing God says about who they are.

James 1:6-8 talks about the man who is double-minded. He asks but doesn't receive what he asks for because he doesn't believe what God has said. Being double-minded happens when the mind believes something, but the heart hasn't accepted it as real. We don't want our clients to be double-minded; this is what causes failure. When we doubt ourselves or think we are unworthy or not good enough, we will fail even when we want to believe we are good enough.

When both mind and heart are in harmony, that's when change occurs. This is why the head and the heart must be in unison and focused on what God says is true. We must help our clients to focus on everything that is true, good, and lovely (Philippians 4:8). Remember, whatever is good comes from God (James 1:17). Through godly meditation, we help our clients to "experience" being loved, good enough, and doing the good things they desire.

A True Prophecy

When we speak edifying words over our client in the form of a godly blessing, which is what I also refer to as a godly meditation, we are really practicing true prophecy. "*But the one who prophesies speaks to people for their strengthening, encouraging and comfort. Anyone who speaks in a tongue edifies themselves, but the one who prophesies edifies the church*" (1 Corinthians 14:3-4 NIV).

A true prophecy is not something that redirects you. Rather, it is a confirmation of a direction that God has already given to you. He has given every prophecy we will ever need in His Word, the Bible. Like the whole concept of YKI, we believe "you know it." You know somewhere within what God is leading you to do, and so does your client. A true prophecy confirms a truth. Our job as a Christian coach is to speak truth to our clients according to God's Word about who our client is in Christ—to encourage them with the hope of Christ and to let them know He has good plans for them. Like God, we want to give our clients the good desires of their heart because we believe that if their desires are good, then God has placed those desires there in the first place.

Ephesians 4:29 (NIRV) says, "*Say only what will help to build others up and meet their needs. Then what you say will help those who listen.*" As coaches for Christ, we are to bless others and say only what is good and helpful to those with whom we speak.

Using Power Words

How do we speak a true prophecy, something that truly blesses our clients? We use what I refer to as "power words," which are words that influence, persuade, and motivate our client in a positive way. These words are powerful tools for the professional coach. Using them as part of our coaching technique will help us to naturally and easily influence, persuade, and motivate our clients to achieve abundant success.

A power word is a word that plants a positive seed for growth. It helps our client create a vision for a good future. Some examples of power words include:

Abundance, accomplish, achieve, aware, calm, capable, centered, clarity, confident, courageous, create, discover, easily, energized, enhanced, exceed, expanding, experience, focused, generate, grace, harmonious, imagine, immediate, impact, increasing, infinite, insightful, inspired, joyful, loved, naturally, now, peaceful, possibilities, purpose, realizing, self-controlled, strong, thoughtful, trusting, worthy...

And the list goes on! Our vocabulary is so vast that we have many, many positive power words that can encourage our clients to move forward and accomplish much.

Let me give you a brief example of how we can add these words to a godly meditation. Imagine we have a client who is seeking to feel comfortable at her new job and to excel in it. After we have given her the relaxation portion of the meditation, we would then slowly share something like this with our client:

"You are *able* to *easily accomplish* the skills necessary for your new job. Because you are *aware* of what needs to be done, you *create* new ways of doing the task *efficiently*. You are *filled* with *purpose* that *exceeds* your *expectation*, and you are leaving an *impact* for *good* on those around you. You are *inspired* and *naturally gifted*. You are *realizing* more of your skills and life *experience* each day. You are now *filled* with *possibilities* for the future, exemplifying great *grace* and *confidence*."

We would then end the meditation with a post-relaxation time. There are sample meditations available for you in the appendix. (We will look more closely at a sample meditation later in this chapter.)

Did you notice all the power words used in just that brief meditation above? These words, planted into the client's mind and heart, will cause her to excel at her new job. When I create a meditation such as this for a client, I record it so that the client can take the meditation with them and hear these words often. The process of listening over and over to these positive words of blessing help our clients to speed up the process of developing a new narration. Faith comes by hearing (Romans 10:17). Our clients then can "experience" the word pictures in their mind's eye, helping them to achieve success. Learning and knowing happens through experience. We all learn best by experience. In fact, the very word "learned" means you have repeatedly done something in order to know it. When our client repeatedly "experiences" herself doing these things during the meditation, she will learn them faster.

We use power words to fill voids in our client's life. And we continue to add positive power words to our client's new narration in every coaching session.

Depending upon our client and their purpose and goals, we will begin to personalize the words we speak to them, painting a picture for each individual's personal vision statement and God's blessing for their life.

Remember, as Christian coaches, we are filled with the Holy Spirit, and as a result, God will continue to fill us with words for our own narration as well as words for our clients. As we learn to rely on the Holy Spirit to give us vision, we will easily paint a word visual for each client so they can achieve good and godly goals.

Keep in mind, too, that power words and positive statements of blessing can be used not only for meditation, but also for prayer, anchoring, encouragement, and more. This will become a new way of speaking for us as coaches and for our clients, changing our life and the lives around us.

Help Clients Edit Out Poison Words

We've spoken about poison words before, but it bears repeating here because these words may come up in our client's conversations. Remember that some words can poison our minds with discouragement and defeat. Poison words can destroy our confidence, energy, and self-esteem, and we must not meditate on them. We must help our clients not to meditate on them as well.

We must be careful not to plant seeds of doubt or discouragement through our words and our tone of voice. As we offer a meditation to our client, we must be careful to avoid words that could be discouraging, such as: but, can't, could have, if only, maybe, might, have to, don't, never, must, do this, I want you to, you should, you shouldn't, someday, sometime, try, what if, would have, loss.

Keep in mind that poison words are words or phrases that trigger the inability to accomplish a goal. They create regret, depression, suspicion, or mistrust. The list of these negative words is as endless as the list of positive, power words we can use. The context in which we use words is also very important. *Must* could be considered a poison word, and yet we *must* give careful consideration when using any of the words we speak to our client.

For example, the word "loss" is often a poison word, as it causes people to mourn. Even when someone is grieving the death of a loved one, a coach for Christ would be careful not to use this word. Let me give you an example. There was a client who came to our YKI coaching ministry because she was going through great difficulty in her marriage. At the time, she and her husband were separated. One of her friends said to her, "I am so sorry for your loss." This caused great distress in the client, all due to the use of a single word, *loss*.

As we learn to use our words carefully in our coaching, we can find ways to express our thoughts without using poison words. In a case such as the above situation, we can simply say, "I am so sorry." Or if the client is going through any difficulty, we could say, "I am sorry you are going through this." The expression of empathy and understanding remains. What is absent is the use of a word that could be distressing.

Crafting a Blessing for Our Client

When formulating a blessing for our client, we want to make sure that it is worded the way God would speak. We use positive, power words to create our client's meditation. We take care not to include poison words or phrases. Anything negative is to be eliminated. Even stated in a positive way, negative words are not used in a meditation. Remember, God's words fill the empty areas in our lives. So, as coaches for Christ, we want to make sure that the meditation we offer to our client is a powerful affirmative statement about our client's goals, dreams, desires, and life purpose. We want to help our clients to reprogram their subconscious mind, giving them a new narrator that speaks as God speaks.

In addition, a godly meditation uses our client's personal language—meaning we mirror and match the positive words that our client uses, or we use the exact opposite of the negative words and feelings they have expressed to us. We want our words to be as close in context to our client as possible, as it will feel natural to them. This may move us as a coach out of our comfort zone, as the words a client uses may differ from ours, but we are here as servants to our client. Therefore, we use the word that is most closely related to their style. For example, I had a client who used the word "inadequate." This is not a word I normally use, but I used the word "adequate" for her in her blessing as this was the antonym of how she felt, and the word adequate was how she desired to feel.

The meditation's goal is to help the client move toward a goal rather than moving away from their goal. The meditation will use internal motivation and could also use some external motivation when speaking about how loved they are.

When writing a blessing for a client, make sure to only use positive phrases. Write the blessing in the present, the now, as if the client has already experienced this blessing and it is already actively at work in their life.

God Himself follows this approach when He speaks to us. He did this when He called Peter a rock when he was really a coward. He called Gideon a mighty warrior when he was hiding in the wine press. It's interesting that these two became exactly who God called them to be. They heard a truth within their heart and became who they were designed to be.

We do the same with our clients when we speak to their true identity. Blessings are an opportunity for our clients to have us paint a word vision that speaks to their truth. They then can experience the good goals they desire, first in their minds, then in their hearts, then in their lives.

If we write a blessing that is for tomorrow, it feels to our minds as if it hasn't happened. A blessing set in the future does not allow the client the opportunity to experience, right now, how to do things and how to feel things.

For example, if I say to you, "You will be forgiven," you are likely to feel a little hopeless because you want to be forgiven *now*. It is when we experience the good that we become equipped to change and do good. A good choice word for the future is "becoming" because becoming is also happening now, like a rose becoming more fragrant each day. I like to use the word "more" as well; for example: "You are becoming more loving, more patient and more kind each day."

Remember, we are working with our client's conscious choices to help them reprogram their subconscious mind, which will give them a new narrator. Think of it like this: change occurs because one's desire has been captured in one's mind. When our client feels and experiences God's love through us, they will desire more of God and more of His blessings.

Notice the differences between these two statements: "You *will be* loved," versus "You *are* loved." Or, "You *will be* more loving," versus "You *are becoming more loving* each day." Do you sense the difference? One feels like it might happen, one day, hopefully. The other sounds and feels true, right now. We can ground ourselves in what is true right now. This gives us substance to build our lives upon.

As coaches for Christ, we are to be like God. That means we are to call people according to their true identity and bless them with words God would use. This does not mean speaking something that doesn't exist into existence. Rather, we are creating an opportunity for our client to visualize their goals and dreams according to what God's Word, the Bible, already says is true about them. We are offering hope, but not false hope, because we are not proclaiming or prophesying anything over our clients that God has not already said about them. When we bless our clients, we are blessing them according to their true identity, something God has already said about them, such as they are loved, forgiven, and worthy.

Our blessing is based on the good goals our client feels inspired to obtain. Because their goals feel true for them on the inside, as coaches we help them experience their goal during a meditation so they can live out what is already true within. We must trust our client to know and to be inspired if their goal or dream is right for them. Our role is to come alongside and help them to accomplish their godly goals. As long as their goal is not sinful, we trust them to know what is best for them.

How to Give a Blessing

Remember, a blessing can take the form of a godly meditation, a prayer, a compliment, encouragement, and more. It is the new way we are learning to speak to our clients. A blessing can be given anytime, anywhere, for any length of time.

Our clients will benefit from a personalized, recorded godly meditation that they can listen to again and again to encourage themselves and build up their vision for the goals they want to achieve. As coaches, we create these meditations with the purpose and intention of helping our client fulfill their God-given destiny. Write down the godly words you have carefully chosen, play relaxing music, begin with a relaxation portion, and speak out the meditation words slowly to your client. You will end with a post relaxation. This will allow your client the opportunity to renew their mind for that which is good and of God.

The format we use to create the godly meditation, or God's blessing, for our client looks like this:

Step One: Relaxation

We begin with leading the client into a more relaxed frame of mind. The relaxation portion of this process is very important. It allows our client to get comfortable and prepare their mind to receive the positive words we will speak.

Set the tone by turning on soft, slow, instrumental music. It's fine to use what is available through any music channel. Or download music by searching for things like spa or meditation music.

As you lead the client into a relaxed state, speak slowly. (Examples are provided in the appendix.) It has been shown that people are more likely to listen to someone who has a deeper voice, so create a soft, deep tone to your voice. Keep your sound and speech natural, of course, but avoid a high-pitched voice, because high-pitched tones have been shown to create a question in the mind and are not relaxing.

You have the ability to change and alter your voice simply by training yourself to do so. To grow more comfortable using a fitting tone of voice and a slow, steady pace, practice listening to yourself. This is a great skill to learn in general because people will listen to you more when they like the sound of your voice.

Remember, some clients take longer to relax than others. Our words of power and blessing might not be well received until the client has had ample time to relax. By helping our client to relax their body and calm their mind, we can speak to their spirit more directly, allowing the Holy Spirit to work better in their life. Also keep in mind that because we are body, mind, and spirit, many of our client's ailments will be relieved by merely blessing them with God's words of relaxation and love.

Step Two: God's Blessing

Begin slowly speaking out the words you have written down for your client's goals. Create the location you have determined for your client to be, painting them with great word pictures, describing in great detail, and using all the senses. Give them word pictures for their purpose, goals, and dreams. Use as many of the six areas of their life as possible to firmly establish all they desire.

Use as much information as you can to create a beautiful, godly meditation that will truly bless your client. Use as many power words as you can to create change and bless their lives. Fill in any void your client is experiencing with words God would tell your client biblically.

This visualization is very important. The more you can mentally help your client visualize their goal coming to pass, the greater their success. This is the same concept as the lemon exercise you did back in chapter 6. Your client will experience their good goals through you. When your client listens to this blessing or meditation, it will reduce self-sabotage and naturally help them to change their lives in a positive way.

Step Three: Post Relaxation

The final portion of the godly blessing or meditation is to bring your client gently back to their present awareness, allowing them a few moments to open their eyes, centering and refreshing them so they can continue their day. Remember your words matter, even in the end. I like to end by allowing the client to take a few inhales and exhales. Then I say, "You are centered in Christ, refreshed and restored, and when you are ready, you can open your eyes."

(There are more examples in the appendix.)

A Final Thought

Every client's meditation is unique to them. It is based on who they are, their true identity. This is what God's blessing, godly meditation, and vision statements are all about. They work by helping our client recognize what is true and experience their good and godly goals, according to God's Word—even those clients who don't yet know God.

We will anchor these concepts in our next chapter, Godly Anchoring.

Chapter 10

THE "I AM" RULE AND GODLY ANCHORING

We have this hope as an anchor for the soul, firm and secure. It enters the inner sanctuary behind the curtain, where our forerunner, Jesus, has entered on our behalf. He has become a high priest forever, in the order of Melchizedek.
~Hebrews 6:19-20 NIV~

In the previous chapter, we discussed how we as coaches can create a godly blessing for ourselves and our clients as a way to help bring out positive changes in our lives. We discussed the concept of choosing the right words to craft that blessing. In this chapter, I will show you how to take those godly blessings and affirm them daily. We must take what we have learned and actively reinforce it on a daily basis, which allows us to continue in the changes we have begun.

133

The Bible tells us, *"As for God, His way is perfect: / the LORD's word is flawless; / he shields all who take refuge in him"* (2 Samuel 22:31 NIV). Christ is perfect, and when we join with Him, we become perfected. Therefore, by equipping ourselves and our clients with our true identity in Christ every day, we are further solidifying the godly blessings we have received in Him. We remain grounded in what is true, so that we can hold onto what we have gained, rather than losing it through disuse and returning to our old, unhealthy thought patterns.

We do this through creating affirmations and anchors that help root us and connect us to who we are in Christ. This identity in Him is who we truly are. We may not always realize it. We may need to be reminded of it often. We need to internalize that truth so we can begin to live it out. But we must start with knowing who He has made us to be.

Coaching our clients, giving them positive affirming words to use in their "I AM" statements, and showing them how to use godly anchoring in a biblical way will help to draw our client to that which is good, which in turn will draw them to God.

The Great "I AM"

To understand who we are and who God has made us to be, we first begin with knowing who God is. In Exodus 3:14, God tells Moses, "I Am who I Am." He is called the "Great I Am." And throughout Scripture, He declares who He is using "I AM" statements. *"I Am the Alpha and the Omega,' says the Lord God, 'who is and who was and who is to come, the Almighty"* (Revelation 1:8 ESV). Jesus is the beginning and end.

God is the great I Am, and we are created by God in His image. *"God created mankind in his own image, / in the image of God he created them; / male and female he created them"* (Genesis 1:27 NIV). He created us to be like Him.

Deuteronomy 31:8 (NIV) says, *"The LORD himself goes before you and will be with you; he will never leave you nor forsake you. Do not be afraid; do not be discouraged."* Because God is the great I Am, we could say this as, "The great I Am Himself goes before us."

Isn't it interesting that the words "I Am" go before us? Jesus goes ahead of us, leads us, cares for us, and makes a way for us. He prays for us, and His prayers are powerful in opening the way ahead of us for good things to come about. (See John 17:20-24 for an example of one of His amazing prayers for us.)

Using Godly "I AM" Statements

Since we are created in the image of God, how we identify ourselves needs to be in alignment with who God says we are. We must therefore be cautious with our words, making sure that who we declare ourselves to be is exactly who God says we are. And since He goes before us, when we use the words I AM, we need to make sure we are declaring that we are who Christ says we are. In this way, we can align ourselves with what is already true according to God's Word, which is something He can bless and bring about. By declaring that we are who He says we are, we are setting ourselves up for success.

This is an important concept because, so often, we as human beings fall into self-sabotage instead. People in general have a tendency to say things like, "I am sad. I am forgetful. I am a loser." Those things are not our true identity in Christ. God never says we are any of those things. Those are expressions of how we feel about ourselves—our self-doubts and self-criticisms. They are not the truth of who God has made us to be.

As Christians, we are taught not to base our sense of self on our feelings. And this is theologically correct. Feelings shift and change; therefore, when we express a feeling, we should name it as such: "I am feeling sad," instead of "I am sad."

Our true self is based on who God has declared us to be, and it is a firm and unwavering truth. We are not our feelings. The problem is humans are very vulnerable to our feelings. We can easily be swayed by what we feel, which can change rapidly. If we or our clients are basing our beliefs about ourselves on who we *feel* we are at any given moment, and if those feelings aren't positive and true, it will hinder our progress toward our good and godly goals.

It's important to consider and be aware of how we are speaking to ourselves and thinking about ourselves. As we've discussed in chapter 9, our narrator (our inner voice) matters because we tend to gravitate toward what we believe about ourselves and begin unconsciously proving ourselves right. On a certain level, we get satisfaction from being able to say, "See? I was right." Therefore, as coaches, our goal is to lead our clients into a pattern of proving themselves right about the positive truths God has declared and not the negative thoughts and feelings that have trapped them in unsatisfying patterns of life.

Colossians 3:9-10 (NIV) says, "*Do not lie to each other, since you have taken off your old self with its practices and have put on the new self, which is being renewed in knowledge in the image of its Creator.*" This means we need to identify ourselves and others in light of the truth of who they were created to be—our true identity. We do this both in words and actions.

Therefore, we must teach our clients to know their true identity by using the words that God would use, saying who He would say they are, teaching them to anchor themselves in what is true. What would He say? We find those "I AM" statements in the Bible. We teach our clients to declare who they are in Christ, according to God's Word: "I am an overcomer. I am worthy. I am joyful in the Lord. I am forgiving. I am loving."

Let us encourage our clients to identify themselves with who God says they are. To help with this, in the appendix, I have included a list of words with Scriptures on our true identity in Christ. And there are many great Christian resources you can use as well. For example, a great book on identity is Neil T. Anderson's *Who I Am in Christ*. Make use of such resources as well as this book to help craft godly blessings and affirmation statements for your clients to use.

The Power of Godly Affirmations

Godly blessings are tools we use as coaches to speak positive truths over our clients. Hand in hand with the godly blessing is a tool we can teach our clients to use over themselves— godly affirmations.

In secular terms, affirmations are words we speak over ourselves to foster positive thinking and beliefs. But as Christians, when we use godly affirmations, we are doing more than simply saying good things about ourselves. We use affirmations that are based in what God says about us in His Word, the Bible.

So, they are *already* true. We are agreeing with what is already true for us so that we can begin to change our thinking and our mental patterns.

Simply put, our godly affirmations, expressed with faith, are a way to anchor ourselves in Christ. As we anchor ourselves in His truths about who we are, it is easier for us to keep our minds steady on the Lord. This helps us to maintain our healing process and keep our focus as we move forward into our good and godly goals. The more we call out in others their true identity as God has created them to be, the more they will desire to become those things. They will also thirst after what we have to say.

Before we get deeper into how we share godly affirmations with our clients, it's important to place it in proper theological context. Using affirmations is not a "name it, claim it" approach to life. Nor is it a "fake it until you make it" philosophy. These truths depend fully on what God has already declared to be true. They aren't something we have to force into being. But they are also something that we cannot and would not have without God.

Ultimately, we are dependent upon God for all the good things in our lives. He is the source of all that is good. Second Corinthians 3:5-6 (NIV) reminds us, "*Not that we are competent in ourselves to claim anything for ourselves, but our competence comes from God. He has made us competent as ministers of a new covenant—not of the letter but of the Spirit; for the letter kills, but the Spirit gives life.*" The source of all we accomplish is God! As coaches, and as our own clients, we do well to remember this in all we do.

Because of Jesus's sacrifice, we have been freed from the penalty of death. Remembering His sacrifice on the cross and all that He has done for us will keep our focus on Jesus! It is only because of Him that we are not only freed from death and sin, but we are made perfect through Him. "*I am the vine; you are the branches. If you remain in me and I in you, you will bear much fruit; apart from me you can do nothing*" (John 15:5 NIV).

In other words, we were not created to live apart from God. And it is only through God's Holy Spirit living within us that we are able to be or do anything of true value. The right intent and the purpose of bringing our client to the Lord is something we must adhere to when teaching our client to anchor themselves with I AM statements! Remember, pride is what will cause one to fall. The goal is not to get the client thinking about who they are in themselves—which creates pride—but who they are when grounded in God, which leads to truth that sets us free.

"I AM" Statements Apply to Non-Christians Too

At times, we will have clients who are not Christians. The good news is our clients do not need to be Christian in order for us to teach them how to apply godly principles to bless their lives. God's principles are true, no matter who is using them. They work for everyone. Givers will receive back. Sowers will reap. Speaking a kind word helps turn away wrath. These godly principles are always true.

This gives us confidence as coaches. When we know godly principles that lead to good, we can guide any client to those principles, no matter their current spiritual beliefs. These principles work because they were created by God!

As a coach, we adapt to where our client is at right now, and we help them grow in their godly identity. If the client is not a Christian, that is okay; we can teach them the use of I AM statements and anchoring anyway, without Christianizing it. We simply remove the Christian terminology that might trip them up, so they can begin to experience good things in their lives.

Though we do not use Christian language for nonbelievers, it is okay to teach them to say things like, "I am loved. I am forgiven." We can teach them such expressions because they are true about our client. Remember that Jesus died for sinners, the ones who didn't yet accept Him, because He loved them!

It is also okay to teach our clients to say any of the positive I AM statements for the purpose of anchoring themselves to those positive feelings. In this way, we will be helping our clients to gain positive, good beliefs about themselves so they can achieve success. As they develop confidence and begin to walk in God's love toward themselves and others, their lives will improve. The more our client achieves success, the more they will trust us and allow us to speak into their life, opening the way for us to share the good news of Jesus Christ and the gospel.

Helping Our Clients Discover Who They Truly Are

How do we identify the right I AM statements to encourage our clients to focus on? After all, our goal as coaches is to help them reach their specific goals. This means their I AM statements, meditations, godly blessings—all of these tools—should be personalized to fit the individual client and meet them where they are at in their lives.

Using the skills you learned earlier on the subject of asking great questions and listening will help you to discover your client's true identity and purpose, even if your client does not yet know what their true identity is. As you attentively listen to their responses, you will find out about their passions and dreams, and discover their skills and life experiences, along with some characteristics they would like to develop.

Here are some starter questions you can use to help your client discover their true identity. We can ask them in a coaching session, or we can encourage them to use these questions in their personal time.

- Who are you as a person?
- What do you like to do?
- What passions do you have?
- What thoughts and patterns do you have?
- What thoughts and patterns would you like to have?
- Who did God create you to be?

As we listen attentively to their answers to questions such as these, we can hear both how they see themselves right now and how they would like to see themselves in the future. We can then guide them into creating I AM statements that express where they want to go.

For example, a client may say, "I am a poor decision-maker. I would like to be a better decision-maker." For this client, we might create I AM statements based on James 3:17: "I am wise and gentle. I know what I need to do." For a Christian, we might add, "I am wise and gentle because the Holy Spirit lives within me."

In addition to creating a specific set of I AM statements that bless our client's specific needs and goals, we can also add general positive encouragements about how God sees them. Remember, people long to hear words of love. Our world is starving for grace and God's love. And whether a client is Christian or not, it is still true that they are loved, accepted, and created in the image of God.

The Concept of Anchoring

Once we have created the I AM statements for our clients, we can then guide them in the process of using these statements to anchor themselves. Anchoring is an NLP technique that encourages the association between an internal response and an external trigger. By learning to associate an external action with an internal thought, we can use that external action to prompt us to think a certain thought or feel a certain feeling we desire to think and feel.

Because anchoring is a way to retrieve a positive emotion, it is a powerful tool we can use to help our clients get back to a state of confidence, peace, and power. We all have a God-given ability to visualize and prepare ourselves for success in addition to a personal power that resides within us.

When used properly, anchoring can help our client to quickly switch over to a positive state, such as content, peaceful, and relaxed. It is an effective tool that helps our clients move out of the thoughts and behavior patterns they wish to change so they can move toward the goals they have.

Remember, feelings are powerful. They were given to us by God for a purpose. Feelings can tell us when we are in situations that need to change, and they can persuade us to act in certain ways. The problem is that the subconscious mind replays our feelings from past negative situations, even if the situation has changed. For example, if we have experienced a frightening situation, we may feel that fear long after we have returned to safety.

For example, I had a client who was attacked one night in a parking lot. She was able to lock herself in her car, call for help, and be rescued. Fear was a reasonable emotion at the time. The experience was traumatic, and even though she made it out safely, her subconscious mind continued to reproduce the fear in an attempt to keep her safe. For this client, I helped her to divinely "edit" her inner narration. I also gave her I AM statements that she was safe, protected, and at peace, and then taught her to anchor herself with these words so that she was no longer experiencing fear in situations when the fear was unwarranted.

God created our feelings. We just need to be master over those feelings and decide how we want and need to feel. We want our feelings to work for us. Anchoring helps us achieve this.

The secular concept of anchoring is to think of a positive thought, such as "I am capable and successful," as we touch an area of our body, such as our ear. That way, we can begin to connect touching our ear with the positive thought. The more we follow this same process, the more automatic it will be for us to think of ourselves as capable and successful whenever we touch our ear.

As coaches for Christ, we adapt this technique by using what I call godly anchoring, which makes use of anchoring the thoughts that focus on our true identity—which is who God says we are! We do this because according to the Bible, our true God-given identity is what keeps us grounded and rooted into His truth, which is what yields growth and fruit. So, we use our true identity as given to us by God to anchor ourselves in Christ. This gives us a sense of peace and strength as we move toward new goals, and it helps us to better receive God's blessings.

Using Our Senses to Anchor Ourselves in Christ

YKI's method for helping clients develop their personal power uses a Christ-centered approach. We have been blessed with senses by God, and we can use our senses in a godly way to take our thoughts captive and honor the Lord by anchoring ourselves in Him. As Christians, we understand that thoughts can either work for us or against us, so we must take them captive and make them obedient to Christ (2 Corinthians 10:5). Godly anchoring helps us to do this in a tangible, practical way.

Therefore, when it comes to anchoring techniques, we instruct our clients to anchor their positive, godly I AM statements by using the palms of their hands as their external, physical anchoring trigger.

The reason we have chosen the inside of our palms as a way to anchor is that it helps us to remember the nails driven into Jesus's hands as He died for us. Because of His death on the cross, when we accept Him as Lord, we have been made perfect through Him. Touching our hands is a reminder of this. We touch the center of our palms to remind ourselves of the Lord's crucifixion and everything it means to us. *"And the people all tried to touch him, because power was coming from him and healing them all"* (Luke 6:19 NIV). Because Christ lives in us, practicing this simple exercise will help us to remember that God lives within us and is ever present as we touch our palms and remember His touch is in our lives.

Using the hands as our anchor position is also helpful because we can use essential oils to lock in the sense of smell too, further anchoring the thoughts and feelings that we desire to have. The sense of smell is closely linked with memory. When we smell something, it takes us right back to the feelings we had when we experienced that smell before. Therefore, when we anoint ourselves with a certain scent and then anchor ourselves with I AM statements, every time we smell that scent in the future, we will be reminded of who we are in Christ. This anchors us further into His likeness.

Using the sense of smell that God gave to us in this way creates a positive trigger and helps us to reprogram our minds. It is a very powerful tool that we can teach to our clients, which further perpetuates their success.

We also use the sense of internal sight and our imagination to help create an anchor. We do this by helping a client to envision what their life looks like or what a specific situation in their life looks like when they are anchored, relaxed, and confident.

Even if our client is not a Christian, we can still teach them to anchor in the palm of their hands so they too can experience that which is good. I had a client who was not a Christian who I taught this method of anchoring to. Her desired goal was to feel more secure in herself. "Secure" was her choice word (along with other positive words), so I used her desired feeling to help her create I AM statements that would be meaningful to her. She would say the words, "I am secure," (and more) while anchoring in the palms of her hands with her scent of rosemary, which she loved. She became very confident and felt more secure in herself through this process.

This client later came to know the Lord through our coaching. After that, the anchoring process done in her palms had a much greater meaning to her. She then understood more clearly her security in Christ and also how anchoring in the palms connected her with all Christ had done for her on the cross. This was an exciting and joy-filled experience! It is what I live for as a coach!

It is so exciting to teach our clients to use this tool to anchor themselves with positive words, vision, and emotions, especially when they are moving into a new comfort zone. For example, anchoring can be very effective when a client is facing something that can be anxiety provoking, such as when they are getting ready to speak publicly and want to calm themselves with their good vision and emotions for speaking, when they are going to court and need to feel at peace, or when they are planning a move or interviewing for a new job and want to feel calm instead of tense. This godly anchoring will reduce self-sabotage and help your client to change their mind so they can change their life and accomplish their goals.

What the Act of Anchoring Looks Like

Some people have never experienced a state of personal power or the feelings of confidence. This is where we as their coach will help them develop and tap into their own vision to develop the feelings of confidence, peace, and safety that will help them move toward their goals and gain success.

In godly anchoring, we are leading our client through several steps that help them to visualize how their life will be different as they are anchored in Christ. We guide them in recognizing their true identity, using their imagination to create the true feelings of security in Christ. We encourage them to embrace the feeling of security and their vision of it and hold on to it through anchoring it in the palm of the hands. We encourage them to imagine themselves constantly anchoring themselves in Christ. As they do so, they visualize, listen, and feel in the clearest detail how different things are when we know Christ is with us.

For my own personal use, I use the same oil each day, creating a consistent trigger of good thoughts in my life. I place the oil in the palm of my hand, remembering Jesus Christ and all He has done for me. I smell the oil, and then I speak out loud my prayer of thanks to the Lord. I begin stating my true identity and the thoughts, feeling, and characteristics I wish to have.

During this process, I also like to visualize the cross and remember the relationship I have with the Lord, as He is first in my life. I visualize this vertical relationship between He and I, and I see myself as a clear vessel for the Lord to pour into. I then visualize the cross extending out horizontally and imagine that love I have been given from God extending out to others.

Anchoring Script

Here is a sample of what anchoring looks like. It may be adjusted in ways that fit with the client's specific situation and goals.

Anoint the palms of your hands with your preferred essential oil…

Breathe in this smell to anchor your mind with the sense of smell and the feelings you desire, thinking of Christ and all He empowers you to be. Affirm yourself with your desired feelings: "I am loved, content and at peace. I am filled with God's Holy Spirit that empowers me. I am kind, forgiving, and filled with His love … etc."

Move into visualization…

Visualize yourself as a clear vessel with God pouring into you all the words of life that He has for you. Visualize whatever it is you desire to do. Speaking kindly to your family, forgiving others, speaking at your meeting, conducting yourself with grace … etc.

Next, move into the anchoring process…

Press into the palms of your hands as you continue to visualize all you wish to achieve. Visualize all the details of how you are feeling, looking, standing, moving. Whatever is before you, you will experience it with ease, confidence, and strength. Embrace this feeling, and visualize yourself with this feeling.

Now, imagine a time in the future when you will want to activate this feeling. You are stepping out of your comfort zone into a situation that in the past may have been uncomfortable. Maybe you are on stage. Maybe you are before an authority figure, or maybe you are taking an exam … Now, imagine the feeling and vision that you anchored earlier.

For a Christian client...

I anchor this feeling by touching the inside of my palms to remember everything that Christ has done for me. He has overcome the world and given me power through the cross and the Holy Spirit who now lives within me.

As a Christian, we imagine Christ going before us, everything He has done for us, and that with Him, all things are possible. Use your anchor and activate it now. That's right ... Remember exactly how you felt, and what you imagined, heard, and saw as you increase your vision even more. Maybe you feel yourself sitting or standing taller. You feel more alive as you feel the strength, the confidence, the energy, the enthusiasm wash over your entire being.

God has given you this power as a believer in Jesus Christ.

This is an amazing process. By touching your anchor, you are creating a trigger to remind you of who you are. You can activate this godly power anytime and then walk into any situation knowing you will be at your personal best, powerful, and strengthened in Christ. By using your anchor, you will experience the confidence and power that you have discovered. Activate this state of godly power and you'll be able to easily and naturally handle whatever comes your way with confidence and enthusiasm!

Traumatic Triggers and Flashbacks

Before we close out this chapter, let's talk about traumatic triggers and flashbacks. I've mentioned triggers in the discussion on godly anchoring as a positive thing. It's important to note that some triggers can actually be good and useful to us. When we smell our chosen essential oil during anchoring, we are triggered positively into the good thoughts, the positive I AM statements, and vision of success that we have worked hard to create for ourselves or our clients.

Of course, triggers can also be associated with negative experiences. I'm not talking about small issues here, but trauma. It's important to distinguish between these two things. We can all fall into negative speech patterns. We all have "buttons" that, when pushed, cause us to react in not so good ways.

Triggers from trauma are more extreme than this button-pushing reaction. Triggers are a response to something environmental that occurred when something disturbing happened. It's the event that causes us pain, but it becomes associated with something sensory.

Here are some examples of negative sensory triggers:

- Sight — someone resembles the abuser, objects, colors
- Sounds — raised voices, whispering, sirens, whistling, words
- Smell — tobacco, foods, odors, alcohol
- Touch — anything resembling abuse, standing close, approach, animals
- Taste — anything related to abuse, foods, alcohol, spices

All of these senses can be reprogrammed to allow the client to think of something good. This takes diligent work but can certainly be done.

We must always honor our client and understand how real flashbacks are for them. Help them to be patient with themselves and nurture and care for themselves. Allow them to take the time to recover. Sometimes flashbacks are very powerful. Teach them to give themselves time to make the transition from any form of trauma, even if it has been years. Just continue to have vision for your client that they will be victorious, and they will heal completely.

God gave us a memory for a reason—to protect us. Sometimes it is helpful to remember that something bad has happened and could happen again. And sometimes we are safe and need not worry or fear, yet our mind is working against us to create worry and fear anyway. Traumatic triggers and flashbacks may plague the mind of a client, and we must understand how to address them.

As we learned earlier in the theory of the mind, our brain can and does change. It is our job as coaches to help our clients to reprogram the brain so that it can think good, healthy thoughts. We have the ability to use our memory for good and God's glory. The key is to take the things that negatively trigger an individual and help them to create a positive trigger out of it. This is what I like to refer to as divine editing!

The Power of Divine Editing

As Christians, we realize that true power comes from the Lord and His Holy Spirit. As we work with people and meet them where they are at, we can help them to realize their God-given power so they can align themselves with His will in order to live a balanced, Christ-centered life. Learning to visualize is a way to help our client into not just a state of mind, but a state of being, where they can comfortably, easily, and naturally walk through something that might have in the past caused them anxiety and stress or led to a fight or flight response.

Remember, triggers can be positive or negative. People who have been traumatized have negative triggers. When we are helping our clients to anchor themselves in Christ, we are creating a positive trigger for them. We do this by using the senses of touch, smell, sight, hearing, and even taste so our clients can be empowered to move toward what is good. Through divinely helping them to edit their triggers, we equip them so that when they find themselves in a situation that once caused them to feel distressed, they will now have affirmative feelings instead because of the positive triggers that have been created.

For example, if someone was hurt while hearing an alarm, every time they hear that alarm, they become negatively triggered. We can help them to create a positive trigger for the alarm that will instead help them to feel safe. No longer will they feel traumatized each time they hear the sound, but instead they will feel protected. This allows them to move forward instead of remaining stuck.

To create this positive trigger, we begin by asking the client what good and helpful things they do know about an alarm. Get them to fill in the blanks with as many positives as possible. When needed, we can offer a suggestion and see if they agree with it. We will use these new, powerful, and true words to establish their new positive trigger and narration. At this time, we teach them the I AM tool and anchoring, as well as offer them a guided, godly meditation.

The really great news is that just by filling their mind with their true identity and with words like, "You are courageous, safe, content, and at peace," they will begin focusing on the good in their life and heal naturally.

Using Compartmental and Enmeshed Thinking for Good

Compartmental and enmeshed thinking are great tools to understand, especially when dealing with trauma and reprogramming the brain. Both can be used for good or bad, so let's take a closer look at how we can use them productively.

Enmeshed thinking is like wires that all connect. Each emotion and thought one has is connected, and so they move into every area of our lives. Here's an example of using enmeshed thinking that is harmful in our life: If we have experienced a terrible event and begin associating other people and situations with the event, we are enmeshing the negative in our life. This type of thinking indicates a need for healing in a particular area so that we can learn to compartmentalize the trauma, put it away, and live a healthy and whole life.

Here's another example: A client's husband has an affair; she discovers that the woman had blonde hair. Now, when the client turns on the news and sees a reporter with blonde hair, she is hurt and angry. This client is no longer watching the news or considering the reporter for who she is; instead, the client is enmeshing the reporter with past grievances that are totally unrelated to her. This is unhealthy enmeshed thinking.

There is a positive and healthy way to use enmeshed thinking, however. For example, let's use our belief in God. If it is enmeshed into every area of our lives, we will have great integrity, and like wires entwining themselves into every fiber of our being, we will act according to our belief in God. We can take positive words that God gives us and enmesh them into every area as well. If your client is a nonbeliever, you can teach them the concept of positive words enmeshing throughout their life.

Compartmental thinking is different. Just like its name indicates, it puts everything into compartments. An example of an unhealthy compartmental way of thinking is going to church on Sundays and then on Wednesdays doing something contrary to your Sunday beliefs. Here's another example: A client gets married, and they see their spouse as being someone they love and care for when they are at home. Yet when they are away, they no longer think about home at all, which affects their decisions in unhealthy ways, such as having an affair.

As with enmeshed thinking, there is a healthy way to use compartmental thinking too. For example, with trauma, a client may work hard to move forward and be free of the trauma's effects. After the client has gone through healing, they can use compartmental thinking to place that traumatic event in a single compartment where it belongs, thus separating it from their current life.

Identifying trauma from childhood dysfunction and compartmentalizing it can help a client to live a healthy and fulfilled life.

Of course, as mentioned earlier, healing is first necessary so the client can successfully compartmentalize the trauma. When working with our clients, we allow them to process by discovering the impact that abuse had on their lives. As they discover truth and recognize their true identity and value, they can then move toward the goals they have for their lives in each area, including and especially emotional wellness. You can learn more about this in my upcoming book, *Complete Healing from Any Form of Abuse.*

Both compartmental and enmeshed thinking in their positive form can be adapted in many areas of an individual's life. This can help the client enjoy God's greatest blessings of complete healing and wholeness. These techniques, along with I AM statements, godly anchoring, God's blessings, and our other coaching tools, help us to use God's words to reprogram the mind and create a new narration in our client's thinking. This is what transforms an individual, bringing them great success and the abundant life God intended!

Chapter 11

HOW THE YKI METHODS
WORK TOGETHER

And we know that all things work together for good to those who love God,
to those who are the called according to His purpose.
~Romans 8:28 NKJV~

N ow that we have taken a look at the individual tools we use as coaches
for Christ in working with our clients, it's time to examine the ways
in which all of these YKI coaching methods work together for good
in actual coaching sessions. These tools weave together to create a tapestry that
helps people grow, move toward what is good and godly, and gain success that
makes their lives better. Together, YKI methods create a balanced life filled with
passion and vision for our futures.

Keep in mind that as we coach our clients over the course of time, they will continue to grow and find new areas of their lives to work on. Our client's needs are going to change day by day and week by week, so we will often circle back to the various tools and techniques we've learned throughout this book, revisiting them whenever needed.

We will constantly be discovering new truths about ourselves as we grow, and our clients will experience this same thing. They will learn new truths about themselves, and they will need to set new goals based on what they learn. As we work with them through this process of new growth, we will utilize all of the YKI methods in new ways, adjusting to their latest discoveries and goals as we help our clients accomplish more and more successes. The YKI methods are designed to adapt to these changes, which are a natural part of life and coaching.

As our clients achieve success, we celebrate with them and help them to continually grow by reevaluating their lives and learning new truths, thus establishing new goals. This creates an ongoing circle of positive changes and experiences with many blessings that they can share with others. In this way, the YKI coaching methods allow us the opportunity to maintain a professional relationship with our clients, allowing them to reap the benefits of having a coach who will continue to grow and adapt to their changes and experiences as they reap the abundant life God intended.

Let's look at some of the practical aspects of how to set up our coaching sessions for success.

How to Organize a Coaching Session

Now that we've reviewed how the YKI method, its tools, and its techniques work together to help our clients move toward that which is good and godly, we can look at the structure of how a coaching session is shaped. These sessions are the "meat" of coaching. This is where we help our client to strategize which goals to tackle first, devise a plan, conquer obstacles, and stay focused on the tasks at hand. It's imperative that we keep our client motivated, inspired, and wanting to move forward.

As we gain more experience coaching, we will learn how to be intuitive and flexible according to our client's needs. Here is a basic structure for our approach to coaching for Christ. First, we establish rapport. Then we do the client evaluation, set goals, and discover their purpose. We establish the Five Keys to Success, form a new narration, teach the I AM Rule, and teach godly anchoring. Next, we offer a godly meditation and then continue to coach and offer new ways for our client to grow!

Now, let's take a look at the professional aspect of coaching and learn how to manage the timing and activities of our hourly sessions with our client. Overall, I recommend timing each session as follows:

First 5-10 minutes — Develop rapport. Remember, rapport is the most important element to establish in any given session with a client. Take time to say hello, ask how things are going, find out what's new, etc.

Next 30 minutes — Walk your client through the evaluation. This should be a natural conversation and will continue each week. Through this practice, you will gain the information necessary for their godly meditation that will edify and encourage them. Remember to ask great questions, listen to what your client is saying, and take notes of what you are hearing your client say. Consider: What need do they have? Where do they lack? In what areas can I bless them so they can get closer to their true identity? What is their vision for their goals and dreams? Write these things down in as much detail as possible! I create a section in my client file entitled "Meditation," and I continue to add words and goal setting information in this section during each session with my client.

At the 40-minute mark of the session, schedule the next appointment. Never leave the session without having a future appointment set. It is often most convenient to do it at this point of the session, so it is done and there is nothing else to concentrate on but the final meditation period.

The final 20 minutes — This time is spent on godly meditation and prayer with a Christian client or meditation and visualization with a non-Christian client. This is a time to deliver positive, encouraging words that leave the client in a good place as they leave the session and continue along with the rest of their day.

Keep in mind, timing is important! As we guide the session, we must make sure our client feels important and cared for, yet we must also stay on time. This can be difficult on occasion, but time *must* be managed. We are training our client as we also stay on task. If we run over the hour-long session, their time is not respected, and neither is our own. Be sure to end the session within an hour.

By the way, this structure for listening and engaging with others works for more than our clients. It is also a wonderful way to interact with any friend or family member. We might spend less than an hour with our personal relationships or even more than an hour at times. But if we will follow the structure of developing rapport, catching up, listening and gaining information, and then encouraging and blessing them, we will find our relationships with friends and family thriving, which will, in turn, help us to thrive!

Working with a New Client

When we first begin working with a new client, we are laying the groundwork for a successful ongoing client relationship. It's so important to spend time developing rapport, especially in our first few sessions. This enables us to build trust with our client.

These early sessions are also where we are first giving the client their evaluation, walking them through the Circle. We are getting to know our client for the first time, and our first objective is to find out where the client is at and where they wish to go. Our listening skills need to be sharp and ready. Note taking is crucial. We will be listening to not only the words that they say but also listening for the underlying beliefs, messages, and thoughts that they might be holding onto. We are listening for their purpose and goal. As we do so, we are keeping biblical principles that apply to our client in mind, all while remembering that we do not counsel!

As we get to know our clients, we can then help them discover goals for each area of their lives. Many people have not yet identified their objectives, as they are still unclear about where they are at in life. Therefore, it is important to be patient with the process and keep rapport as your number one objective until you can establish their goals.

Ongoing Sessions with the Client

Once we have worked through the initial client evaluation, our ongoing sessions with our client allow us to continue with the Five Keys to Success. We continue to gain additional information, discover new truths, set additional goals, and plan. We hold our clients accountable as they work toward their goals and then celebrate success with them as we help them learn how to give back.

This process will be ongoing as we continue to help our client to set new goals. We offer them new godly meditations, use relevant I AM statements, and teach our clients how to anchor themselves with their new positive narration. This process of further anchoring our client's godly identity into their heart and establishing a new way of thinking and speaking for them is continual.

In these ongoing sessions, we continue to help our client to find their purpose. We do this through practical activities in each session that help our client grow. This includes encouraging them to reflect on their week. Did they do their homework? If not, what kept them from doing it? What has changed for them during the week?

As we listen and ask questions, we look for patterns in their thinking and behaviors, discerning when to push and when to offer grace. We stay focused on their best interests. We encourage them to stay focused on their global picture while looking at the specifics in each area. We help our client to see the positive, offering new perspectives and feeding them godly principles. And we lead them in godly meditation and prayer.

Setting Goals with Clients

When setting goals with a client, keep in mind that the client's goal needs to be focused and very specific. Their goal needs to be attainable, meaning it must be possible and practical. Their goal needs to be internally motivated, meaning it must come from them, not us. We cannot set goals for other people because we cannot control them. Goals can only be set for oneself. Our client's goal must be trackable, meaning that we can create action steps with them that can take the form of homework, which can then be checked to see if it has been done.

Remember, a client's God-given purpose drives the goal they will pursue. As a coach, we help our client to discover the purpose behind their goals, which will help them to stay focused. This is what makes Christian coaching so powerful! It speaks to the true identity of an individual and their higher purpose.

Remember, the more questions we ask in our coaching sessions, the more we will know and the more we will be able to help our client establish new godly goals, creating balance and success in each of the key areas of their life. We will continue to develop new godly goals for our client as we see them regularly.

Delivering God's Blessing Through Meditation

Once we have gained information about our client, developed at least one goal for our client to work on, written down many words of encouragement and written down great details for them to visualize themselves succeeding, it is then time to deliver a godly meditation for our client to help them renew their mind and gain their new narrator. The meditation that we develop for our client should include the purpose of their goal.

During this phase, we help our client to understand the importance of spending time visualizing their goals each day. We ask them if they would be interested in having us offer them a godly guided meditation. I have not had a client say no yet! Most everyone is in need of taking the time to relax and visualize their success. This will instill hope and will give them great encouragement to succeed! Your personalized meditation will bless your client into success.

Allow your client the opportunity to prepare for their meditation by creating a calming and peaceful environment. Also, enlighten your client about how visualization will help them to renew their mind and develop a new narrator so they can accomplish their godly desires. For their meditation, use relaxing music and remember to speak in a slow, calming, and naturally deep voice.

If your client is not a Christian, stay focused as a coach on their goals, and offer their meditation to them in a way that meets them where they are at. Maybe they don't desire or have time for a meditation, so instead you offer them a vision statement to keep them focused on their goals, making them real and possible in their mind's eye. This will elevate their comfort zone and raise the bar on what they can accomplish. As we continue to speak of that which is good, we will help our client to achieve success, while staying within godly boundaries.

Have fun and enjoy the meditation that you are offering to your client! I am blessed each time I deliver a meditation for my client. "*The one who blesses others is abundantly blessed; / those who help others are helped*" (Proverbs 11:25 MSG).

Preparing the Client for Success

There are several steps we can take to prepare our clients to be successful after a session is over.

First, remind the client that it is important that they keep regular appointments in order to renew their mind and develop their new patterns. This is the path to change. Make sure to set or confirm your next appointment!

Next, make sure the client is clear about the steps they need to take during the week to move them closer to their goal. Give them homework that will keep them focused on their purpose. Teach them how to use affirmations and anchor themselves to that which is good.

Aim to be a blessing in every session! Now, let's look at an example of a coaching session to see how all these elements work together in real life.

Chapter 12

AN EXAMPLE OF
A COACHING SESSION

But when he, the Spirit of truth, comes, he will guide you into all the truth.
~John 16:13 NIV~

I met with my friend and client, Zoey, to discuss how she is doing and to demonstrate a sample coaching session for you to learn from. If you'd like to know more or see the recorded coaching session, I recommend you sign up for the Christ Centered Coach Training found on my site, *https://ykicoaching. com/coachtraining/*. After you sign up, I highly encourage you to watch the video to observe all the elements of great coaching that we have discussed throughout this book.

When Zoey came to me about six years ago, she was experiencing depression and anxiety. To sum it up quickly for you, she received her complete healing along with the desire of her heart, which was to gain full custody of her daughter, as mentioned in chapter 4. Zoey's life-changing experience through YKI coaching led her to partner with us and to also become one of our board of directors. She believes wholeheartedly in our approach to healing.

Everyone can use a coach in their life, and I am grateful to be Zoey's coach and safe place to turn to when she needs help working through things.

A Deeper Look at a Coaching Session

In the session with Zoey, I first took the time to talk with her about her week. I also asked her permission if we could get started in the evaluation. This allows both coach and client to get into the mind frame of beginning the session, while also establishing good rapport.

Zoey, like most of us, had new things going on in her week. For her, it happened to be fasting. She wanted the opportunity to get closer to the Lord. Many things were opening up for her. I didn't want to rush her as she shared. Even though she was serving as an example client for training purposes, and I wanted to get through the entire evaluation for my audience, I still felt the need for rapport. Following a natural, conversational format, we began with an evaluation of her spiritual life. That is what she was going through for the week, which is why I began there.

I usually do begin in the spiritual area for a client because it gives me great information and a foundation for how I will proceed. But not always. I may make exceptions to this rule as needed to help the client express their most pressing concern at the moment. For example, if a client comes to me stressed about a relationship, I will allow them to share and will take a mental note as well as writing things down in the relationship section. Remember, the goal for any evaluation is to gain information, and you do this through conversation, keeping it as natural as possible each and every time you meet.

Note in the spiritual section of our discussion, I asked Zoey to rate it. In doing so, she filled me in with all the information needed. We established a truth about what she was doing as well as establishing a goal, the purpose, and plan for this area.

If you view the video, you will notice body language and how I mirrored and matched Zoey, how I followed her lead, her mood. When she laughed, I laughed. When she was intent, I was listening. In the session, I did most of the listening. I was mostly quiet and allowed her story to be the main focus.

In our discussion, Zoey shared about her desire to see her daughter baptized, as well as some concerns and pain from her past experiences with her father. Notice that the spiritual section and the relationship section of her evaluation—her life Circle—began overlapping for Zoey. Her overt message was fasting and baptism. Her covert message was the reason for her fasting, which was the pain her dad has caused her most of her life.

I did not assume that was true; rather, I allowed her to speak. She solved her own problem, without me advising her. On her own, Zoey set spiritual goals for herself: reading the Word, getting baptized, spending more time with God. I helped her create a plan of when she would do these things. I allowed the time to feel right for her! She decided to do it at 5 a.m. for thirty minutes. This will be something we can discuss in future sessions to see how well she is sticking with her goal.

We then proceeded to the relationship section for Zoey, where she shared about her daughter in detail. I asked questions to gain clarity. She had a deletion *here*—she said she felt resentment but didn't say who towards, so I clarified by asking, "Towards who?" As she explained, I complimented her for her honesty and repeated back to her what I was hearing her saying so she could confirm. *I asked* a great question (remember, we don't advise!). I asked her if she thought forgiveness was needed. As I was giving a suggestion, I phrased it as "one of the things I find helpful." This encourages the client to choose what they will do.

Next, I helped Zoey to create a positive trigger of compassion *as opposed to the negative trigger she was having with her daughter. I then asked,* "Does that feel right for you?" Zoey created a goal in relationships for a deeper connection with her daughter. I asked *if she would like some suggestions in the planning stages* and gave some "maybe examples" to see if any felt right for her.

Zoey stated she was beginning to feel okay with herself as a mom. She brought up her dad again as a source of pain in relationships. Saying loving words is challenging for her, as she wasn't brought up this way. She talked about her desire to be an even better mother. I continued to just listen, allowing her to give me the information I needed.

We moved into the area of emotional health and the idea of rating herself on a scale of 1 to 10. Here, Zoey wanted clarity for what that meant. It's great to take the time to explain when a client has a question, especially concerning something that is an essential part of the coaching session. Once she gained the clarity she needed, she rated her emotional health at an 8. I then added some of the good words she was currently feeling to the meditation list I would use for her godly meditation later in the session and in future sessions.

In viewing the video recording of this session, you will notice how I made her feel safe in the financial section—she didn't have to give me financial numbers. She rated this area a 5, as she wants to do better financially, to be able to manage the money she is given. She would like to tithe more. We discussed what her financial actions look like right now, and I asked her how often *(this is part of planning) she would like to look at her finances.*

Next, we discussed her career area. Zoey wanted to work in the film industry. She was trusting for opportunities to open up. I was honest with her and asked questions because I don't understand the film industry, and I wanted to know what her career plan looked like. As coaches, we do not need to act like we know everything about every goal. Instead, we ask questions. Remember, these are your client's goals, and it is all about their planning, visualization, and moving into a new comfort zone.

As you study the video session, notice how some sections of our discussion move faster than others. This is perfectly acceptable, as each coaching session will differ and the client will sometimes have more to discuss in an area and sometimes less. Remember, an evaluation is for you, for your clients, and for use with your friends as a way to engage in conversation. When doing an evaluation, you might not get through the entire Circle in every session, although sometimes you might. It is important to trust the process and keep the rapport, which is the most important thing to establish and maintain.

As Zoey was speaking, I was writing her meditation. These are the notes you can see me taking in the video of this session. When she spoke of things that she lacked in, I wrote down the opposite word that would heal and satiate that area. I also added the positive words that she used, like *thankful, connected to God, clear, focused,* etc. I additionally added words that were in harmony with her goals, like *understanding her purpose,* that *she is a great mom, knows what needs to be done, honest, real, trusting,* etc.

Also, notice how she said she didn't want to be hungry or desperate in the film industry. In her meditation, I would not use these words, even stated in a positive way. I removed those words and replaced them with positive words like *trusting* and *courageous.*

Before I began the meditation, I first asked Zoey for her permission if she would like to receive a meditation. I also asked her if she would like to record the session. My goal is for my clients to be healed, healthy, and whole, so it is important that they listen to their new narration often. She recorded the meditation so she would have access to it whenever she desired to play it again.

Then I made space for calm. I played relaxing music and allowed her the time to just slow down and breathe. Because she is a Christian, I was able to pray with her and invite the Holy Spirit to be present in our meditation time. With a non-Christian, I would simply ask if they would like a meditation and then apply godly words without Christianizing the meditation.

With Zoey, I painted the word pictures of all that she was doing and was going to be doing, visualizing her time with her daughter, word pictures of her blessing her daughter, positive triggers for her to focus on when seeing her daughter—which would bring healing, compassion, love, kindness, and God's goodness. I used words of what she would be doing in the film industry, how she was emotionally well, visualizing herself managing her money well, and more. The meditation is only about eight minutes long, yet it is so powerful, as it focuses on all the goals Zoey mentioned in the session.

Note: I find when meditations are shorter, clients listen to them often. Remember that faith comes by hearing (Romans 10:17).

When I asked Zoey how she felt after the meditation was completed, I was not prepared for her to say she was fearful. Notice I didn't let this throw me. I came in instead with a question—"Tell me more about that." She proceeded to explain that she now knew that her goals will come to pass for her, as other things she has meditated on and prayed for have happened. This was actually an opportunity to help her see that God will prepare her for success. This also opened the door for another opportunity of a future session to work on the courage needed to walk in what she has been called to do. We then set our next appointment for that to happen.

Notice how I asked Zoey about her state of mind after the session and her will in the process of meditation. She affirmed that she was still aware and discerning. Zoey shared how she was able to visualize and picture her goals. I then gave her a bottle of Thankful essential oil so she could anchor herself in the Lord and in her goals that she had set. She affirmed how well these godly principles work. She has lived these principles and loves them!

As you consider this example coaching session (and watch the video many times!), I encourage you to notice the Five Keys in each section of the sessions. Everything was from within Zoey; she determined her goals, based on what she knew to be true within her. There is always something more to work on with our clients, and we continue to point them to their ultimate life coach, Jesus Christ!

Notice also how we acknowledged the growth that she has had. Rating each area of the Circle with numbers allowed her the opportunity to see this growth, as she would probably not have been aware of where she was at prior to coaching.

When she was speaking and mentioned "the demons in her," I didn't interrupt her. This was a distortion. Notice how I didn't operate in pleasing to the point of not correcting, but I made a note to bring it up at the right time and gently offer her another way to view this. Culturally, she has had to break many patterns. I offered her a suggestion, and she heard truth and accepted it.

A Few Additional Thoughts

There will be times, as coaches, when we will do the same evaluation process with a non-believer. As a coach, much of the flow of the session will be similar to what I have described above with Zoey. We would just eliminate any Christian language while using godly principles, painting word pictures for our client to help them achieve their goals. Remember that the intention of a Christian coach is to bring our non-Christian client to the Lord. We simply do that slowly so that we increase our chances of doing so.

Knowing how to do the coaching evaluation is an important skill that can also be used with friends and family members. To use it in that setting, we would tone it way down to a conversation style *so that* it doesn't feel like an evaluation but instead offers great ways of communicating and showing interest. We can also use the blessing portion with family and friends by just encouraging them with the words we know and hear they need!

Congratulations on all your great work so far! Next, we will be discovering more about your client, and then in the following chapter we will be talking about how to lead them to the Lord and how to offer a sinner's prayer.

Chapter 13

DISCOVERING MORE ABOUT YOUR CLIENT

For we are God's handiwork, created in Christ Jesus to do good works, which
God prepared in advance for us to do.
~Ephesians 2:10 NIV~

I n the previous chapter, we took an in-depth look at a complete coaching session with my friend and client Zoey. Perhaps you have watched the video of this session as well. (If not, remember that you can always sign up for the video classes, which are a useful complement to this book!)

In Zoey's session, we saw firsthand that even after a complete evaluation and a godly meditation, there was still more work to be done in her life and her coaching sessions, as she is now moving into an area of growth and will need to develop a new comfort zone. She has in the past established many goals in her life and accomplished them through our coaching. Because of that, she knew that she would accomplish the new goals set for herself. I didn't expect Zoey to say that she felt fear in establishing these new goals, but she was able to be honest with herself and with me because of our good rapport. This disclosure now gives us a new area of truth to work on in our next session.

As coaches, we will continue to discover new truths about our clients, and we will need to be prepared for things we do not expect. We must remain flexible and open to God's help in order to be ready for new insights that come up in each session. This is a skill we can work on and practice.

To help us be adaptable as coaches, we will look at additional tools to help us go deeper in a client's life, which will help them to continue to discover new truths and develop new goals.

Build on What We Have Already Learned

One good thing to remember is that each session with a client builds upon and draws from what was discussed and discovered in previous sessions. There is no need to do a complete evaluation each time we meet with our client; instead, we add onto what we have already learned from previous sessions. This allows us to work with them to create a trajectory of growth, rather than reinventing the wheel.

There is so much to explore in just one area of an individual's life. Using the Five Keys to Success and our great questioning skills, we will be able to dive deeper into each area of a client's life and our own! Remember, you are your most important client! Each of us as coaches can apply this concept of "discovering more" to ourselves, our family, and our friends, as well as our clients.

As we use the techniques we have learned, we will be discovering where our client's roadblocks are—in other words, the thoughts and beliefs and situations that are keeping our client from succeeding. Through questions, we will get to the heart of the matter. We will discover the lies they have believed and their fears. This is where breakthroughs and new growth that leads our client to good will come from!

Remember that each area of an individual's life will overlap. If they are not doing well in one area, often those issues will be overlapping into another area of their life as well. For example, if a client is not doing well relationally, it will impact how they are doing emotionally. If they are not doing well physically, it may affect how they are doing relationally. This is true for each area, as they all overlap.

Building Long-Term Success

Our main objective for asking great questions of our client is to gain information about their roadblocks and areas of need so we can lead our client to success. As we've already discussed, everything pertaining to success is rooted in the mind and our mental patterns. It is all about the mind. The more we can help our clients change their mind and their thinking patterns, the better we can help them change their lives. This is what makes the meditation portion of our coaching so successful.

In our ongoing sessions with our client, our goal will be to continue to discover the truth in each area of the Circle, to help them to set new goals and discover the purpose behind their goals, and to plan and strategize together with our client on how they are going to achieve these goals. We hold our client accountable to take the action that will move them toward their goals. And then we celebrate their success while also helping them discover ways to give back!

In this way, we are helping our client to achieve that which is good in their life, thus bringing them closer to the Lord each time we meet with them. What a tremendous blessing and privilege that is!

Keep in mind that there are many practical steps we can take in our ongoing sessions to equip our client for further growth.

First, reflect on the week with the client. Did they do their homework? If not, what kept them from doing it? Look for the roadblocks that could possibly reveal patterns and other insights into how the client is thinking. Discern when to push and when to offer grace. Refer to notes on what the client has said. Do they want to be reminded weekly, biweekly, or monthly about their goals and action steps?

Throughout each session, stay focused on the client's best interest. Remain focused on the larger goal while looking at the smaller goals in each area. We might ask what has changed for them during the week. We can also help our client to see the positive, offering new perspective and feeding them godly principles.

Remember to set their next appointment forty minutes into the session. And finally, discern the use of godly meditation and prayer that will bring the session to a positive close. What does our client need to do to continue to move forward? Remember, we are to believe in our client while also helping them to set realistic goals they can envision accomplishing.

Keep in mind that each of our clients has a divine purpose. We only help our clients to set godly goals. Even if they are not a Christian, we can still help them to stay focused on that which is good. To maintain rapport, we respect all faiths.

As people, we must have freedom. Advice is contrary to freedom, so we never tell our clients what to do or advise them. We instead empower them! We can make suggestions and help them to understand their resources. In this way, we equip them for long-term success even when we are not present.

Finally, as coaches we must be discerning in our choice of approach to each client in each session. If we push someone too hard, too soon without hearing them or validating them, they may feel misunderstood and probably won't come back. This is detrimental to their growth, and as much as possible, we must do our part to avoid this. Give your client time to discover their own solutions. We are here to empower them and help them to change their minds so they can change their lives!

Diving Deeper into Spirituality

As we work with our clients to discover more and dive into deeper truths, we are essentially helping them to grow more deeply in each area of the Circle. Let's begin with how we can approach the spirituality sphere of their lives.

One of the questions I often ask my clients is, "What is your spiritual preference?" By opening the discussion this way, we show respect for the client's individual right to have a preference in their religion. It also gives us information as a coach on how we should proceed. This will help us to maintain the rapport necessary so we can discover more about our client and help them to achieve their godly goals.

If we ask a client to rate their spirituality from 1 to 10 and they tell us it is a zero, this is the one area we allow them to say so. They may be agnostic or atheist, and that is their right.

If the client is a Christian, we can go on to explore what their spiritual practices and habits are. We can ask questions: What are their spiritual routines? What routines would they like to have? Do they attend a Bible study or church? Would they like to? How can they plan to implement this into their schedule? Do they pray regularly? Do they practice meditation or visualization? Are they in fellowship with other believers?

Even if our client is not a Christian, they may still have spiritual practices. As we lead them to that which is good, we will help lead them to the truth. For example, a non-Christian can still practice meditation, focusing on that which is good, incorporating the right people in their life, reading from personal development books, and having positive and helpful routines in their area of spirituality, even if they would like to give that area a different title.

To help a client who is in a false religion or no religion, we gain an awareness of their truth. While working with them, we focus on that which is good and slowly question the areas that need improvement. The key is in how we ask questions. Our tone of voice must always reflect that we are on our client's side and that we care for them.

Ask them how they feel about certain false beliefs such as polygamy in Mormonism or multiple levels in Scientology. The Lord will lead us to share our beliefs in a gentle, respectful way to help our client see the truth. When sharing our beliefs, we must remember that they are our own personal beliefs. We must let our tone reflect our respect for our client's right to their beliefs, just as we would want others to respect ours.

As we help our clients to grow in their spirituality, it is important to keep in mind the Five Keys to Success. What is the truth of where they are? What is their goal and purpose? Help them devise a plan with action steps. Celebrate their reward for reaching their goals, and teach them to give back.

These Five Keys will be repeated for every area of the Circle. They do not have to become robotic, nor should they! As we memorize and understand the Five Keys, we will be able to implement them in a natural way with our client through great questions. (Refer to the chapter Asking Great Questions and the appendix for ideas.)

Diving Deeper into Relationships

How are our clients doing in their relationships? Ask them to rate themselves on a 1 to 10 scale. This is an opportunity for them to give us a lot of information about many important aspects of their life. When rating this area, ask them to rate it as a whole, just as you would any other area. They might decide on their own to rate individual relationships and that is fine. The point of this exercise is to gain information for goal setting and improvement.

There are so many areas to expand on in the area of relationships. As a coach who specializes in emotional wellness, I find relationships to be the primary key to emotional health. When our relationships are going well, we as people thrive and every area of our lives improves. As Christians, we know that the most important relationship we have is with Jesus Christ. We certainly learn from His example how to love and do relationships well.

With our clients, the area of relationships provides a lot of information. We learn the foundation of our clients' beliefs, and often their behaviors, by discovering their family of origin. What happened? What programming was instilled? We can find out if there needs to be any forgiveness offered, or if the client needs to forgive themselves.

We can then find out about the relationships that are closest to them and how they are operating in them. Are they married? How is their marriage going? Is there fun and romance in their marriage? What can they do to plan for more of these things? Are they kind? Do they take responsibility? How are they communicating?

This is what we call discovering truth, the first key to success. We have to know where we are before we can know where we wish to go.

In the area of communication alone, many people are unaware of how they actually communicate, which can dramatically impact how their relationships are going. Coaching with us is an opportunity for our clients to gain this much-needed awareness. Often in communication, the approach that our client takes doesn't match their intent. In other words, they can intend to love someone, but their approach on how they love isn't causing the other person to feel loved.

Often in relationships, people get caught up in a need for agreement. They expect others to agree with them and are upset when they do not, which can cause relationship stress. But what if agreement was no longer the goal and, instead, connection became the goal? We can have love and connection without agreement, which can strengthen the client's relationships.

Communication, therefore, is an important area where we can dive deeper and explore with our client how to love in a way that helps the other individual in their life feel loved.

Another important area to explore in relationships is the roles we play. How are we playing our roles as parents, spouses, children, friends, and so on? How are others playing their roles? Are the roles being played in a healthy manner? Is there dysfunction?

There will be some relationships that will require distance to help protect the client. The amount of distance and whether or not this relationship can be reconciled will be based on each individual and their discernment and wisdom as to what is right and healthy for them. Remember, we never advise! We simply explore options, suggest resources, and help our client realize the possible long-term outcomes of their decisions.

Again, we are applying the Five Keys to Success in the area of relationships. We are discovering the truth, devising a goal, identifying a purpose for that goal, creating a plan to achieve it, and taking the action steps necessary. If our client isn't taking the action steps, the discovery of what is preventing them from taking those steps becomes a new area of truth. We are always learning truth and discovering new things about our clients!

The relationship rewards will come as these first four keys are adhered to, and we will have the opportunity to celebrate success with our client! We then help them learn what to do with their reward by learning to give back in the area where they have achieved success, further perpetuating more rewards and blessings in their life. An example of this would be that if a client has received restoration in their marriage, they would then look for opportunities to help others struggling in their marriage. This not only blesses the individual receiving support, but also further perpetuates the success of our client's marriage.

Diving Deeper into Emotional Wellness

Let's now look at the area of emotional wellness. Ask the client how they would rate this area on a scale of 1 to 10. If our client says that they are so depressed that they give this area a zero, listen to them and let them talk for just a moment. Then praise them for being there and reaching out, and because they came to the session, ask them if they will allow you to bump that number up to a 1 or 2. Then give them hope that this number will increase! We are here to help our client. We would never want anyone to walk away from our time together thinking that they are a zero emotionally. We want to make sure they know that they are going to be okay.

As I mentioned earlier, relationships are a major factor for how well clients are doing emotionally. The feeling of being out of control is another major cause of depression and anxiety. Therefore, it is important to help our clients get back to being in the driver's seat of their lives. God has told us to have self-control, and there is so much we can do to be in control of our emotions. Our emotions were made to bless us, not to harm us!

Here are some tools we can use to help our client get back their sense of self-control.

First, ask them if they are getting outside. Nature has such a great way of lifting our spirits and helping to lift depression. Even just a ten minute walk outside will do great things for our client's mood.

Next, ask if our client is sleeping well. If not, we can help them to set a goal of sleeping well. We can suggest options to consider as they come up with a plan and routines that will help our client to get the sleep that they need to lift their mood. This will be something to add to their meditation, speaking it as though it already happened. For example, we would say in their meditation: "When you lie down at night, you are able to relax and go into a deep sleep, bringing you great rest and restoration to your body, mind, and spirit."

Another thing we should look for in any of our clients with depression is how they are using their words. Do they speak of depression as if it were their identity? Help them with some anchoring tools and I AM statements so they can get back to their true identity of being filled with joy!

Does your client practice meditation and visualization? What are their passions? What dreams need to be restored? What are their spiritual habits? Would they like to establish some to help them? What is their diet like? Remember, everything overlaps, so if they are not doing well physically, it will affect them emotionally. Help them to establish some healthy eating habits that are right for them.

What is going on with our client's relationships? What perspectives can we give to them to help them? Do they need to offer forgiveness? To be forgiven? Do they need to let some things go?

How is their financial health? What can they do to improve it?

The more we can help our clients with the other areas of their lives, the more their emotional wellness will improve. As coaches, we help them to see that there is hope and that they have the ability to design their life for good. God desires this ability for your client. Healing and restoration are what Jesus came to offer!

Diving Deeper into Physical Health

God desires for us to be healthy and strong! He desires us to take care of our bodies the way He intended. He created the foods for us that would help us to overcome illness. There are many books and materials out there we can use to educate ourselves on health. One of the great ones that I like is *The Daniel Plan* by Daniel Amen, Mark Hyman, and Rick Warren. This idea comes from the book of Daniel in the Old Testament of the Bible. And there are plenty of other resources we can suggest to our clients for their consideration as well.

Here are some things to find out as we walk through the area of physical health with our clients: How is their hydration? Are they getting enough water? How is their diet? Do they take the time to prepare healthy foods? How can they incorporate healthy eating habits into their schedule? Do they exercise? Are they taking the time for self-nurturing? Do they need vitamins and supplements? Do they get enough rest?

Remember, our clients truly know the answers to these questions. We do not advise! Instead, we help to bring out in them what they need to do to feel better physically. Perhaps they need to see a nutritionist or doctor. These truths come out through questions. It is our job as a coach to ask great questions and listen well. This will help us coach our clients into planning their goals and action steps, and it will help us to prepare a meditation that is fitting.

Diving Deeper into Career

Is our client happy in their career? What can they do to either get happy in their career or prepare for a change? What are their strengths? What skills or talents do they possess? Do they need to go back to school or gain additional education? What would that look like for them? What are their passions and desires? Do they need to market themselves better? Or perhaps create a network to improve their current position?

The important things to remember when coaching a client on the career section of their life are: Is this career goal obtainable? What income do they need to make while making a transition, if any? Do they need a new career or maybe just a hobby?

Are they viewing their current position as an opportunity for ministry? Often, people feel stuck because they feel a lack of value in what they do. Many times, they just need a new perspective for where they are at. We can all do ministry wherever we are placed.

Diving Deeper into Financial Health

In the coaching session that I did with Zoey (see the previous chapter), I first made her feel safe by reminding her that she did not need to give me any specific numbers. Financial planners seek numbers. But we do not need the numbers unless our client desires to give them to us and seeks our help in that area.

As a coach, our job is to bring balance to our clients' lives and to help them live their best lives! One of the things that will help them to do that is to make sure they are managing their money well. As we saw in the coaching session, Zoey knew that she needed to do better in the area of tithing and good financial stewardship of her money. This is where budgeting comes in and savings. What could our client do to improve those areas? Are they insured? Have they set aside money for retirement? For travel? For ministry? Do they need to set aside money for their children, for college funds?

There are many areas to explore in finances. Our client truly knows the answers. As a great coach, we can bring those answers out of them, helping them to live a rewarding and abundant future!

Using Timelines for Goal Setting

As we continue to coach our clients, we will both discover new truths and set new goals with them. An additional tool we can use to help with this is a timeline.

A timeline is something that will help our client explore their life as a whole, regardless of their age. Where are they now on the timeline? If they are young, this gives them an even greater opportunity to see what lies ahead. When will they be driving? Dating? Going to college? When would they like to marry? What kind of spouse will support them in their dreams? When will they die? What kind of legacy would they like to leave behind?

A timeline is a very helpful tool for many scenarios! I have used this tool with people going through divorce, helping them to see their future and to devise a plan on how to get there. I use this tool for all situations and ages. One client I used it for thought she wanted a divorce until we looked at all that a divorce would entail, including the healing from a divorce. She decided to heal within her marriage.

Get creative and help your client see where they are at, where they wish to go, and what kind of legacy they will leave behind.

Using Journaling to Discover More

Statistics show that those who write their goals down have a higher percentage of achieving success! With this in mind, I have my clients bring in a journal, and I encourage all coaches to do the same. If our clients do not have a journal, we can always have blank paper and a pen for them to use in our sessions.

Journals are a great way for our clients to keep track of anything from a session that they want to remember or think about. We can also give our clients assignments to write down, such as their passions and talents, their true identity in Christ, their words of affirmations, and more.

If a client does not wish to write, we do not force it. We simply offer them paper and a pen and allow them to choose for themselves. We can also offer them the opportunity to take a picture of the meditation section we write for them to use in their anchoring. Since our practice is so very positive and visual, I do not mind sharing my notes with my client.

Using the Prince or Princess List to Discover More

Another tool that can help clients to discover more and develop new goals is something I like to call the "Prince or Princess" list. We could also call this a future husband or wife list. This is a great exercise for our single clients or children. It helps them to gain a perspective of what they would like to see in their future spouse.

Some of those characteristics are: a Christian, one who is loving, kind, loyal, generous, helpful, committed, fun, adventurous, calm, responsible, authentic, caring, etc. The list goes on! This is a wonderful tool to use! And this list also helps our clients to become like the person they are seeking to attract, as like attracts like.

Practicing Premarital and Marital Coaching

YKI coaching also offers premarital and marital coaching, and this may be something you as a coach will want to add to your practice. Here are some tips.

The more alike that two people are in each area of the Circle, the better they will get along. This is why eHarmony works so well. They pair up people who are more alike than different. This does not mean that the two people are the same! Obviously, a man and woman are going to be very different. The idea is to be working toward unity and the same goals in addition to supporting one other in their individual goals. This is why God tells us to be equally yoked.

If, however, two people are married and they are of different religions, we can still help them to stand on common ground and unity. As couples, we can find commonality by using the Five Keys to Success in each of the areas. We can help them as a couple to see what blocks them from achieving unity and their goals.

In premarital coaching, I take both the man and the woman together through each area of the Circle, beginning with spirituality, as this is the most important area to discuss. If they do not agree spiritually, everything else will be difficult as one's spiritual life overlaps into each area. If they are different religions, they will need to make difficult decisions like where they will tithe their money, what religion they will raise their children in, and where they will attend church. It is not recommended for people of different religions to marry, and it is very important to be equally yoked. We can help our client to see this through questions, and even though it might be very obvious that they should not marry, being of mixed faiths, we do not advise. We can make them aware, but ultimately the choice will be theirs.

Remember, when coaching couples, continue to use the YKI methods that you have been taught, including the meditation portion. This helps couples focus on their united goals in love.

The Value of Discovering More

At heart, the coaching process involves helping people to let go of beliefs and thinking patterns that don't serve them, so they can be led to that which is good and godly. As we work with our clients, learning more about them and helping them to learn more about themselves, we can guide them through questions to a place where they will desire to connect with the source for an abundant life—their ultimate life coach, Jesus Christ. In the next chapter, we'll look at our sole purpose as a coach for Christ and how to bring people into a saving relationship with Him.

Chapter 14

BRING THEM TO THE LORD

This is good, and it is pleasing in the sight of God our Savior, who desires all
people to be saved and to come to the knowledge of the truth.
~1 Timothy 2:3-4 ESV~

I believe you are going to do great things for our Lord and Savior, Jesus Christ!
As a coach for Christ, you are His disciple. Jesus said in His own words in Luke
14:25-35 that the cost of being His disciple is high! This is why throughout this
book we continually discuss ways of being a servant to our client. We must think
more of others and less of ourselves.

I encourage you to go through the Scripture verses in this book and take
Jesus's counsel to count the cost of following Him. Are you ready to give up your
life for others? Are you ready to call Jesus Lord and surrender to everything He
has to say? If your answer to those questions is yes, then you are ready to take the
oath as a coach for Christ, which is the following three things:

You accept Jesus as your only Lord and Savior.

You are dedicated to serving the Lord and will seek the lost and bring them into a saving relationship with Jesus.

You agree that the Bible is the final word of the Lord and will use the Bible as the final authority in your coaching practice.

Keep these words from Psalm 119:105-106 (NIV) in your heart and mind: *"Your Word is a lamp for my feet, / a light on my path. / I have taken an oath and confirmed it, / that I will follow your righteous laws."*

As you coach others, you are bringing them to that which is good, which ultimately leads them to God. As a result, there will be opportunities for you to present the good news of the gospel to them.

As a Christian, you are already equipped by God to accomplish what He has called you to do, including sharing the gospel (see 2 Timothy 3:17). *"But in your hearts revere Christ as Lord. Always be prepared to give an answer to everyone who asks you to give the reason for the hope that you have. But do this with gentleness and respect"* (1 Peter 3:15 NIV).

If you are wondering how to share the gospel, it doesn't have to be long or complicated. The shortest salvation prayer recorded in the Bible is in Luke 23:42. The thief dying on the cross next to Jesus humbled himself and simply said, *"Jesus, remember me when you come into your kingdom"* (NIV). In this simple prayer, so much is being said that isn't verbalized. The thief was acknowledging that Jesus was Lord and had a kingdom. He was also indicating that Jesus had power and could come back to life and therefore remember him.

As you seek to bring people to the Lord, keep things simple and to the point. The gospel is good news! Trust Jesus to work things out for your client. Just simply point them to Jesus.

One of my clients who I brought to the Lord was an agnostic. She didn't want to talk about God. I kept things very secular for her until the timing was right. Her dad was in the hospital, about to die. She is someone I only worked with on the phone, as she lived in Virginia and I am in California. She was with her family and took some time away to do her coaching session with me.

As she relayed to me her dad's situation, this gave me the opportunity to ask her what she thought happened when people die. I continued to ask her questions and directed her to peace and asked her if she desired this peace in her life. She said yes. I told her that Jesus was her answer to that and briefly explained how God would give her eternal life. I asked her if she wanted to accept Jesus into her life, and she said, "I am with my family right now." I then calmly explained that this was something between just herself and Jesus and that all she had to do was accept Him by saying yes and asking Him to come into her life. She did just that!

She went on to get baptized and is now living the full life that Jesus has for her, all because of one brief question. Coaching is so exciting! Go slow, and meet your client where they are at.

You are now ready to improve lives! You are an evangelist. You have been trained and equipped. Believe in yourself. God believes in you! Remember, you are never alone! God is always with you, and our team is here for you. Email us anytime at info@YKIcoaching.com.

Chapter 15

Marketing Your Coaching Business

Write the vision; make it plain on tablets, so he may run who reads it.
~Habakkuk 2:2 ESV~

B efore we bring this book to a close, let's talk a little bit about marketing yourself as a coach. This is something that can be a bit tricky and must be handled with care. Here's a look at how you can approach this important area of building your business in a way that honors the Lord.

What is Christian Marketing?

Christian marketing is a tricky action as it must be handled with care; otherwise it could be seen as us trying to display our good works instead of offering value and bringing others to the Lord. *"Be careful not to practice your righteousness in front of others to be seen by them. If you do, you will have no reward from your Father in heaven"* (Matthew 6:1 NIV).

But like many things, marketing itself is not an evil. What matters is how we approach it. We are first and foremost coaching for Christ! Everything we do, including marketing, needs to be pleasing to our Lord Jesus Christ.

Our Christian marketing must be consistent with the attitudes, beliefs, and values that the Bible tells us are essential to our Christian walk. Look to the Bible, and let it guide you. Consider Galatians 5:22-23 (ESV): *"But the fruit of the Spirit is love, joy, peace, patience, kindness, goodness, faithfulness, gentleness, self-control; against such things there is no law."* Qualities like these should be evident in your business, including your marketing.

Here are some other essential qualities that a Christian coach should exhibit in their marketing.

Be truthful and trustworthy. Above all, we must demonstrate great integrity when marketing to others. We are never to be deceitful or hiding something in order to attract a client. Trust and honesty are the foundation of productive coaching relationships. And it is honorable to make sure your marketing is beyond reproach.

Add value to an individual's life. With your great skills as a coach, you have great value to add to others. You can help them in the six key areas of their lives. And it is good news to share with others how you can guide them into what is good and godly.

Serve others. If we are only after selfish gain, we will not have the Lord's approval. Great leaders serve others. There are many ways to serve others, including volunteering, which I will mention further in this chapter. Just remember as you market yourself that the foundation of Christian coaching is our servant's heart.

Be relatable. There are many people we desire to reach who are outside of the Christian norm. They will have different beliefs, belong to different religions, and may even be atheists. These are the people we seek to lead to good and bring to God. This is why throughout this book and our YKI training we teach coaches to relate to everyone. We are seeking the lost and therefore must be relatable.

Ask for a commitment the way Jesus did. Jesus knew that what He offered was the best! He wanted His followers to count the cost of following Him. We certainly serve others and help those in need, and at the same time we seek a commitment from them. This is why we ask for regularly scheduled appointments and payments from our clients. This is a good practice to help our clients be committed to the process of their growth, and it benefits both the client and the coach from the service.

Be beautiful and positive. We want to focus on that which is good and lovely and of good report. Our marketing can focus on what is good too. Creating a picture of how life can improve through Christian coaching is a good way to encourage others to connect with us.

Establish a Godly Reputation

Since the Scriptures give us caution about practicing our righteousness before others, our intention and purposes need to be coming from a beautiful heart for the Lord to serve Him and humanity, rather than seeking attention for ourselves. Always seek Him and review things with Him before going public.

How then do you get others to know what you do? You begin to serve! Get out there and begin coaching. Help others, and let your reputation speak for itself! *A good name is to be chosen rather than great riches, / and favor is better than silver or gold* (Proverbs 22:1 ESV).

As you begin to reach out to others, ask yourself what you truly desire. Keep in mind that when you seek God's kingdom first, everything else will be added to you as God promises in Matthew 6:33. Let your light shine so brightly that God receives the glory!

When I started coaching, my method of marketing was that people would become so well and filled with joy that they would share the good news with others! People need to know you and your true character if they are going to work with you.

Finding Your Niche

As you build your life coaching practice through helping others, you will begin to refine what it is that you do. You'll discover more clearly where your unique strengths are. Often, your strength has come out of your greatest weakness! What painful experiences have you endured and overcome through Christ? How can you help others do the same?

Often, this becomes your niche market. By this, I mean the exact purpose of what it is that you do. When others ask you what it is that you do, you will be able to answer in one quick sentence! This is known as your elevator pitch because you only have just a few moments with others in the elevator.

For me, I tell people that I am a life coach, that I help people to achieve their personal goals, and that I specialize in emotional wellness. I usually keep this conversation very secular until I know that they are Christian. Not that I deny being a Christian, but it is my goal to bring non-Christians to the Lord and therefore I don't want to scare them away or cause them to think I cannot relate to them because we are somehow different. I want to meet them where they are at.

When you begin to understand what a short period we have with strangers, you will begin to look for ways to help others, to bless them in just a brief moment. Let your light continually shine!

Growing Your Coaching Practice

As coaches for Christ, we never stop building our audience. People are always watching. As you share with the world what you have to offer, you will continue to build your circle of influence.

To help yourself do this intentionally, ask yourself these three questions:
1. Who do you know?
2. Who do you need to know?
3. Who needs to know you?

This third question of who needs to know you will indicate whether or not you know your value. Once you begin to understand the ability you have to make an impact for good in people's lives, you will begin to think to yourself, "These people need to know me. I can help them!" You will begin to think of the other professionals who can offer your services to their clients, and with great courage, you will reach out to them, letting them know what you offer.

Look for Opportunities to Volunteer

Are you currently volunteering within your church? Your community? Through giving back to others with your coaching skills and your other gifts, you can make a difference.

I volunteer in my church as a greeter because I absolutely love talking to people! I also volunteer weekly at the OC Rescue Mission, teaching life skills, parenting skills, and complete healing from sexual abuse, which I developed the class for. Neither of these volunteer positions do I hold to get something back, but to give.

Nevertheless, it is interesting how clients and students come through these avenues as my heart is displayed to serve. As Luke 6:38 says, when we give, blessings come back to us. God sees us, and He will provide!

As you continue developing your network, think of the people you know who are involved in academics, such as school counselors, academic advisors, principals, and assistant principals. These people may need your help or know others who do.

Think of your church, which may be in need of youth ministers, teen ministers, and the list goes on and on. There are many opportunities where you can make a difference and share what God has given you to help others.

Simply thinking through the network that you would like to establish and writing these networks down is a very powerful exercise that many professionals don't take the time to develop. Yet this is the most powerful thing you can do to build your network.

Marketing Checklist

To help you get creative with how you promote your coaching business, here's a list of things you can do to share what God has equipped you to do. Work on these, and add to the list anything He puts on your heart as a way to reach others. Remember, these actions help you connect with others, which is the first step toward serving them and bringing them to good and to God.

1. Let others know what you do.
2. Get to know the ones who can help your business grow.

3. Offer charity and volunteer in places where you can share your coaching skills.
4. Network with everyone you can.
5. Blog to build your online presence. Share useful tips that bless others.
6. Share your success stories.
7. Create classes both online and in person.
8. Use Meetup.com and other similar groups to connect with others.
9. Make use of Facebook, LinkedIn, and other forms of social media.
10. Speak at libraries, schools, churches, and other places where what you know can be helpful to others.
11. Write reviews and work with people. Be collaborative, not in competition.
12. Write a book that reflects your niche.
13. Continue learning.
14. Join an association that can help you build your practice.

The Value of Being Connected

Starting a business might seem lonely, but it doesn't have to be. God has never called us to go it alone. At YKI coaching, we feel it is very important for Christian coaches to work together as a team. Consider these Scriptures that encourage us to stand together in faith as Christians:

"*For where two or three are gathered in my name, there am I among them*" (Matthew 18:20 ESV).

"*Two are better than one, because they have a good reward for their toil. For if they fall, one will lift up his fellow. But woe to him who is alone when he falls and has not another to lift him up!*" (Ecclesiastes 4:9-10 ESV).

"*From whom the whole body, joined and held together by every joint with which it is equipped, when each part is working properly, makes the body grow so that it builds itself up in love*" (Ephesians 4:16 ESV).

As we collaborate and share ideas and encourage one another, we can help each other to grow as coaches for Christ. And as we grow in our skills and our abilities as coaches, we position ourselves to be more effective at connecting with our clients and equipping them to move toward their good, godly goals.

Remain Accountable

In addition to growing in our skill sets as we collaborate, there is another valuable outcome of staying connected with other coaches. Our connections help us to continue moving faithfully in the right direction. Those we are connected with help us to focus on what is good in our own lives and businesses.

"*And let us consider how to stir up one another to love and good works, not neglecting to meet together, as is the habit of some, but encouraging one another, and all the more as you see the Day drawing near*" (Hebrews 10:24-25 ESV).

"*Iron sharpens iron, / and one man sharpens another*" (Proverbs 27:17 ESV).

"*Therefore we ought to support people like these, that we may be fellow workers for the truth*" (3 John 1:8 ESV).

"*Do nothing from selfish ambition or conceit, but in humility count others more significant than yourselves. Let each of you look not only to his own interests, but also to the interests of others*" (Philippians 2:3-4 ESV).

Without accountability, it is all too easy to miss the mark and not accomplish what God has called us to do. This is the reason for these Scripture verses on working together as Christians. It is vital to our success as coaches for Christ that we remain accountable to ourselves, fellow coaches, and clients. As coaches for Christ, we are servants to Him, and He has called us to work together. Having this accountability through YKI helps us to be successful in this.

Establish Credibility

In order to be effective, we need to have credibility. We have to do a lot of leading by influence, which means we have to do a lot of aligning and engaging and evangelizing. This only works when people trust us. They only trust us if we deliver the service we have promised and are accountable. In our marketing and in our daily practice, we do what we say, and we say what we mean.

One way that we can establish credibility is through becoming certified through a reputable source. One that operates beyond reproach and has a reputation of staying connected and remains accountable and offers qualified training and services. A coach's certification should demonstrate that they have been equipped to handle the task at hand. Therefore, the certification should come from a reputable company—one that has a solid reputation among other coaches, Christians, and clients.

YKI coaching is Here to Help

YKI coaching provides certification for coaches. We believe that your training through this book, our video course, and other resources we offer equips you to be an excellent coach, along with the continued support that we offer. We are a five-star company, and we consider it an honor and privilege to maintain that high rating through proven results and integrity in all we do.

If you are interested in becoming an associate with YKI coaching, I would love to speak with you! Please send me an email at Learl@YKIcoaching.com and let me know your desires and goals as a coach. Most importantly, I would love to learn of your relationship with Jesus Christ and how He has transformed your life, and your desire now to help others come to know Him so He can transform their lives!

CONCLUSION

Congratulations! You have accomplished some very important steps to becoming an effective coach for Christ! Through you, others will begin to experience the love of God and will have the opportunity to gain a transformed life that is filled with purpose and direction as they come to know their Lord and Savior, Jesus Christ!

APPENDIX SECTION

THE FIVE KEYS TO SUCCESS

These are the Five Keys to Success. I encourage you to memorize them and apply them to every area of your life. These five keys are used to discover more in each area of the Circle and to help you and your clients to set goals, plan, and succeed:

1. Truth

   God has said you shall know the truth, and the truth will set you free (see John 8:32). He wasn't just talking about spirituality. Truth is critical for success in every area of our life. We must know the truth about ourselves to begin with. Who are we? We must understand the truth in each and every given situation in order to distinguish what we are to change in order to attain our goal.

2. Purpose

   "For the Scriptures say that God told Pharaoh, 'I have appointed you for the very purpose of displaying my power in you and to spread my fame throughout the earth" (Romans 9:17 NLT). Purpose is the crucial element that drives us in life. Without purpose, we are lost in the world, just consuming oxygen and waiting for it all to end. Our energy becomes

197

depleted as the zest for "what could have been" has slowly faded away. If you are finding yourself disheartened, disappointed, and drained from the hours in the day, then it is quite possible that you are not living out your purpose in life.

3.   Plan

"Plans fail for lack of counsel, / but with many advisers they succeed" (Proverbs 15:22 NIV). Once the light bulb has gone on and your energy and excitement has returned, the next step is creating a plan. God tells us He knows the plans He has for us (Jeremiah 29:11). You see, He has laid it all out in detail. When we are walking in His plans for us with clarity and detail, the joy and energy return.

4.   Action

"Therefore, since we are surrounded by such a great cloud of witnesses, let us throw off everything that hinders and the sin that so easily entangles. And let us run with perseverance the race marked out for us" (Hebrews 12:1 NIV). Without action, your truth, purpose, and planning are nothing more than wasted information. The good news is that once you have established what is truth, found your purpose, and devised the plan, action is easy. With all the newfound energy and excitement that you will gain, starting your day will be a joy.

5.   Success

"All praise to God, the Father of our Lord Jesus Christ. God is our merciful Father and the source of all comfort. He comforts us in all our troubles so that we can comfort others. When they are troubled, we will be able to give them the same comfort God has given us. For the more we suffer for Christ, the more God will shower us with his comfort through Christ" (2 Corinthians 1:3-5 NLT). The rewards from the first four keys will begin to pour into your life. This is the point where the keys then must be repeated. As you reap your harvest, your question becomes, "What is the truth of why I have been blessed? What now is my purpose for this harvest? Who will I help? What plan of action will I take to bless others?" And the circle begins as your keys to happiness, joy, and success have been given to you.

Asking Great Questions: The Circle/Evaluation

This is not an exhaustive list of all the questions possible to ask a client. Rather, it's a beginning list of questions that can help you get started as you work with your clients and develop your skills in coaching and questioning. Feel free to add to this list—always remembering that your goal is to avoid judgment and remain open as you guide the client into discovering the answers within themselves.

Questions to Guide You in Self Evaluation and Client Evaluation (The Circle)

An evaluation on your client should feel natural, like a conversation. Depending on your client, you could also make them aware by asking them if they mind taking an evaluation. Begin by saying something along these lines to your client: "It would be helpful to you if we did an evaluation of the six key areas of your life to gain a little more information and to help you get the balance back in your life along with helping you establish your goals. Is this okay with you?"

Once you have established rapport and received their agreement to move forward with an evaluation, you may begin to ask questions that lead the client through the Circle. Beginning with spirituality, make sure that the client feels respected and has a right to their own spirituality, even if they are not a Christian. I usually like to begin with the question, "What spiritual preference do you have?" This gives them the respect that they deserve to have a spiritual practice of their choosing. Then you can ask them to rate their spiritual life. Simply ask them to rate themselves from one to ten, with ten being when they feel their best. In the area of spirituality, if your client says zero, allow it and move on. Remember to tailor your questions to your client. If they are non-Christian, remove Christian terms from the questions so you can establish rapport with them where they are at.

You will ask your client to rate themselves in each area as you move through the circle. When you are asking them to rate themselves on their emotional health and they give a zero, this is an area where you will listen, validate them, and offer hope. However, never let your client stay at a zero because this would cause them to feel hopeless. Instead, you might say something like, "I am so glad you are here. Because you are able to make wise choices just by being here, and I can see great things in store for you, can we at least give you a 2 or 3?"

Questions about Spirituality:

1. What spiritual preference do you have?
2. How would you rate your spirituality?
3. What causes you to give it this rating?
4. What are your spiritual beliefs?
5. What routines or practices do you have?
6. Is there anyone in your life who is in conflict with your beliefs?
7. How do you feel about God?
8. What kind of relationship do you have with Him?
9. Is it easy or hard for you to talk with the Lord?
10. What are your spiritual plans?

Questions about Relationships:

1. Who are your closest relationships?
2. How would you rate those relationships?
3. How much effort do you put into each of these relationships?
4. In what ways would you like to improve these relationships?
5. Does anyone in particular stand out to you who is causing you grief?
6. Is there anyone you need to spend less time with?
7. Is there anyone you need to forgive?
8. Is there anything you need to be forgiven for?
9. Do you have friends outside of family?
10. What are your relationship plans?

Questions about Emotional Wellness:

1. How would you rate your emotional life?
2. What do you currently do to take care of yourself emotionally?
3. Do you get outside regularly?
4. Do you eat a regular diet?
5. How is your sleep?
6. Is there someone causing you grief?
7. What spiritual practices do you do for your emotional health?
8. Do you practice meditation?
9. Can I offer you some meditation that will help you to relax?
10. Would you like me to reserve time for meditation in each session?

Questions about Physical Wellness:

1. How would you rate yourself physically?
2. Do you consider yourself an attractive person?
3. What type of exercise do you like the most?
4. Do you have any routines to keep your physical health in good shape?
5. Would you like to work on any physical goals?
6. Do you consider yourself healthy?
7. What is your diet like?
8. Would you like to work on your diet and set some goals?

9. Are you physically attracted to your spouse?
10. Do you judge people based on their physical appearance? How does that affect you?

Questions about Financial Wellness:

Remember, you do not need to know specific numbers to evaluate financial wellness. Make sure your client feels safe before proceeding.

1. How would you rate your finances?
2. What makes you say that?
3. Do you currently work with someone to help you with financial planning?
4. Would you like to set some financial goals?
5. What are your retirement plans?
6. Do you have a tithing or charity account?
7. Would you like to learn more about that?
8. What do you feel the purpose of your finances is?
9. Do you feel financially free or tied up by your finances?
10. If you had all the money in the world, what would you do?

Questions about Career:

1. What type of work do you do?
2. How do you like it?
3. If you could do anything, what would you do?
4. What do you feel your strengths and talents are?
5. What are you passionate about?
6. Do you consider your current job as serving someone?
7. Do you feel obligated or pressured to work?
8. Would you hire yourself?
9. How would you like your work associates to remember you?
10. Do you plan to stay at your current job or seek something new?

Questions about Ministry:

(when appropriate)

1. How do you feel about working for the Lord?
2. Are you able to brighten or bless someone through your work?
3. What are your ministry plans?
4. If the Lord were to call you, what do you think He would have you do?
5. What questions would you ask Jesus?
6. What type of needs do you like fulfilling?
7. What breaks your heart in the world?
8. If you could fulfill any need for others, what would it be?
9. Do you like teaching others about the Lord?
10. Would you like to travel and serve or stay local?

ADDITIONAL QUESTIONS FOR USE IN CLIENT SESSIONS

These questions can provide starting off points for you as you invite your client to share more about their life, their goals, and their needs in each coaching session.

Alternative viewpoints and perspectives:

1. What are alternative ways of looking at this?
2. Who benefits from this?
3. What is the difference between ... and ... ?
4. What makes ... better than ... ?
5. What are the strengths and weaknesses of ... ?
6. How are ... and ... similar?
7. How could you look at this another way?
8. Another way of looking at this is ... Does this seem reasonable?
9. What would ... say about it?
10. What if you compared ... and ... ?

Anticipation:

1. What is possible?
2. What if it works out exactly as you want it to?
3. What is your dream?
4. What is exciting to you about this?
5. What is the urge?
6. What does your intuition tell you?
7. What do you anticipate will happen?
8. Do you think your child will make the right decision?
9. When do you anticipate your boss will speak to you?
10. At what point are you expecting things to change?

Assessment:

1. What do you make of this situation?
2. What do you think is best for all involved?
3. How does this situation look to you?
4. How do you feel about the current situation?
5. What resonates for you?
6. How will their choice affect you?
7. How does this choice compare with that choice?
8. What is the positive outcome for all?
9. What is the negative outcome for all?
10. How would your life change if you made that choice?

Assumptions:

Be careful not to use phrases like this:

1. Are you possibly assuming ... ?
2. How did you choose those assumptions?
3. Instead, gain more information:
4. Could you tell me more about ... ?
5. How can you verify or disprove what your thoughts are   on that?
6. What would happen if ... ?
7. Do you agree or disagree with ... ?

8. What do you mean by …?
9. Could you explain … another way?
10. What is your end goal?
11. Could you give me some background on this?
12. How long has this been a problem?
13. What makes you feel that way?

Clarification:

1. What do you mean?
2. What does it feel like?
3. What is the part that is not yet clear?
4. Can you say more?
5. What do you want?
6. What do you think is happening?
7. How do you think they feel?
8. What causes you to say that?
9. How long have you been thinking about that?
10. Do others support you in your decision?

Communication:

1. Are you quick to listen?
2. Are you slow to speak?
3. Are you slow to become angry?
4. Would Jesus approve of the way you speak?
5. What needs to change in the way you speak?
6. Have you spoken to them about that?
7. How would others say you communicate?
8. Do you feel connected to others in conversation?
9. Have you built up an inventory of questions?
10. Do you work on your communication skills?

Difficult situations:

1. Do you think God wants you in this situation?
2. Do you believe God desires the best for you in your life?
3. Are there other resources you have not checked?
4. Have you learned about …?
5. Do you believe this person will change?
6. Do you think having stronger boundaries will help you?
7. Do you think God has boundaries?
8. What will this mean for your family/children?
9. Do you believe great things can happen for you?
10. What is the difference between a confident person and one who is not?
11. Do you believe your thoughts matter?
12. What would happen if you began to think like … ?
13. Are you open to reprogramming (or renewing) your mind for change?

Elaboration:

1. Can you tell me more?
2. What else?
3. What other ideas/thoughts/feelings do you have about it?
4. What is your biggest challenge with this?
5. What goals and objectives do you have for this?
6. What has caused you to look into this now?
7. In a perfect world, what would you like to see happen?
8. What options have you tried?
9. What is the biggest problem you are facing in this?
10. Is there anything you might have overlooked?

Evaluation:

1. What is the opportunity here?
2. What is the challenge here?
3. How does this fit with your plans/way of life/values?
4. What do you think that means?
5. What is your assessment?

6. What do you feel is the correct solution?
7. How will your finances be affected?
8. Do you feel emotionally equipped to handle this?
9. Does your current career offer you long-term benefits?
10. Are there any moves you would like to make to change things?

Example:

1. What is an example?
2. For instance?
3. Like what?
4. Such as?
5. What would it look like?

Exploration:

1. What is here that you want to explore?
2. What part of the situation have you not yet explored?
3. What other angles can you think of?
4. What is just one more possibility?
5. What are your other options?

Fun:

1. What does fun mean to you?
2. What was humorous about the situation?
3. How can you make this more fun?
4. How do you want it to be?
5. If you were to teach people how to have fun, what would you say?

Gaining more information:

1. Could you tell me more about ... ?
2. How can you gain more information?
3. What would happen if ... ?
4. Do you agree or disagree with ... ?
5. What makes you feel that way?

6. What exactly does this mean?
7. How do you think this relates?
8. Could you give me an example?
9. Could you tell me more?
10. How could you rephrase that?

Goal-setting and vision casting:

1. What are your dreams and passions?
2. What are your goals?
3. What do you think is the right thing to do?
4. Is that what is best for you?
5. What is holding you back?
6. How can I help you with this?
7. Where do you see yourself in five years?
8. Is that decision going to give you the results you desire?
9. What is God calling you to do?
10. Who are the important people in your life?
11. What are your favorite things to do?
12. Where are your favorite places to go?
13. What would you do if ... ?
14. If money were no object, what would you do?
15. What do you feel God is calling you to do?
16. How would you do it?
17. Where would you go?
18. What would it look like, feel like, sound like?
19. Who, what, where, when, how much?

Helping others:

1. Who do you think needs your example?
2. What areas in their life could you nurture?
3. What is your time commitment to that individual?
4. Does your lifestyle—your work, play, buying habits, giving—help or hurt people who have less than you do?

5.   What one thing could you do this week to help a helpless person?

History:

1.   What caused it?
2.   What led up to it?
3.   What have you tried so far?
4.   What do you make of it all?
5.   How long has this been going on?

Implementation:

1.   What is the action plan?
2.   What will you have to do to get the job done?
3.   What support do you need to accomplish it?
4.   What will you do?
5.   When will you do it?

Implications and consequences:

1.   Then what would happen? ... And then what would happen?
2.   What are the consequences of that assumption?
3.   What are the implications of ... ?
4.   How does this fit with what we learned before?
5.   What is the best solution for ... ? What makes it the best?
6.   What makes ... important?
7.   Do these ... make sense? Are they desirable?
8.   How could ... be used to ... ?
9.   How does ... affect ... ?

Influence:

1.   What influences you?
2.   Are your television shows bringing you closer to your transformation?
3.   Are your friendships encouraging you to do better?
4.   What books help you to become a better person?
5.   Does your social media cause you to think on what is good?

6. How much time do you spend on your positive transformation?

Integration:

1. What will you take away from this?
2. How do you explain this to yourself?
3. What was the lesson?
4. How can you make sure you remember what you have learned?
5. How would you pull all this together?

Learning:

1. If your life depended on taking action, what would you do?
2. If you had free choice in the matter, what direction would you take?
3. If the same thing came up again, how would you respond?
4. If we could wipe the slate clean, how would you do things differently?
5. If you had it to do over again, what would you change?

Options:

1. What are the possibilities?
2. If you had your choice, what would you do?
3. What are possible solutions?
4. What will happen if you do, and what will happen if you don't?
5. What options can you create?
6. If you could do it over again, what would you do differently?
7. If it had been you, what would you have done?
8. How else could a person handle this?
9. If you could do anything you wanted, what would you do?
10. What is your choice in the matter?

Outcomes:

1. What do you want?
2. What is your desired outcome?
3. If you got it, what would you have?
4. How will you know you have reached it?

5.   What would it look like?

Perspective:

1.   When you are 95 years old, what will you want to say about your life?
2.   What will you think about this situation five years from now?
3.   How does this relate to your life purpose?
4.   In the bigger scheme of things, how important is this?

Planning:

1.   What do you plan to do about it?
2.   What is your game plan?
3.   How do you suppose you could improve upon the situation?
4.   What amount of time are you willing to put into this?
5.   What sacrifices will you need to make?
6.   What daily habits will you adhere to?

Predictions:

1.   How do you suppose it will all work out?
2.   What will that get you?
3.   Where will this lead?
4.   What are the chances of success?
5.   What is your prediction?

Questions about the question:

1.   Could you explain to me the purpose of your question?
2.   What does your question mean?
3.   Do you understand the reason I asked you this question?

Rationale, reasons, and evidence:

1.   What do you think is causing that to happen?
2.   How do you know this?
3.   Show me ... ?
4.   Can you give me an example of that?

5. What do you think causes ... ?
6. What is the nature of this?
7. Are these reasons good enough?
8. What facts can you give me about ... ?
9. What evidence have you seen?
10. Are there any connections to anything from your past?
11. Could you tell me what is causing you to feel that way?
12. Do you believe there is a reason this happened?
13. Are these reasons enough to confirm your belief?

Resources:

1. What resources do you need to help you decide?
2. What do you know about it now?
3. How do you suppose you can find out more about it?
4. What kind of picture do you have right now?
5. Do you know your available resources?

Starting the session:

1. What's occurred since we last spoke?
2. What would you like to talk about?
3. What's new/the latest/the update?
4. How was your week?
5. Where are you right now?

Substance:

1. What seems to be the trouble?
2. What seems to be the main obstacle?
3. What is stopping you?
4. What concerns you the most about ... ?
5. What do you want?

Summary

1. What is your conclusion?
2. How is this working?
3. How would you describe this?
4. What do you think this all amounts to?
5. How would you summarize the effort so far?

Taking action

1. What action will you take?
2. And after that?
3. What will you do?
4. When will you do it?
5. Is this a time for action? What action?
6. Where do you go from here? When will you do that?
7. What are your next steps?
8. By what date or time will you complete these steps?

Thinking critically and with clarity:

1. What makes you say that?
2. What exactly does this mean?
3. What is the nature of this?
4. What do we already know about this?
5. Can you give me an example?
6. How does this relate to what we have been talking about?
7. Are you saying ... or ... ?
8. Can you rephrase that, please?
9. What makes you feel that way?
10. How do you think this relates?
11. Could you tell me more?
12. How could you rephrase that?

Thinking more deeply:

1. What do you want out of life?
2. What is the purpose of your life?
3. If you had a magic wand, what would you want?
4. What legacy do you wish to leave behind?
5. Are you living a life for yourself or others?

Transformation of self:

1. In which areas of your life do you find yourself most in need of transformation?
2. Whom could you seek to emulate?
3. Who in your life can mentor you and help you with this transformation?
4. What do you admire about them?
5. What characteristic would you like to see in your life that they possess?
6. What would you want to resist?

QUESTIONS JESUS ASKED

Note how Jesus is helping His listener to gain awareness and understanding on their own. He used questions to help one critically think and to empower them by giving them freedom instead of explaining or advising.

Italics are used when the word "why" has been restated as the word "what" or otherwise rephrased. Otherwise, these quotes are taken from the NIV.

1. Matthew 5:13 — "You are the salt of the earth. But if the salt loses its saltiness, how can it be made salty again?"

2. Matthew 5:46-47 — "If you love those who love you, what reward will you get? ... And if you greet only your own people, what are you doing more than others?"

3. Matthew 6:25 — "Is not life more than food, and the body more than clothes?"

4. Matthew 6:26 — "Look at the birds of the air; they do not sow or reap or store away in barns, and yet your heavenly Father feeds them. Are you not much more valuable than they?"

5. Matthew 6:27 — "Can any one of you by worrying can add a single hour to your life?"

6. Matthew 6:30 — "If that is how God clothes the grass of the field, which is here today and tomorrow is thrown into the fire, will he not much more clothe you—you of little faith?"

7. Matthew 6:31 — "So do not worry, saying, 'What shall we eat?' or 'What shall we drink?' or 'What shall we wear?'"

8. Matthew 7:4 — "How can you say to your brother, 'Let me take the speck out of your eye,' when all the time there is a plank in your own eye?"

9. Matthew 7:9-10 — "Which of you, if your son asks for bread, will give him a stone? Or if he asks for a fish, will give him a snake?"

10. Matthew 8:26 — He replied, *"You of little faith, what is causing you to be so afraid?"*

11. Matthew 9:4 — Knowing their thoughts, Jesus said, *"What is causing you to entertain evil thoughts in your hearts?"*

12. Matthew 10:29 — "Are not two sparrows sold for a penny? Yet not one of them will fall to the ground outside your Father's care."

13. Matthew 11:16 — "To what can I compare this generation?"

14. Matthew 12:11 — He said to them, "If any of you has a sheep and it falls into a pit on the Sabbath, will you not take hold of it and lift it out?"

15. Matthew 12:26 — "If Satan drives out Satan, he is divided against himself. How then can his kingdom stand?"

16. Matthew 12:34 — "You brood of vipers, how can you who are evil say anything good? For the mouth speaks what the heart is full of."

17. Matthew 12:48 — He replied to him, "Who is my mother, and who are my brothers?"

18. Matthew 14:31 — Immediately Jesus reached out his hand and caught him. "You of little faith," he said, *"what is causing you to doubt?"*

19. Matthew 16:8-11 — Aware of their discussion, Jesus asked, *"You of little faith, what is the reason you are talking among yourselves about having no bread? Do you still not understand? Don't you remember the five* loaves for the five thousand, and how many basketfuls you gathered? Or the seven loaves for the four thousand, and how many basketfuls you

gathered? How is it you don't understand that I was not talking to you about bread?"

20. Matthew 16:26 — "What good will it be for someone to gain the whole world, yet forfeit their soul? Or what can anyone give in exchange for their soul?

21. Matthew 18:12 — "If a man owns a hundred sheep, and one of them wanders away, will he not leave the ninety-nine on the hills and go to look for the one that wandered off?"

22. Matthew 18:33 — "Shouldn't you have had mercy on your fellow servant just as I had on you?"

23. Matthew 19:17 — *"What is the reason you ask me about what is good?"* Jesus replied.

24. Matthew 20:6 — "About five in the afternoon he went out and found still others standing around. He asked them, *'What is the reason you have been standing here all day long doing nothing?'"*

25. Matthew 20:22 — "You don't know what you are asking," Jesus said to them. "Can you drink the cup I am going to drink?"

26. Matthew 20:32 — Jesus stopped and called them. "What do you want me to do for you?" he asked.

27. Matthew 22:12 — He asked, "How did you get in here without wedding clothes, friend?"

28. Matthew 22:18 — But Jesus, knowing their evil intent, said, *"You hypocrites, what is the reason you are trying to trap me?"*

29. Matthew 23:17 — "You blind fools! Which is greater: the gold, or the temple that makes the gold sacred?"

30. Matthew 23:33 — "You snakes! You brood of vipers! How will you escape being condemned to hell?"

31. Matthew 26:53 — "Do you think I cannot call on my Father, and he will at once put at my disposal more than twelve legions of angels?"

32. Matthew 26:54 — "But how then would the Scriptures be fulfilled that say it must happen in this way?"

33. Mark 2:8 — *"What is causing you to think these things?"*

34. Mark 2:9 — "Which is easier: to say to this paralyzed man, 'Your sins are forgiven,' or to say, 'Get up, take your mat and walk'?"

35. Mark 3:4 — Then Jesus asked them, "Which is lawful on the Sabbath: to do good or to do evil, to save life or to kill?"

36. Mark 3:23 — So Jesus called them over to him and began to speak to them in parables: "How can Satan drive out Satan?"

37. Mark 4:30 — Again he said, "What shall we say the kingdom of God is like, or what parable shall we use to describe it?"

38. Mark 4:40 — He said to his disciples, *"What is causing you to be so afraid?* Do you still have no faith?"

39. Mark 5:30 — At once Jesus realized that power had gone out from him. He turned around in the crowd and asked, "Who touched my clothes?"

40. Mark 5:39 — He went in and said to them, *"What is the reason for all this commotion and wailing?* The child is not dead but asleep."

41. Mark 7:18 — "Are you so dull?" he asked. "Don't you see that nothing that enters a person from the outside can defile them?"

42. Mark 8:5 — "How many loaves do you have?" Jesus asked.

43. Mark 8:12 — He sighed deeply and said, *"What is causing this generation to ask for a sign?"*

44. Mark 8:23 — When he had spit on the man's eyes and put his hands on him, Jesus asked, "Do you see anything?"

45. Mark 8:27 — Jesus and his disciples went on to the villages around Caesarea Philippi. On the way he asked them, "Who do people say I am?"

46. Mark 8:29 — "But what about you?" he asked. "Who do you say I am?"

47. Mark 9:12 — *"What is the reason then is it written that the Son of Man must suffer much and be rejected?"*

48. Mark 9:16 — "What are you arguing with them about?" he asked.

49. Mark 9:19 — "O unbelieving generation," Jesus replied, "how long shall I stay with you? How long shall I put up with you?"

50. Mark 9:33 — When he was in the house, he asked them, "What were you arguing about on the road?"

51. Mark 10:3 — "What did Moses command you?" he replied.

52. Mark 10:36 — "What do you want me to do for you?" he asked.

53. Mark 10:38 — "You don't know what you are asking," Jesus said. "Can you drink the cup I drink or be baptized with the baptism I am baptized with?"

54. Mark 11:30 — "John's baptism—was it from heaven, or of human origin? Tell me!"

55. Mark 12:15 — But Jesus knew their hypocrisy. *"What is the reason you are trying to trap me?"* he asked.

56. Mark 12:24 — Jesus replied, "Are you not in error because you do not know the Scriptures or the power of God?"

57. Mark 12:35 — While Jesus was teaching in the temple courts, he asked, *"How is it that the teachers of the law say that the Christ is the son of David?"*

58. Mark 12:37 — "David himself calls him 'Lord.' How then can he be his son?"

59. Mark 14:6 — "Leave her alone," said Jesus. *"What is the reason you are bothering her?"*

60. Mark 14:14 — "Say to the owner of the house he enters, 'The Teacher asks: Where is my guest room, where I may eat the Passover with my disciples?'"

61. Mark 14:37 — Then he returned to his disciples and found them sleeping. "Simon," he said to Peter, "are you asleep? Couldn't you keep watch for one hour?"

62. Mark 14:41 — Returning the third time, he said to them, "Are you still sleeping and resting? Enough!"

63. Mark 14:48 — "Am I leading a rebellion," said Jesus, "that you have come out with swords and clubs to capture me?"

64. Mark 15:34 —And at three in the afternoon Jesus cried out in a loud voice, "Eloi, Eloi, lama sabachthani?" (which means, *"My God, my God, for what have you forsaken me?"*).

65. Luke 2:49 — *"What is the reason you were searching for me?"* he asked. "Didn't you know I had to be in my Father's house?"

66. Luke 5:22 — Jesus knew what they were thinking and asked, *"What is the reason you are thinking these things in your hearts?"*

67. Luke 5:23 — "Which is easier: to say, 'Your sins are forgiven,' or to say, 'Get up and walk'?"

68. Luke 6:9 — Then Jesus said to them, "I ask you, which is lawful on the Sabbath: to do good or to do evil, to save life or to destroy it?"

69. Luke 6:34 — "And if you lend to those from whom you expect repayment, what credit is that to you? Even sinners lend to sinners, expecting to be repaid in full."

70. Luke 6:39 — He also told them this parable: "Can the blind lead the blind? Will they not both fall into a pit?"

71. Luke 6:42 — "How can you say to your brother, 'Brother, let me take the speck out of your eye,' when you yourself fail to see the plank in your own eye?"

72. Luke 6:46 — *"What is the reason you call me, 'Lord, Lord,' and do not do what I say?"*

73. Luke 7:24 — After John's messengers left, Jesus began to speak to the crowd about John: "What did you go out into the wilderness to see? A reed swayed by the wind?"

74. Luke 7:25 — "If not, what did you go out to see? A man dressed in fine clothes? No, those who wear expensive clothes and indulge in luxury are in palaces."

75. Luke 7:26 — "But what did you go out to see? A prophet?"

76. Luke 7:31 — "To what, then, can I compare the people of this generation? What are they like?"

77. Luke 7:42 — "Neither of them had the money to pay him back, so he forgave the debts of both. Now which of them will love him more?"

78. Luke 8:25 — "Where is your faith?" he asked his disciples.

79. Luke 8:30 — Jesus asked him, "What is your name?"

80. Luke 8:45 — "Who touched me?" Jesus asked.

81. Luke 9:18 — Once when Jesus was praying in private and his disciples were with him, he asked them, "Who do the crowds say I am?"

82. Luke 9:20 — "But what about you?" he asked. "Who do you say I am?"

83. Luke 9:25 — "What good is it for someone to gain the whole world, and yet lose or forfeit their very self?"

84. Luke 10:36 — "Which of these three do you think was a neighbor to the man who fell into the hands of robbers?"

85. Luke 11:11 — "Which of you fathers, if your son asks for a fish, will give him a snake instead?"
86. Luke 11:12 — "Or if he asks for an egg, will give him a scorpion?"
87. Luke 11:19 — "Now if I drive out demons by Beelzebul, by whom do your followers drive them out?"
88. Luke 11:40 — "You foolish people! Did not the one who made the outside make the inside also?"
89. Luke 12:6 — "Are not five sparrows sold for two pennies? Yet not one of them is forgotten by God."
90. Luke 12:14 — Jesus replied, "Man, who appointed me a judge or an arbiter between you?"
91. Luke 12:17 — "He thought to himself, 'What shall I do? I have no place to store my crops.'"
92. Luke 12:20 — "But God said to him, 'You fool! This very night your life will be demanded from you. Then who will get what you have prepared for yourself?'"
93. Luke 12:26 — *"Since you cannot do this very little thing, what good would it do you to worry about the rest?"*
94. Luke 12:42 — "Who then is the faithful and wise manager, whom the master puts in charge of his servants to give them their food allowance at the proper time?"
95. Luke 12:51 — "Do you think I came to bring peace on earth? No, I tell you, but division."
96. Luke 12:56-57 — "Hypocrites! … How is it that you don't know how to interpret this present time? Why don't you judge for yourselves what is right?"
97. Luke 13:2 — Jesus answered, "Do you think that these Galileans were worse sinners than all the other Galileans because they suffered this way?"
98. Luke 13:4-5 — "Or those eighteen who died when the tower in Siloam fell on them—do you think they were more guilty than all the others living in Jerusalem? I tell you, no!"

99. Luke 13:7 — "So he said to the man who took care of the vineyard, 'For three years now I've been coming to look for fruit on this fig tree and haven't found any. Cut it down! *For what reason should it use up the soil?*'"

100. Luke 13:15 — The Lord answered him, "You hypocrites! Doesn't each of you on the Sabbath untie your ox or donkey from the stall and lead it out to give it water?"

101. Luke 13:16 — "Then should not this woman, a daughter of Abraham, whom Satan has kept bound for eighteen long years, be set free on the Sabbath day from what bound her?"

102. Luke 13:18 — Then Jesus asked, "What is the kingdom of God like? What shall I compare it to?"

103. Luke 13:20 — Again he asked, "What shall I compare the kingdom of God to?"

104. Luke 14:3 — Jesus asked the Pharisees and experts in the law, "Is it lawful to heal on the Sabbath or not?"

105. Luke 14:5 — Then he asked them, "If one of you has a child or an ox that falls into a well on the Sabbath day, will you not immediately pull it out?"

106. Luke 14:28 — "Suppose one of you wants to build a tower. Won't you first sit down and estimate the cost to see if you have enough money to complete it?"

107. Luke 14:31 — "Or suppose a king is about to go to war against another king. Won't he first sit down and consider whether he is able with ten thousand men to oppose the one coming against him with twenty thousand?"

108. Luke 15:4 — "Suppose one of you has a hundred sheep and loses one of them. Doesn't he leave the ninety-nine in the open country and go after the lost sheep until he finds it?"

109. Luke 15:8 — "Or suppose a woman has ten silver coins and loses one. Doesn't she light a lamp, sweep the house and search carefully until she finds it?"

110. Luke 16:11-12 — "So if you have not been trustworthy in handling worldly wealth, who will trust you with true riches? And if you have not been trustworthy with someone else's property, who will give you property of your own?"

111. Luke 17:7 — "Suppose one of you has a servant plowing or looking after the sheep. Will he say to the servant when he comes in from the field, 'Come along now and sit down to eat'?"

112. Luke 17:8 — "Won't he rather say, 'Prepare my supper, get yourself ready and wait on me while I eat and drink; after that you may eat and drink'?"

113. Luke 17:9 — "Will he thank the servant because he did what he was told to do?"

114. Luke 17:18 — "Has no one returned to give praise to God except this foreigner?"

115. Luke 18:7-8 — "And will not God bring about justice for his chosen ones, who cry out to him day and night? Will he keep putting them off? I tell you, he will see that they get justice, and quickly. However, when the Son of Man comes, will he find faith on the earth?"

116. Luke 18:19 — "*What is the reason you call me good?*" Jesus answered. "No one is good—except God alone."

117. Luke 18:41 — "What do you want me to do for you?"

118. Luke 19:22 — "His master replied, 'I will judge you by your own words, you wicked servant! You knew, did you, that I am a hard man, taking out what I did not put in, and reaping what I did not sow?"

119. Luke 19:23 — "*What is the reason you didn't put my money on deposit, so that when I came back, I could have collected it with interest?*'"

120. Luke 20:15 — "So they threw him out of the vineyard and killed him. What then will the owner of the vineyard do to them?"

121. Luke 20:17 — Jesus looked directly at them and asked, "Then what is the meaning of that which is written: / 'The stone the builders rejected / has become the cornerstone'?"

122. Luke 20:41 — Then Jesus said to them, "*How is it said that the Messiah is the Son of David?*"

123. Luke 20:44 — "David calls him 'Lord.' How then can he be his son?"

124. Luke 22:27 — "For who is greater, the one who is at the table or the one who serves? Is it not the one who is at the table? But I am among you as one who serves."

125. Luke 22:35 — Then Jesus asked them, "When I sent you without purse, bag or sandals, did you lack anything?"

126. Luke 22:46 — *"What is the reason you are sleeping?"* he asked them.

127. Luke 22:48 — But Jesus asked him, "Judas, are you betraying the Son of Man with a kiss?"

128. Luke 22:52 — Then Jesus said to the chief priests, the officers of the temple guard, and the elders, who had come for him, "Am I leading a rebellion, that you have come with swords and clubs?"

129. Luke 23:31 — "For if people do these things when the tree is green, what will happen when it is dry?"

130. Luke 24:38 — He said to them, *"What is causing you to be troubled, and what is the reason you are allowing doubts to rise in your minds?"*

131. Luke 24:41 — And while they still did not believe it because of joy and amazement, he asked them, "Do you have anything here to eat?"

132. John 1:38 — Turning around, Jesus saw them following and asked, "What do you want?"

133. John 2:4 — *"Woman, what is the reason you are involving me?"* Jesus replied. "My hour has not yet come."

134. John 3:10 — "You are Israel's teacher," said Jesus, "and do you not understand these things?"

135. John 3:12 — "I have spoken to you of earthly things and you do not believe; how then will you believe if I speak of heavenly things?"

136. John 4:7 — When a Samaritan woman came to draw water, Jesus said to her, "Will you give me a drink?"

137. John 4:35 — "Don't you have a saying, 'It's still four months until harvest'? I tell you, open your eyes and look at the fields! They are ripe for harvest."

138. John 5:6 — When Jesus saw him lying there and learned that he had been in this condition for a long time, he asked him, "Do you want to get well?"

139. John 5:44 — "How can you believe since you accept glory from one another but do not seek the glory that comes from the only God?"

140. John 5:47 — "But since you do not believe what he wrote, how are you going to believe what I say?"

141. John 6:5 — When Jesus looked up and saw a great crowd coming toward him, he said to Philip, "Where shall we buy bread for these people to eat?"

142. John 6:61 — Aware that his disciples were grumbling about this, Jesus said to them, "Does this offend you?"

143. John 6:67 — "You do not want to leave too, do you? "Jesus asked the Twelve.

144. John 6:70 — Then Jesus replied, "Have I not chosen you, the Twelve? Yet one of you is a devil!"

145. John 7:19 — "Has not Moses given you the law? Yet not one of you keeps the law. Why are you trying to kill me?"

146. John 7:23 — *"Now if a boy can be circumcised on the Sabbath so that the law of Moses may not be broken, what is causing you to be angry with me for healing a man's whole body on the Sabbath?"*

147. John 8:10 — Jesus straightened up and asked her, "Woman, where are they? Has no one condemned you?"

148. John 8:43 — *"What is the reason my language is not clear to you?"*

149. John 8:46a — "Can any of you prove me guilty of sin?"

150. John 8:46b — *"If I am telling the truth, what is the reason you don't believe me?"*

151. John 9:35 — Jesus heard that they had thrown him out, and when he found him, he said, "Do you believe in the Son of Man?"

152. John 10:32 — But Jesus said to them, "I have shown you many good works from the Father. For which of these do you stone me?"

153. John 10:34 — Jesus answered them, "Is it not written in your Law, 'I have said you are "gods"'?"

154. John 10:35–36 — "If he called them 'gods,' to whom the word of God came—and the Scripture cannot be set aside—what about the one whom the Father set apart as his very own and sent into the world? *What is the reason then you accuse me of blasphemy because I said, 'I am God's Son'?"*

155. John 11:34 — "Where have you laid him?" he asked.

156. John 11:40 — Then Jesus said, "Did I not tell you that if you believe, you will see the glory of God?"

157. John 12:27 — "Now my soul is troubled, and what shall I say? 'Father, save me from this hour'? No, it was for this very reason I came to this hour."

158. John 13:12 — When he had finished washing their feet, he put on his clothes and returned to his place. "Do you understand what I have done for you?" he asked them.

159. John 13:38 — Then Jesus answered, "Will you really lay down your life for me?"

160. John 14:9 — Jesus answered: "Don't you know me, Philip, even after I have been among you such a long time? Anyone who has seen me has seen the Father. How can you say, 'Show us the Father'? Don't you believe that I am in the Father, and that the Father is in me?"

161. John 16:19 — Jesus saw that they wanted to ask him about this, so he said to them, "Are you asking one another what I meant when I said, 'In a little while you will see me no more, and then after a little while you will see me'?"

162. John 18:4 — Jesus, knowing all that was going to happen to him, went out and asked them, "Who is it you want?"

163. John 18:7 — Again he asked them, "Who is it you want?"

164. John 18:11 — Jesus commanded Peter, "Put your sword away! Shall I not drink the cup the Father has given me?"

165. John 18:21 — *"What is the reason you question me?* Ask those who heard me. Surely they know what I said."

166. John 18:23 — "If I said something wrong," Jesus replied, "testify as to what is wrong. *But if I spoke the truth, what is the reason you struck me?"*

167. John 18:34 — "Is that your own idea," Jesus asked, "or did others talk to you about me?"

168. John 20:15 — He asked her, *"Woman, what is the reason you are crying?* Who is it you are looking for?"

169. John 21:5 — He called out to them, "Friends, haven't you any fish?"

170. John 21:15 — When they had finished eating, Jesus said to Simon Peter, "Simon son of John, do you love me more than these?"

171. John 21:16 — Again Jesus said, "Simon son of John, do you love me?"

172. John 21:17 — The third time he said to him, "Simon son of John, do you love me?"
173. John 21:22 — Jesus answered, "If I want him to remain alive until I return, what is that to you? You must follow me."

REPLACING NEGATIVE FEELINGS OR LIES ONE HAS BELIEVED WITH GOD'S TRUTH

When you are listening to your client, remember you are listening for patterns, fears, triggers, and the lies that they believe. As you hear any of these words, be sure to replace them with words that are God's truth and closely resembling the antonym of what they believed. You can even ask your client what they would like to feel instead and use that word. Trust that your client knows the answers because God speaks to them.

Below is a brief list of lies and truths. Keep in mind the list is endless, and there are many more words to be included. This is just a starting point with some of the most common lies that clients may have been taught to believe.

The positive words are what you will use in creating meditations to help your client to reprogram their mind and develop a new internal narrator. Use these words to bless people into who they were created to become: their true identity in Christ.

Remember, the enemy uses these lies to condemn and keep people stuck. Never in our practice do we use the negative word, even stated in a positive

231

way. Even in our questions, we must be careful to not plant negative seeds or suggestions. Simply ask how they are feeling about something or how they would like to feel. Ask how God feels about them, and what He would say to them. If it is negative, it isn't what God would say.

Lies	Truths
Abandoned	Cared For, Cherished, Connected, Included
Abused	Adored, Cherished, Loved, Respected, Treasured
Accused	Absolved, Vindicated, Innocent, Understood
Afraid	Confident, Content, Peaceful, Powerful, Unafraid
Aggravated	Calm, Content, Happy, Peaceful
Agony	Comfort, Content, Healthy, Peaceful, Joyful
Alienated	Accepted, Cherished, Loved
Alone	Bonded, Cared For, Connected, Cherished, Loved
Aloof	Caring, Kind, Interested, Loving, Warm
Angry	Calm, Content, Forgiving, Loving, Merciful, Peaceful

Anxiety	Calm, Content, Faithful, In Control, Peaceful, Powerful, Trusting
Apathetic	Caring, Compassionate, Concerned, Empathetic, Loving
Argumentative	Accepting, Agreeable, Flexible, Grace Filled, Harmonious, Peaceful
Arrogant	Accepting, Compassionate, Grace Filled, Humble, Loving, Teachable
Ashamed	Clean, Forgiven, Glorified, Powerful, Pure, Righteous
Attacked	Defended, Protected, Supported, Upheld
Avoidant	In Control, Dedicated, Facing, Helpful, Permitting, Purposeful
Awful	Content, Good, Happy, Joyful, Loving, Peaceful
Awkward	Bold, Confident, Content, Graceful, Smooth, Powerful
Bad	Good, Loved, Priceless, Treasured, Worthwhile, Valuable
Beaten Down	Elevated, Excited, Happy, Powerful, Purposeful, Joyful
Betrayed	Confident, Defended, Loved, Powerful, Protected, Respected, Supported
Bitter	Content, Forgiving, Loving, Peaceful, Purposeful, Useful
Blocked	Directed, Driven, Joyful, Passionate, Productive, Purposeful
Boastful	Grateful, Humble, Modest, Sincere
Bondage	Free, Liberated, Powerful, Released, Independent, Joyful

Bored	Creative, Excited, Passionate, Purposeful, Involved
Careless	Accurate, Attentive, Careful, Detailed, Thoughtful
Chaotic	Calm, Methodical, Ordered, Organized, Peaceful, Purposeful, Quiet
Cheap	Cherished, Priceless, Treasured, Valuable, Worthwhile
Childish	Mature, Sensitive, Thoughtful, Understanding, Wise
Clingy	Content, Independent, Powerful, Self-Assured, Surrendered, Unattached
Closed-Minded	Accepting, Flexible, Humble, Teachable, Wise
Comparison	Adored, Assured, Content, Cooperative, Cherished, Independent, Unique
Complaining	Approval, Appreciative, Grateful, Thankful
Compromised	Faithful, Honest, Honoring, Loyal, Obedient, Steadfast
Compulsive	Accepting, Content, Flexible, Grace Filled, Peaceful, Relaxed
Conceited	Caring, Empowering, Grace Filled, Humble, Teachable
Conflict	Agreeable, Content, Forgiving, Peaceful

Controlling	Accepting, Flexible, Humble, Pliable, Relaxed, Submissive
Cynical	Accepting, Believing, Optimistic, Trusting
Confused	Clarity, Comprehend, Directed, Powerful, Purposeful, Wise
Deceitful	Honest, Honorable, True
Defeated	Successful, Victorious, Renewed, Tenacious
Deficient	Capable, Competent, Sufficient
Defiled	Clean, Purified, Renewed, Restored
Degraded	Dignified, Honored, Praised, Valued
Dependent	Capable, Independent, Self-Reliant
Depressed	Energized, Enthused, Excited, Joyful, Passionate, Purposeful
Despair	Assured, Courageous, Faithful, Hope Filled, Trusting
Despising	Caring, Faithful, Forgiving, Loving
Destroyed	Protected, Restored, Renewed, Saved
Different	Authentic, Equal, Equivalent, Kindred, Similar
Disappointed	Accepting, Content, Hopeful, Peaceful
Disappointing	Encouraging, Helpful, Pleasing, Satisfactory

Dumb	Bright, Intelligent, Smart, Wise
Egotistical	Humble, Selfless, Teachable
Embarrassed	Confident, Courageous, Proud
Empty	Filled with Joy, Full Of life, Joyful
Enraged	Calm, Forgiving, Peaceful, Relaxed
Envious	Accepting, Charitable, Generous, Kind
Exhausted	Energized, Enthused, Invigorated
Failing	Accomplished, Capable, Competent, Successful
Faithless	Faithful, Loyal, Steadfast
Fearful	Brave, Courageous, Faithful, Trusting
Forced	Able to Choose, Free, Liberated
Forgetful	Able to Remember, Aware, Careful, Mindful, Thoughtful
Forgotten	Included, Remembered, Treasured
Forsaken	Favored, Indispensable, Saved
Frantic	Calm, Collected, Relaxed
Frustrated	Content, Delighted, Pleased

Gloomy	Bright, Excited, Happy, Light-Hearted
Greedy	Charitable, Generous, Unselfish
Grieved	Comforted, Consoled, Healed, Restored, Soothed
Guilty	Absolved, Forgiven, Pardoned, Peaceful, Unashamed
Hard-Hearted	Caring, Loving, Meek, Soft, Tender
Hateful	Affectionate, Forgiving, Gracious, Loving, Sweet
Haunted	Protected, Safe, Secure, Sheltered
Heartbroken	Consoled, Comforted, Cheerful, Healed
Hesitant	Assertive, Eager, Enthusiastic, Productive
Hopeless	Assured, Faithful, Great Future, Trusting
Humiliated	Esteemed, Favored, Honored, Loved
Hurried	Easygoing, Organized, Relaxed
Hurt	Comforted, Forgiveness, Honored, Revered
Impatient	Accepting, Calm, Patient, Relaxed
Impossible	Believing, Faithful, Possible, Trusting
Impulsive	Aware, Mindful, Slow, Thoughtful
Inadequate	Adequate, Capable, Competent, Qualified

Inconsiderate	Concerned, Considerate, Kind, Loving, Thoughtful
Indecisive	Clear, Decisive, Directed, Resolute
Indifferent	Attentive, Concerned, Mindful, Thoughtful
Ineffective	Effective, Meaningful, Productive, Successful
Insane	Balanced, Competent, Sane, Stable
Intense	Accepting, Calm, Grace Filled, Peaceful, Relaxed
Intimidated	Assured, Calm, Confident, Reassured
Jealous	Accepting, Benevolent, Esteemed, Well Meaning
Lacking	Abounding, Complete, Enough, Sufficient
Lazy	Alive, Ambitious, Energized, Motivated
Left Out	Cared About, Embraced, Honored, Included
Less Than	Equal To, Esteemed, Important, Talented
Let Down	Built Up, Edified, Elevated, Hope Filled
Livid	Calm, Forgiving, Loving, Merciful, Peaceful
Lonely	Accepted, Comforted, Connected, Fulfilled, Loved

Longing	Accepting, Content, Hopeful, Peaceful, Trusting
Lost	Clarity, Directed, Focused, Found, Purposeful
Low Self-Esteem	Confident, Secure, Self-Assured, Sure, Upbeat
Lustful	Disciplined, Integrity, Moral, Pure, Self-Controlled
Lying	Authentic, Forthright, Honest, Trustworthy, Truthful
Mad	Forgiving, Happy, Joyful, Loving, Peaceful
Manipulated	Discerning, Perceptive, Prudent, Thoughtful, Wise
Manipulative	Decent, Forthright, Genuine, Honest, Proper
Martyr	Cared for, Independent, Strong, Valued, Wise
Materialistic	Generous, Giving, Godly, Humble, Spiritual
Mean	Caring, Considerate, Gentle, Kind, Loving, Virtuous
Melancholy	Blissful, Cheerful, Delighted, Happy, Sunny
Misunderstand	Comprehend, Enlightened, Grasp, Understand, Wise
Misunderstood	Admired, Appreciated, Heard, Seen, Understood, Valued
Moody	Cheerful, Constant, Happy, Stable, Steadfast

Morbid	Caring, Good Natured, Healthy, Sane, Sound
Naughty	Agreeable, Behaved, Disciplined, Good, Obedient
Negative	Cheerful, Happy, Optimistic, Positive, Upbeat
Neglected	Attended To, Cared For, Cherished, Remembered
Negligent	Attentive, Aware, Caring, Thoughtful, Responsible
Nervous	Calm, Composed, Confident, Peaceful, Relaxed, Stable
No Good	Adored, Priceless, Valued, Special, Treasured
Not Enough	Exceptional, Important, Very Loved, Worthy
Novice	Excellent, Expert, Praiseworthy, Proficient, Skillful
Numb	Alive, Energized, Invigorated, Passionate, Refreshed
Obnoxious	Agreeable, Charming, Delightful, Enjoyable, Pleasant
Obsessive	Balanced, Content, Healthy, Relaxed, Secure, Stable, Steady
Offended	Calm, Content, Peaceful, Satisfied, Secure, Thankful
Opinionated	Accepting, Compliant, Flexible, Pliable, Tolerant

Opposing	Helping, Like-Minded, Obliging, United, Willing
Outcast	Accepted, Friend, Honored, Included, Insider, Restored
Out of Control	Calm, Centered, Composed, Grounded, Self-Controlled
Oversensitive	Accepting, Confident, Forgiving, Resilient, Strong
Old	Healthy, Purposeful, Significant, Vital, Youthful
Pained	Comforted, Eased, Peaceful, Pleased, Soothed, Tranquil
Purposeless	Decided, Determined, Purposeful, Significant
Perfectionist	Accepting, Allowing, Forgiving, Grace Filled, Loving
Perplexed	Clear, Discerning, Directed, Knowing, Understanding, Wise
Persecuted	Acquitted, Exonerated, Forgiven, Pardoned, Welcomed
Pessimistic	Cheerful, Enthusiastic, Hopeful, Optimistic, Trusting
Powerless	Dynamic, Impressive, Mighty, Powerful, Strong
Prejudiced	Accepting, Admire, Appreciated, Loving, Welcoming
Prideful	Contrite, Humble, Modest, Simple, Teachable

Quarrelsome	Good-Natured, Harmonious, Peacemaker
Quitting	Committed, Resolute, Steadfast, Uncompromising
Rage	Calm, Forgiveness, Kind, Love, Merciful, Peace
Refusal	Cooperative, Flexible, Soft, Teachable
Regret	Accepting, Content, Forgiveness of Self, Onward, Peace, Progressive
Resentment	Friendship, Forgiveness, Love, Peace, Unity
Ridiculed	Approved, Applauded, Commended, Praised
Rude	Considerate, Gracious, Kind, Sympathetic, Warm-Hearted
Sad	Cheerful, Comforted, Healed, Joyful, Peaceful, Restored
Self-Conscious	At Ease, Confident, Self-Assured, Trusting Self
Selfish	Caring, Charitable, Considerate, Generous, Selfless
Shallow	Deep, Essential, Meaningful, Purposeful, Worthwhile
Shameless	Chaste, Dignified, Modest, Quiet, Reserved
Shocked	Comforted, Renewed, Unaffected, Unshaken
Shy	Affectionate, Assertive, Friendly, Neighborly, Receptive
Sinful	Apologetic, Chaste, Contrite, Honest, Repentant, Virtuous

Sinking	Buoyed-Up, Elevated, Invigorated, Uplifted
Slave	Appreciated, Free, Independent, Liberated, Renewed, Saved, Valued
Stressed	Calm, Composed, Peaceful, Relaxed, Tranquil
Suicidal	Assured, Full of Life, Hopeful, Loved, Loving, Passionate, Purposeful, Trusting
Tempted	Committed, Devoted, Loyal, Steadfast, Strong, True
Threatened	Guarded, Protected, Safe, Secure, Sheltered, Treasured
Tired	Alert, Dynamic, Energetic, Spirited, Vigorous, Vital
Traitor	Committed, Dependable, Honest, Loyal, Steadfast, True, Virtuous
Ugly	Beautiful, Graceful, Handsome, Pretty, Lovely
Unappreciated	Acknowledged, Appreciated, Loved, Valued, Revered, Treasured
Unforgiving	Exonerated, Forgiving, Merciful, Loving, Tender, Understanding
Unproductive	Beneficial, Effective, Useful, Productive, Prolific, Successful
Unthankful	Blessed, Grateful, Happy, Joyful, Pleased, Thankful

Unsure	Certain, Clear, Confident, Convinced, Resolute, Sure
Useless	Effective, Good, Important, Useful, Worthwhile
Victim	Champion, On Top, In Control, Victorious, Triumphant
Void	Complete, Energetic, Filled, Full, Hopeful, Joyful, Passionate
Wallowing	Directed, Fulfilled, Focused on Good, Purposeful
Weak	Energetic, Firm, Healthy, Powerful, Resolute, Strong
Why	Direction, Faith, Hope, Powerful, Purpose, Strong, Trusting
Worry	Assured, Calm, Faithful, Hopeful, Trusting
Yearning	Blessed, Content, Fulfilled, Grateful, Gratified, Satisfied

WHO I AM IN CHRIST – REFERENCE SCRIPTURES

Adored	1 John 3:1
Authentic	John 8:32
Beautiful	Ecclesiastes 3:11
Brave	Philippians 4:13
Calm	Isaiah 43:2
Capable	James 1:5
Caring	Galatians 6:10
Cheerful	1 Thessalonians 5:16-18
Comforting	2 Corinthians 1:3-4
Committed	Ruth 1:16-18
Compassionate	James 1:27
Confident	Hebrews 4:16

Content	Hebrews 13:5
Daughter	Galatians 3:26
Dedicated	Revelation 14:12
Dependable	1 John 2:5-6
Determined	2 Timothy 4:7
Disciple	Isaiah 50:4
Disciplined	1 Peter 1:13
Discreet	Proverbs 8:12
Edifying	Romans 15:2
Energetic	Romans 12:8
Faithful	Psalm 23:6
Flexible	2 Timothy 2:15
Focused	Proverbs 4:25
Forgiving	Matthew 6:14-15
Free	2 Corinthians 3:17
Friend	Proverbs 17:17
Full of Light	Matthew 6:22
Full of Love	Philippians 1:9
Fun	Ecclesiastes 5:18-20
Generous	Psalm 37:21
Good	1 Timothy 4:4
Grace Filled	2 Thessalonians 3:18
Grateful	Psalm 66:8
Great Listener	Exodus 19:5
Grounded	Ephesians 3:17

Happy	Psalm 9:2
Hard Working	Proverbs 10:4
Helpful	Proverbs 31:15
Holy	John 17:17
Honorable	Romans 12:17
Hopeful	2 Corinthians 5:6
Hospitable	1 Timothy 5:10
Humble	James 4:10
Intelligent	James 3:13
Inspired	2 Peter 1:21
Joyful	Psalm 5:11
Kind	3 John 1:5
Leader	Psalm 18:43
Loved	John 13:34
Loyal	2 Kings 18:6
Merciful	Psalm 103:8
Modest	1 Timothy 5:2
Motherly	Titus 2:4
Non-Judgmental	Matthew 7:1
Nurturing	1 Peter 5:2
Obedient	Isaiah 1:19
Passionate	1 Peter 3:13
Patient	Proverbs 14:29
Peaceful	Proverbs 3:17
Persevering	Psalm 51:10

Persuasive	1 Corinthians 9:20
Positive	Proverbs 18:20
Powerful	2 Timothy 1:7
Prayerful	1 Thessalonians 5:17
Prepared	Philippians 1:10
Productive	Proverbs 21:5
Protective	John 15:13
Proud	1 Corinthians 1:31
Pure	Philippians 4:8
Quiet	Exodus 14:14
Relatable	1 Corinthians 9:20
Reliable	Proverbs 12:5
Resourceful	James 1:5
Responsible	1 Timothy 5:8
Reverent	Titus 2:3
Romantic	Genesis 2:18
Royal	James 2:8
Self-Controlled	2 Peter 1:6
Selfless	Mark 12:33
Sense of Humor	Proverbs 31:25-26
Servant	2 Timothy 1:3
Simple	James 5:12
Skilled	Exodus 35:31
Soft	Proverbs 25:15

Strong	Philippians 4:13
Successful	Romans 8:28
Supportive	Hebrews 10:24-25
Sweet	Psalm 133:1
Tender	1 Peter 3:8
Thankful	Psalm 100:4
Thoughtful	Philippians 4:10
Tolerant	Colossians 3:13
Transparent	Philippians 1:10
True	3 John 1:3
Trusting	Proverbs 30:5
Understanding	1 Kings 2:3
Victorious	Romans 8:37
Virtuous	Proverbs 31:10
Warrior	1 John 5:4
Wholesome	Ephesians 4:29
Wise	Ecclesiastes 7:12

CHRIST CENTERED COACH TRAINING SCRIPTURE REFERENCES

Equipped

- That the man of God may be complete, equipped for every good work. — 2 Timothy 3:17 ESV
- But in your hearts revere Christ as Lord. Always be prepared to give an answer to everyone who asks you to give the reason for the hope that you have. But do this with gentleness and respect. — 1 Peter 3:15 NIV

Discipling Others

- Go therefore and make disciples of all nations, baptizing them in the name of the Father and of the Son and of the Holy Spirit. — Matthew 28:19 ESV
- Him we proclaim, warning everyone and teaching everyone with all wisdom, that we may present everyone mature in Christ. — Colossians 1:28 ESV

Relying on God

- Trust in the Lord with all your heart, / and do not lean on your own understanding. —Proverbs 3:5 ESV
- Trust in the Lord forever, / for the Lord God is an everlasting rock. —Isaiah 26:4 ESV

Five Keys to Success

- Truth:
  - Then you will know the truth, and the truth will set you free. —John 8:32 NIV
- Purpose:
  - For the Scriptures say that God told Pharaoh, "I have appointed you for the very purpose of displaying my power in you and to spread my fame throughout the earth." — Romans 9:17 NLT
- Plans:
  - Plans fail for lack of counsel, but with many advisers they succeed. — Proverbs 15:22 NIV
- Action:
  - Therefore, since we are surrounded by such a great cloud of witnesses, let us throw off everything that hinders and the sin that so easily entangles. And let us run with perseverance the race marked out for us. — Hebrews 12:1 NIV
- Success:
  - All praise to God, the Father of our Lord Jesus Christ. God is our merciful Father and the source of all comfort. He comforts us in all our troubles so that we can comfort others. When they are troubled, we will be able to give them the same comfort God has given us. For the more we suffer for Christ, the more God will shower us with his comfort through Christ. — 2 Corinthians 1:3-5 NLT

The Ultimate Goal

- Who desires all people to be saved and to come to the knowledge of the truth. — 1 Timothy 2:4 ESV

- If you declare with your mouth, "Jesus is Lord," and believe in your heart that God raised him from the dead, you will be saved. — Romans 10:9 NIV
- To put off your old self, which belongs to your former manner of life and is corrupt through deceitful desires, and to be renewed in the spirit of your minds, and to put on the new self, created after the likeness of God in true righteousness and holiness. — Ephesians 4:22-24 ESV
- For though I am free from all, I have made myself a servant to all, that I might win more of them. To the Jews I became as a Jew, in order to win Jews. To those under the law I became as one under the law (though not being myself under the law) that I might win those under the law. To those outside the law I became as one outside the law (not being outside the law of God but under the law of Christ) that I might win those outside the law. To the weak I became weak, that I might win the weak. I have become all things to all people, that by all means I might save some. I do it all for the sake of the gospel, that I may share with them in its blessings. — 1 Corinthians 9:19–23 ESV

YKI – Your Kingdom Inheritance/ You Know It

- "Thy kingdom come, thy will be done in earth, as it is in heaven." — Matthew 6:10 KJV
- "And now I entrust you to God and the message of his grace that is able to build you up and give you an inheritance with all those he has set apart for himself." — Acts 20:32 NLT
- Even Gentiles, who do not have God's written law, show that they know his law when they instinctively obey it, even without having heard it. They demonstrate that God's law is written in their hearts, for their own conscience and thoughts either accuse them or tell them they are doing right. — Romans 2:14-15 NLT
- "But when he, the Spirit of truth, comes, he will guide you into all the truth. He will not speak on his own; he will speak only what he hears, and he will tell you what is yet to come." — John 16:13 NIV

The Christ-Centered Life

- "Seek the Kingdom of God above all else, and live righteously, and he will give you everything you need." — Matthew 6:33 NLT

- This is good, and it is pleasing in the sight of God our Savior, who desires all people to be saved and to come to the knowledge of the truth. — 1 Timothy 2:3-4 ESV

- For we are his workmanship, created in Christ Jesus for good works, which God prepared beforehand, that we should walk in them. — Ephesians 2:10 ESV

- "I don't speak on my own authority. The Father who sent me has commanded me what to say and how to say it." — John 12:49 NLT

- As for you, the anointing you received from him remains in you, and you do not need anyone to teach you. But as his anointing teaches you about all things and as that anointing is real, not counterfeit—just as it has taught you, remain in him. — 1 John 2:27 NIV

- Therefore, if anyone is in Christ, he is a new creation. The old has passed away; behold, the new has come. — 2 Corinthians 5:17 ESV

- When Christ, who is your life, appears, then you also will appear with him in glory. — Colossians 3:4 NIV

- "Blessed is the man who trusts in the LORD, / whose trust is the LORD. / He is like a tree planted by water, / that sends out its roots by the stream, / and does not fear when heat comes, / for its leaves remain green, / and is not anxious in the year of drought, / for it does not cease to bear fruit." — Jeremiah 17:7-8 ESV

- Search me, God, and know my heart; / test me and know my anxious thoughts. / See if there is any offensive way in me, / and lead me in the way everlasting. — Psalm 139:23-24 NIV

God's Blessing/ Vision Statement/ Godly Meditation

- The tongue has the power of life and death, / and those who love it will eat its fruit. —Proverbs 18:21 NIV

- The key to change is the heart. — Sirach 37:17 CEB (Catholic book in the OT)

- But the one who prophesies speaks to people for their strengthening, encouraging and comfort. Anyone who speaks in a tongue edifies themselves, but the one who prophesies edifies the church. — 1 Corinthians 14:3-4 NIV
- Let no corrupting talk come out of your mouths, but only such as is good for building up, as fits the occasion, that it may give grace to those who hear.— Ephesians 4:29 ESV
- And the LORD answered me: / "Write the vision; / make it plain on tablets, / so he may run who reads it." —Habakkuk 2:2 ESV
- Do not conform to the pattern of this world but be transformed by the renewing of your mind. Then you will be able to test and approve what God's will is—his good, pleasing and perfect will. — Romans 12:2 NIV
- Finally, brothers and sisters, whatever is true, whatever is noble, whatever is right, whatever is pure, whatever is lovely, whatever is admirable—if anything is excellent or praiseworthy—think about such things. — Philippians 4:8 NIV
- "The Spirit of the Lord is on me, / because he has anointed me / to proclaim good news to the poor. / He has sent me to proclaim freedom for the prisoners / and recovery of sight for the blind, / to set the oppressed free, / to proclaim the year of the Lord's favor." — Luke 4:18-19 NIV
- May these words of my mouth and this meditation of my heart / be pleasing in your sight, / LORD, my Rock and my Redeemer. — Psalm 19:14 NIV
- My mouth will speak words of wisdom; / the meditation of my heart will give you understanding. —Psalm 49:3 NIV

The I AM Rule

We were not created to live apart from God. Clarity and purpose must be adhered to. This rule is not intended to create a life apart from God or to think one can do anything apart from God. When working with non-Christians, teach godly principles and follow the Spirit's lead in order to bring the individual to Christ.

- "I am the vine; you are the branches. Whoever abides in me and I in him, he it is that bears much fruit, for apart from me you can do nothing." — John 15:5 ESV
- "I am the true vine, and my Father is the vinedresser." — John 15:1 ESV
- "This is the bread that comes down from heaven, so that one may eat of it and not die. I am the living bread that came down from heaven. If anyone eats of this bread, he will live forever. And the bread that I will give for the life of the world is my flesh." The Jews then disputed among themselves, saying, "How can this man give us his flesh to eat?" So Jesus said to them, "Truly, truly, I say to you, unless you eat the flesh of the Son of Man and drink his blood, you have no life in you. Whoever feeds on my flesh and drinks my blood has eternal life, and I will raise him up on the last day." — John 6:50-54 ESV
- Therefore, there is now no condemnation for those who are in Christ Jesus. — Romans 8:1 NIV
- Who is the man who desires life / And loves *length of* days that he may see good? / Keep your tongue from evil / And your lips from speaking deceit. — Psalm 34:12-13 NASB
- Do not lie to one another, since you laid aside the old self with its *evil* practices, and have put on the new self who is being renewed to a true knowledge according to the image of the One who created him. — Colossians 3:9-10 NASB
- The tongue has the power of life and death, / and those who love it will eat its fruit. —Proverbs 18:21 NIV

Rapport

- Though I am free and belong to no one, I have made myself a slave to everyone, to win as many as possible. To the Jews I became like a Jew, to win the Jews. To those under the law I became like on under the law (though I myself am not under the law), so as to win those under the law. To those not having the law I became like one not having the law (though I am not free from God's law but am under Christ's law), so as to win those not having the law. To the weak I became weak, to win the weak. I have become all things to all people so that by all possible means I might save some. I do all this for the sake of the gospel, that I may share in its blessings. — 1 Corinthians 9:19–23 NIV

- Let your reasonableness be known to everyone. The Lord is at hand. — Philippians 4:5 ESV

Listen

- My dear brothers and sisters, take note of this: Everyone should be quick to listen, slow to speak and slow to become angry. — James 1:19 NIV
- If one gives an answer before he hears, it is his folly and shame. — Proverbs 18:13 ESV
- Where there is no guidance, the people fall, / But in abundance of counselors there is victory. — Proverbs 11:14 NASB
- If anyone thinks he is religious and does not bridle his tongue but deceives his heart, this person's religion is worthless. — James 1:26 ESV
- Whoever restrains his words has knowledge, / and he who has a cool spirit is a man of understanding. — Proverbs 17:27 ESV
- And he said to them, "Pay attention to what you hear: with the measure you use, it will be measured to you, and still more will be added to you." — Mark 4:24 ESV

Questions

- The one who has knowledge uses words with restraint / ... Even fools are thought wise if they keep silent, / and discerning if they hold their tongues. — Proverbs 17:27-28 NIV
- Judge not, that ye be not judged. — Matthew 7:1 KJV
- If any of you lacks wisdom, let him ask God, who gives generously to all without reproach, and it will be given him. — James 1:5 ESV
- Therefore be imitators of God, as beloved children. — Ephesians 5:1 NASB

Discernment

- I say this because many deceivers, who do not acknowledge Jesus Christ as coming in the flesh, have gone out into the world. Any such person is the deceiver and the antichrist. Watch out that you do not lose what we have worked for, but that you may be rewarded fully. — 2 John 7, 8 NIV

- Anyone who runs ahead and does not continue in the teaching of Christ does not have God; whoever continues in the teaching has both the Father and the Son. — 2 John 9 NIV

Breaking Patterns

- Don't copy the behavior and customs of this world, but let God transform you into a new person by changing the way you think. Then you will learn to know God's will for you, which is good and pleasing and perfect. — Romans 12:2 NLT
- Jesus looked at them and said, "With man this is impossible, but not with God; all things are possible with God." — Mark 10:27 NIV

The Mind Attached to the Senses/ Discovering Reality/ Conscious vs Subconscious/ Faith

- He answered, "Whether he is a sinner I do not know. One thing I do know, that though I was blind, now I see." — John 9:25 ESV
- Make me to know your ways, O LORD; / teach me your paths. — Psalm 25:4 ESV
- Now faith is the assurance of things hoped for, the conviction of things not seen. For by it the people of old received their commendation. By faith we understand that the universe was created by the word of God, so that what is seen was not made out of things that are visible. By faith Abel offered to God a more acceptable sacrifice than Cain, through which he was commended as righteous, God commending him by accepting his gifts. And through his faith, though he died, he still speaks. By faith Enoch was taken up so that he should not see death, and he was not found, because God had taken him. Now before he was taken, he was commended as having pleased God. — Hebrews 11:1-5 ESV
- Jesus gave parables to help people relate to His message through word pictures and "experience" them through the mind, as in Matthew 13:31-32 (NASB): "He presented another parable to them, saying, 'The

kingdom of heaven is like a mustard seed, which a man took and sowed in his field; and this is smaller than all *other* seeds, but when it is full grown, it is larger than the garden plants and becomes a tree, so that THE BIRDS OF THE AIR COME AND NEST IN ITS BRANCHES.'"

NLP- Neuro: Thoughts, Mind; Linguistics: Words; Programming

- The Teacher sought to find just the right words to express truths clearly. — Ecclesiastes 12:10 NLT
- Let the words of my mouth, and the meditation of my heart, be acceptable in thy sight, O LORD, my strength, and my redeemer. — Psalm 19:14 KJV

Learning Styles

- Seeing the crowds, he went up on the mountain, and when he sat down, his disciples came to him. And he opened his mouth and taught them, saying: "Blessed are the poor in spirit, for theirs is the kingdom of heaven. / Blessed are those who mourn, for they shall be comforted. / Blessed are the meek, for they shall inherit the earth." — Matthew 5:1-5 ESV
- Let the wise hear and increase in learning, / and the one who understands obtain guidance. — Proverbs 1:5 ESV
- My brothers, show no partiality as you hold the faith in our Lord Jesus Christ, the Lord of glory. — James 2:1 ESV
- But as for you, teach what accords with sound doctrine. — Titus 2:1 ESV
- Here there is not Greek and Jew, circumcised and uncircumcised, barbarian, Scythian, slave, free; but Christ is all, and in all. — Colossians 3:11 ESV

Poison Words vs. Edifying

- Death and life are in the power of the tongue, / and those who love it will eat its fruits. —Proverbs 18:21 ESV
- There is one whose rash words are like sword thrusts, / but the tongue of the wise brings healing. — Proverbs 12:18 ESV

- And the tongue is a fire, a world of unrighteousness. The tongue is set among our members, staining the whole body, setting on fire the entire course of life, and set on fire by hell. — James 3:6 ESV
- Whoever keeps his mouth and his tongue / keeps himself out of trouble. — Proverbs 21:23 ESV

Christ-Centered Life

- For I do not speak on my own, but the Father who sent me commanded me to say all that I have spoken. — John 12:49 NIV
- As for you, the anointing you received from him remains in you, and you do not need anyone to teach you. But as his anointing teaches you about all things and as that anointing is real, not counterfeit—just as it has taught you, remain in him. — 1 John 2:27 NIV
- Therefore, if any man be in Christ, he is a new creature: old things are passed away; behold, all things are become new. — 2 Corinthians 5:17 KJV
- When Christ who is your life appears, then you also will appear with him in glory. —Colossians 3:4 ESV
- "Blessed is the man who trusts in the LORD, / whose trust is the LORD. / He is like a tree planted by water, / that sends out its roots by the stream, / and does not fear when heat comes, / for its leaves remain green, / and is not anxious in the year of drought, / for it does not cease to bear fruit." — Jeremiah 17:7-8 ESV
- Search me, God, and know my heart; / test me and know my anxious thoughts. / See if there is any offensive way in me, / and lead me in the way everlasting. — Psalm 139:23-24 NIV

Perfected in Christ

- "God's way is perfect. / All the LORD's promises prove true. / He is a shield for all who look to him for protection." — 2 Samuel 22:31 NLT
- For it is by grace you have been saved, through faith—and this is not from yourselves, it is the gift of God—not by works, so that no one can boast. — Ephesians 2:8-9 NIV

- Not as though I had already attained, either were already perfect: but I follow after, if that I may apprehend that for which also I am apprehended of Christ Jesus. — Philippians 3:12 KJV
- For by a single offering he has perfected for all time those who are being sanctified. —Hebrews 10:14 ESV

Godly Anchoring

- Not that we are competent in ourselves to claim anything for ourselves, but our competence comes from God. He has made us competent as ministers of a new covenant—not of the letter but of the Spirit; for the letter kills, but the Spirit gives life. — 2 Corinthians 3:5–6 NIV
- We have this as a sure and steadfast anchor of the soul, a hope that enters into the inner place behind the curtain. — Hebrews 6:19 ESV
- I therefore, a prisoner for the Lord, urge you to walk in a manner worthy of the calling to which you have been called, with all humility and gentleness, with patience, bearing with one another in love, eager to maintain the unity of the Spirit in the bond of peace. There is one body and one Spirit—just as you were called to the one hope that belongs to your call—one Lord, one faith, one baptism. — Ephesians 4:1-5 ESV
- And to the centurion Jesus said, "Go; let it be done for you as you have believed." And the servant was healed at that very moment. — Matthew 8:13 ESV
- Then God said, "Let us make man in our image, after our likeness. And let them have dominion over the fish of the sea and over the birds of the heavens and over the livestock and over all the earth and over every creeping thing that creeps on the earth." So God created man in his own image, / in the image of God he created him; / male and female he created them. And God blessed them. And God said to them, "Be fruitful and multiply and fill the earth and subdue it, and have dominion over the fish of the sea and over the birds of the heavens and over every living thing that moves on the earth." — Genesis 1:26–28 ESV

- If ye abide in me, and my words abide in you, ye shall ask what ye will, and it shall be done unto you. —John 15:7 KJV
- Therefore I tell you, whatever you ask in prayer, believe that you have received it, and it will be yours. — Mark 11:24 NIV
- Pray then like this: "Our Father in heaven, / hallowed be your name. / Your kingdom come, / your will be done, / on earth as it is in heaven. / Give us this day our daily bread, / and forgive us our debts, / as we also have forgiven our debtors. / And lead us not into temptation, / but deliver us from evil." — Matthew 6:9-13 ESV
- So we fix our eyes not on what is seen, but on what is unseen, since what is seen is temporary, but what is unseen is eternal. — 2 Corinthians 4:18 NIV

Ongoing Sessions

- As for you, brothers, do not grow weary in doing good. — 2 Thessalonians 3:13 ESV
- Bear one another's burdens, and so fulfill the law of Christ. — Galatians 6:2 ESV
- Not domineering over those in your charge, but being examples to the flock. — 1 Peter 5:3 ESV
- "Give, and it will be given to you. A good measure, pressed down, shaken together and running over, will be poured into your lap. For with the measure you use, it will be measured to you." — Luke 6:38 NIV
- Beloved, if God so loved us, we ought also to love one another. — 1 John 4:11 KJV
- For God gave us a spirit not of fear but of power and love and self-control. Therefore, do not be ashamed of the testimony about our Lord, nor of me his prisoner, but share in suffering for the gospel by the power of God. — 2 Timothy 1:7-8 ESV

Scriptures to Solve Problems or Fill Needs

Abandoned
- For the Lord your God is a merciful God; he will not abandon or destroy you or forget the covenant with your ancestors, which he confirmed to them by oath. — Deuteronomy 4:31 NIV
- No one will be able to stand against you all the days of your life. As I was with Moses, so I will be with you; I will never leave you nor forsake you. — Joshua 1:5 NIV
- Psalm 27:10, Acts 2:27, 2 Corinthians 4:9

Anger
- Don't sin by letting anger control you. / Think about it overnight and remain silent. — Psalm 4:4 NLT
- A gentle answer turns away wrath, but a harsh word stirs up anger. — Proverbs 15:1 NIV
- Proverbs 16:32, Ecclesiastes 7:9, Ephesians 4:26-27

Anxiety/Worry

- Cast your cares on the Lord / and he will sustain you; / he will never let / the righteous be shaken. — Psalm 55:22 NIV
- "Don't let your hearts be troubled. Trust in God, and trust also in me." — John 14:1 NLT
- John 14:27, Philippians 4:6-7, 1 Peter 5:7

Believe

- Therefore I tell you, whatever you ask for in prayer, believe that you have received it, and it will be yours. — Mark 11:24 NIV
- For God so loved the world that he gave his one and only Son, that whoever believes in him shall not perish but have eternal life. — John 3:16 NIV
- John 7:38, John 11:40, John 20:27

Betrayal

- A gossip betrays a confidence, / but a trustworthy person keeps a secret. — Proverbs 11:13 NIV
- A false witness will not go unpunished, / and he who breathes out lies will not escape. — Proverbs 19:5 ESV
- Matthew 24:10, Psalm 41:9, Matthew 7:12

Bitterness

- See to it that no one fails to obtain the grace of God; that no "root of bitterness" springs up and causes trouble, and by it many become defiled. — Hebrews 12:15 ESV
- Let all bitterness and wrath and anger and clamor and slander be put away from you, along with all malice. — Ephesians 4:31 ESV
- Acts 8:23, Mark 11:25, Romans 12:17

Blessings

- I will bless those who bless you, / and whoever curses you I will curse; / and all peoples on earth / will be blessed through you. — Genesis 12:3 NIV

- The LORD bless you and keep you; / the LORD make his face to shine upon you and be gracious to you; / the LORD lift up his countenance upon you and give you peace. — Numbers 6:24-26 ESV
- Romans 12:14, Ephesians 1:3, Romans 10:12

Boundaries

- The LORD is my chosen portion and my cup; / you hold my lot. / The lines have fallen for me in pleasant places; / indeed, I have a beautiful inheritance. / I bless the LORD who gives me counsel; / in the night also my heart instructs me. / I have set the LORD always before me; / because he is at my right hand, I shall not be shaken. / Therefore my heart is glad, and my whole being rejoices; / my flesh also dwells secure. — Psalm 16:5-9 ESV
- Do not be unequally yoked with unbelievers. For what partnership has righteousness with lawlessness? Or what fellowship has light with darkness? — 2 Corinthians 6:14 ESV
- Proverbs 22:24, Psalm 147:14, 1 Corinthians 15:33

Comfort

- Blessed be the God and Father of our Lord Jesus Christ, the Father of mercies and God of all comfort, who comforts us in all our affliction, so that we may be able to comfort those who are in any affliction, with the comfort with which we ourselves are comforted by God. — 2 Corinthians 1:3-4 ESV
- Even though I walk through the valley of the shadow of death, / I will fear no evil, / for you are with me; / your rod and your staff, / they comfort me. — Psalm 23:4 ESV
- Matthew 11:28-30, Psalm 119:50, Romans 8:26-28

Condemnation/Guilt

- Then I acknowledged my sin to you / and did not cover up my iniquity. / I said, "I will confess / my transgressions to the Lord." And you forgave / the guilt of my sin. — Psalm 32:5 NIV

- Jesus straightened up and asked her, "Woman, where are they? Has no one condemned you?" "No one, sir," she said. "Then neither do I condemn you," Jesus declared. "Go now and leave your life of sin." — John 8:10-11 NIV
- Romans 8:1, John 3:17, 1 John 1:9

Confession

- Rather, we have renounced secret and shameful ways; we do not use deception, nor do we distort the word of God. On the contrary, by setting forth the truth plainly we commend ourselves to everyone's conscience in the sight of God. — 2 Corinthians 4:2 NIV
- Nevertheless, God's solid foundation stands firm, sealed with this inscription: "The Lord knows those who are his," and, "Everyone who confesses the name of the Lord must turn away from wickedness." — 2 Timothy 2:19 NIV
- James 5:16, Psalm 32:5, Proverbs 28:13

Confidence

- I remain confident of this: / I will see the goodness of the LORD / in the land of the living. / Wait for the LORD; / be strong and take heart / and wait for the LORD. — Psalm 27:13-14 NIV
- But blessed are those who trust in the Lord / and have made the Lord their hope and confidence. — Jeremiah 17:7 NLT
- Philippians 1:6, 1 John 3:21-22, 1 John 4:16-17

Confusion

- For God is not a God of confusion but of peace. — 1 Corinthians 14:33 ESV
- For where envy and self-seeking *exist,* confusion and every evil thing *are* there. — James 3:16 NKJV
- Psalm 71:1, 2 Timothy 2:7, Galatians 5:10

Deliverance

- He said: / "The LORD is my rock, my fortress and my deliverer." — 2 Samuel 22:2 NIV
- I sought the Lord, and he answered me; / he delivered me from all my fears. — Psalm 34:4 NIV
- Psalm 107:6, Psalm 116:8, Daniel 12:1

Direction

- Show me your ways, LORD, / teach me your paths. / Guide me in your truth and teach me, / for you are God my Savior, / and my hope is in you all day long. — Psalm 25:4-5 NIV
- Direct my footsteps according to your word; / let no sin rule over me. — Psalm 119:133 NIV
- Psalm 25:12, Proverbs 4:11, Isaiah 30:21

Discouraged

- This is my command—be strong and courageous! Do not be afraid or discouraged. For the LORD your God is with you wherever you go." — Joshua 1:9 NLT
- Finally, brothers and sisters, whatever is true, whatever is noble, whatever is right, whatever is pure, whatever is lovely, whatever is admirable—if anything is excellent or praiseworthy—think about such things. — Philippians 4:8 NIV
- Hebrews 4:16, 2 Chronicles 20:17, Hebrews 12:1

Encouragement

- Such things were written in the Scriptures long ago to teach us. And the Scriptures give us hope and encouragement as we wait patiently for God's promises to be fulfilled. — Romans 15:4 NLT
- May our Lord Jesus Christ himself and God our Father, who loved us and by his grace gave us eternal encouragement and good hope, encourage your hearts and strengthen you in every good deed and word. — 2 Thessalonians 2:16-17 NIV

- 2 Timothy 4:2, Joshua 1:9, 1 Corinthians 14:3

Envy/Jealousy

- A heart at peace gives life to the body, / but envy rots the bones. — Proverbs 14:30 NIV
- Love is patient, love is kind. It does not envy, it does not boast, it is not proud. — 1 Corinthians 13:4 NIV
- Titus 3:3, Proverbs 23:17, Mark 7:21-22

Faith

- We do this by keeping our eyes on Jesus, the champion who initiates and perfects our faith. Because of the joy awaiting him, he endured the cross, disregarding its shame. Now he is seated in the place of honor beside God's throne. — Hebrews 12:2 NLT
- Now faith is confidence in what we hope for and assurance about what we do not see. — Hebrews 11:1 NIV
- Romans 10:17, 2 Corinthians 5:7, James 2:17

Family

- Therefore a man shall leave his father and his mother and hold fast to his wife, and they shall become one flesh. — Genesis 2:24 ESV
- Fathers, do not provoke your children to anger, but bring them up in the discipline and instruction of the Lord. — Ephesians 6:4 ESV
- 1 Timothy 3:4, Exodus 20:12, Proverbs 22:6

Fear

- Fear not, for I am with you; / be not dismayed, for I am your God; / I will strengthen you, I will help you, / I will uphold you with my righteous right hand. — Isaiah 41:10 ESV
- For God gave us a spirit not of fear but of power and love and self-control. — 2 Timothy 1:7 ESV
- 1 John 4:18, Psalm 23:4, Psalm 46:1-2

Forgiveness
- Be kind to one another, tenderhearted, forgiving one another, as God in Christ forgave you. — Ephesians 4:32 ESV
- If we confess our sins, he is faithful and just to forgive us our sins and to cleanse us from all unrighteousness. — 1 John 1:9 ESV
- Luke 6:37, Colossians 3:13, Matthew 6:14-15

Freedom
- For freedom Christ has set us free; stand firm therefore, and do not submit again to a yoke of slavery. — Galatians 5:1 ESV
- Now the Lord is the Spirit, and where the Spirit of the Lord is, there is freedom. — 2 Corinthians 3:17 ESV
- John 8:32, Psalm 118:5, 1 Corinthians 6:12

God Hears
- "For the eyes of the Lord are on the righteous, / and his ears are open to their prayer. / But the face of the Lord is against those who do evil." — 1 Peter 3:12 ESV
- But know that the LORD has set apart the godly for himself; the LORD hears when I call to him. — Psalm 4:3 ESV
- Psalm 34:17, Psalm 22:24, 2 Kings 20:5

Godly Character/Integrity
- Whoever walks in integrity walks securely, / but he who makes his ways crooked will be found out. — Proverbs 10:9 ESV
- Whatever you do, work heartily, as for the Lord and not for men. — Colossians 3:23 ESV
- 1 Chronicles 29:17, Psalm 101:2-3, Titus 2:7-8

God's Will
- Do not be conformed to this world, but be transformed by the renewal of your mind, that by testing you may discern what is the will of God, what is good and acceptable and perfect. — Romans 12:2 ESV

- For this is the will of God, that by doing good you should put to silence the ignorance of foolish people. — 1 Peter 2:15 ESV
- Genesis 50:20, Matthew 6:10, Ephesians 5:17

Grace

- But he said to me, "My grace is sufficient for you, for my power is made perfect in weakness." Therefore I will boast all the more gladly of my weaknesses, so that the power of Christ may rest upon me. — 2 Corinthians 12:9 ESV
- For by grace you have been saved through faith. And this is not your own doing; it is the gift of God. — Ephesians 2:8 ESV
- Romans 11:6, John 1:16, Romans 5:8

Healing

- Heal me, O LORD, and I shall be healed; / save me, and I shall be saved, / for you are my praise. — Jeremiah 17:14 ESV
- Behold, I will bring to it health and healing, and I will heal them and reveal to them abundance of prosperity and security. — Jeremiah 33:6 ESV
- Isaiah 53:5, James 5:15, 3 John 1:2

Heart

- Create in me a clean heart, O God, / and renew a right spirit within me. — Psalm 51:10 ESV
- And I will give you a new heart, and a new spirit I will put within you. And I will remove the heart of stone from your flesh and give you a heart of flesh. — Ezekiel 36:26 ESV
- Jeremiah 17:10, Psalm 34:18, Proverbs 21:2

Heaviness/Oppression

- The LORD is a stronghold for the oppressed, / a stronghold in times of trouble. — Psalm 9:9 ESV
- The LORD works righteousness / and justice for all who are oppressed. — Psalm 103:6 ESV

- Psalm 146:7, Psalm 82:3, Acts 10:38

Holy Spirit

- "But the Helper, the Holy Spirit, whom the Father will send in my name, he will teach you all things and bring to your remembrance all that I have said to you." — John 14:26 ESV
- But the fruit of the Spirit is love, joy, peace, patience, kindness, goodness, faithfulness, gentleness, self-control; against such things there is no law. — Galatians 5:22-23 ESV
- Acts 2:38, Acts 1:8, Romans 15:13

Hope

- For I know the plans I have for you, declares the LORD, plans for welfare and not for evil, to give you a future and a hope. — Jeremiah 29:11 ESV
- But they who wait for the LORD shall renew their strength; / they shall mount up with wings like eagles; / they shall run and not be weary; / they shall walk and not faint. — Isaiah 40:31 ESV
- Hebrews 11:1, Psalm 39:7, Romans 5:5

Humility

- The reward for humility and fear of the LORD / is riches and honor and life. — Proverbs 22:4 ESV
- Put on then, as God's chosen ones, holy and beloved, compassionate hearts, kindness, humility, meekness, and patience. — Colossians 3:12 ESV
- Proverbs 11:2, Ephesians 4:2, Luke 14:11

Identity

- So God created man in his own image, / in the image of God he created him; / male and female he created them. — Genesis 1:27 ESV
- See what kind of love the Father has given to us, that we should be called children of God; and so we are. The reason why the world does not know us is that it did not know him. Beloved, we are God's children now, and what we will be has not yet appeared; but we know that when

he appears we shall be like him, because we shall see him as he is. And everyone who thus hopes in him purifies himself as he is pure. — 1 John 3:1-3 ESV

- Galatians 2:20, John 15:5, John 1:2

Joy

- May the God of hope fill you with all joy and peace in believing, so that by the power of the Holy Spirit you may abound in hope. — Romans 15:13 ESV
- Rejoice in the Lord always; again I will say, rejoice. — Philippians 4:4 ESV
- Galatians 5:22, John 16:24, Psalm 118:24

Justice

- Beloved, never avenge yourselves, but leave it to the wrath of God, for it is written, "Vengeance is mine, I will repay, says the Lord." — Romans 12:19 ESV
- Learn to do good; / seek justice, / correct oppression; / bring justice to the fatherless, / plead the widow's cause. — Isaiah 1:17 ESV
- Micah 6:8, Isaiah 61:8, Zechariah 7:9

Listen

- We know that God does not listen to sinners, but if anyone is a worshiper of God and does his will, God listens to him. — John 9:31 ESV
- And a voice came out of the cloud, saying, "This is my Son, my Chosen One; listen to him!" — Luke 9:35 ESV
- Isaiah 51:7, Proverbs 15:31-32, Proverbs 12:15

Lonely

- And my God will supply every need of yours according to his riches in glory in Christ Jesus. — Philippians 4:19 ESV
- For my father and my mother have forsaken me, / but the LORD will take me in. — Psalm 27:10 ESV
- Isaiah 41:10, Psalm 147:3, John 14:18

Love

- Love is patient and kind; love does not envy or boast; it is not arrogant or rude. It does not insist on its own way; it is not irritable or resentful; it does not rejoice at wrongdoing, but rejoices with the truth. Love bears all things, believes all things, hopes all things, endures all things. Love never ends. As for prophecies, they will pass away; as for tongues, they will cease; as for knowledge, it will pass away. — 1 Corinthians 13:4-8 ESV
- Let all that you do be done in love. — 1 Corinthians 16:14 ESV
- 1 John 4:8, 1 Peter 4:8, John 15:13

Marriage-Husbands

- Likewise, husbands, live with your wives in an understanding way, showing honor to the woman as the weaker vessel, since they are heirs with you of the grace of life, so that your prayers may not be hindered. — 1 Peter 3:7 ESV
- Husbands, love your wives, as Christ loved the church and gave himself up for her. — Ephesians 5:25 ESV
- Colossians 3:19, Ephesians 5:33, 1 Peter 4:8

Marriage-Wives

- Wives, submit to your own husbands, as to the Lord. — Ephesians 5:22 ESV
- Wives, submit to your husbands, as is fitting in the Lord. — Colossians 3:18 ESV
- Ephesians 5:33, Matthew 19:6, 1 Peter 4:8

Mercy

- "Blessed are the merciful, for they shall receive mercy." — Matthew 5:7 ESV
- Let us then with confidence draw near to the throne of grace, that we may receive mercy and find grace to help in time of need. — Hebrews 4:16
- Luke 6:36, Psalm 23:6, Psalm 25:6

Mind

- Set your minds on things that are above, not on things that are on earth. — Colossians 3:2 ESV
- You keep him in perfect peace / whose mind is stayed on you, / because he trusts in you. — Isaiah 26:3 ESV
- Do not be conformed to this world, but be transformed by the renewal of your mind, that by testing you may discern what is the will of God, what is good and acceptable and perfect. — Romans 12:2 ESV
- 1 Peter 5:8, 2 Corinthians 5:17, Romans 8:5-6

New Beginnings

- Therefore, if anyone is in Christ, he is a new creation. The old has passed away; behold, the new has come. — 2 Corinthians 5:17 ESV
- To put off your old self, which belongs to your former manner of life and is corrupt through deceitful desires, and to be renewed in the spirit of your minds, and to put on the new self, created after the likeness of God in true righteousness and holiness. — Ephesians 4:22-24 ESV
- 1 Peter 2:10-11, 1 Peter 1:23, Revelations 21:1-27

Obedience

- "If you love me, you will keep my commandments." — John 14:15 ESV
- Whoever keeps his commandments abides in God, and God in him. And by this we know that he abides in us, by the Spirit whom he has given us. — 1 John 3:24 ESV
- Exodus 23:22, John 8:51, Luke 11:28

Parents

- Fathers, do not provoke your children to anger, but bring them up in the discipline and instruction of the Lord. — Ephesians 6:4 ESV
- Fathers, do not provoke your children, lest they become discouraged. — Colossians 3:21 ESV
- Proverbs 29:17, Psalm 103:13, Proverbs 20:7

Patience

- Rejoice in hope, be patient in tribulation, be constant in prayer. — Romans 12:12 ESV
- But if we hope for what we do not see, we wait for it with patience. — Romans 8:25 ESV
- Isaiah 40:31, Psalm 37:7, James 1:19

Peace

- You keep him in perfect peace / whose mind is stayed on you, / because he trusts in you. — Isaiah 26:3 ESV
- If possible, so far as it depends on you, live peaceably with all. — Romans 12:18 ESV
- Hebrews 12:14, 1 Peter 3:11, Romans 8:6

Perseverance

- And let us not grow weary of doing good, for in due season we will reap, if we do not give up. — Galatians 6:9 ESV
- As for you, brothers, do not grow weary in doing good. — 2 Thessalonians 3:13 ESV
- Romans 5:3, James 1:23-25, Hebrews 12:3

Power

- For God gave us a spirit not of fear but of power and love and self-control. — 2 Timothy 1:7 ESV
- I can do all things through him who strengthens me. — Philippians 4:13 ESV
- Luke 10:19, Ephesians 3:20, 1 Corinthians 4:20

Power of Words

- Gracious words are like a honeycomb, / sweetness to the soul and health to the body. — Proverbs 16:24 ESV
- Death and life are in the power of the tongue, / and those who love it will eat its fruits. — Proverbs 18:21 ESV

- Proverbs 25:11, Proverbs 10:19, Isaiah 55:11

Prayer

- "Therefore I tell you, whatever you ask in prayer, believe that you have received it, and it will be yours." — Mark 11:24 ESV
- "If you abide in me, and my words abide in you, ask whatever you wish, and it will be done for you." — John 15:7 ESV
- 1 Thessalonians 5:17, Romans 8:26, Luke 11:9

Pride

- When pride comes, then comes disgrace, / but with the humble is wisdom. — Proverbs 11:2 ESV
- One's pride will bring him low, / but he who is lowly in spirit will obtain honor. — Proverbs 29:23 ESV
- Proverbs 8:13, James 4:6, Proverbs 16:5

Promises

- The Lord is not slow to fulfill his promise as some count slowness, but is patient toward you, not wishing that any should perish, but that all should reach repentance. — 2 Peter 3:9 ESV
- Give your burdens to the Lord, / and he will take care of you. / He will not permit the godly to slip and fall. —Psalm 55:22 NLT
- Isaiah 26:3, Jeremiah 29:13, Psalm 32:8

Protection

- For the LORD loves justice, / and he will never abandon the godly. / He will keep them safe forever, / but the children of the wicked will die. — Psalm 37:28 NLT
- The angel of the LORD encamps / around those who fear him, and delivers them. — Psalm 34:7 ESV
- Psalm 32:7, 2 Thessalonians 3:3, Psalm 138:7

Provision

- And God is able to make all grace abound to you, so that having all sufficiency in all things at all times, you may abound in every good work. — 2 Corinthians 9:8 ESV
- But seek first the kingdom of God and his righteousness, and all these things will be added to you. — Matthew 6:33 ESV
- Psalm 84:11, Proverbs 19:17, Isaiah 58:11

Purity

- "Blessed are the pure in heart, for they shall see God." — Matthew 5:8 ESV
- Create in me a clean heart, O God, / and renew a right spirit within me. — Psalm 51:10 ESV
- Hebrews 8:12, 1 John 2:12, Isaiah 1:18

Purpose

- For I know the plans I have for you, declares the Lord, plans for welfare and not for evil, to give you a future and a hope. — Jeremiah 29:11 ESV
- And Jesus came and said to them, "All authority in heaven and on earth has been given to me. Go therefore and make disciples of all nations, baptizing them in the name of the Father and of the Son and of the Holy Spirit, teaching them to observe all that I have commanded you. And behold, I am with you always, to the end of the age." — Matthew 28:18-20 ESV
- Romans 8:28, Ephesians 2:10, Psalm 138:8

Redemption

- In him we have redemption through his blood, the forgiveness of our trespasses, according to the riches of his grace. — Ephesians 1:7 ESV
- Who gave himself for us to redeem us from all lawlessness and to purify for himself a people for his own possession who are zealous for good works. — Titus 2:14 ESV
- Psalm 111:9, 1 Corinthians 1:30, Romans 10:10

Refresh/Weary

- The generous will prosper; / those who refresh others will themselves be refreshed. — Proverbs 11:25 NLT
- But those who trust in the LORD will find new strength. / They will soar high on wings like eagles. / They will run and not grow weary. / They will walk and not faint. — Isaiah 40:31 NLT
- Philemon 1:7, Philemon 1:20, Hebrews 12:3

Rejection

- "If the world hates you, know that it has hated me before it hated you." — John 15:18 ESV
- For my father and my mother have forsaken me, / but the LORD will take me in. — Psalm 27:10
- Psalm 94:14, John 1:11, Luke 10:16

Repentance

- From that time Jesus began to preach, saying, "Repent, for the kingdom of heaven is at hand." — Matthew 4:17 ESV
- If we confess our sins, he is faithful and just to forgive us our sins and to cleanse us from all unrighteousness. — 1 John 1:9 ESV
- 2 Chronicles 7:14, Luke 13:3, Proverbs 28:13

Rest

- "Come to me, all who labor and are heavy laden, and I will give you rest. Take my yoke upon you, and learn from me, for I am gentle and lowly in heart, and you will find rest for your souls. For my yoke is easy, and my burden is light." — Matthew 11:28-30 ESV
- And he said, "My presence will go with you, and I will give you rest." — Exodus 33:14
- Isaiah 32:18, Jeremiah 6:16, Jeremiah 50:34

Restoration

- Restore to me the joy of your salvation, / and uphold me with a willing spirit. — Psalm 51:12 ESV
- And the LORD restored the fortunes of Job, when he had prayed for his friends. And the LORD gave Job twice as much as he had before. — Job 42:10 ESV
- Revelation 21:1-5, Zechariah 9:12, Galatians 6:1

Safety

- In peace I will both lie down and sleep; / for you alone, O LORD, make me dwell in safety. — Psalm 4:8 ESV
- Put on the whole armor of God, that you may be able to stand against the schemes of the devil. — Ephesians 6:11 ESV
- Proverbs 11:14, 1 Samuel 2:9, Psalm 3:5

Salvation

- For by grace you have been saved through faith. And this is not your own doing; it is the gift of God, not a result of works, so that no one may boast. — Ephesians 2:8-9 ESV
- Because, if you confess with your mouth that Jesus is Lord and believe in your heart that God raised him from the dead, you will be saved. — Romans 10:9 ESV
- Acts 4:12, John 14:6, Psalm 37:39

Seek the Lord

- You will seek me and find me, when you seek me with all your heart. — Jeremiah 29:13 ESV
- And without faith it is impossible to please him, for whoever would draw near to God must believe that he exists and that he rewards those who seek him. — Hebrews 11:6 ESV
- Matthew 6:33, John 14:12, Hebrews 10:22

Self-Control

- For this very reason, make every effort to add to your faith goodness; and to goodness, knowledge; and to knowledge, self-control; and to self-control, perseverance; and to perseverance, godliness; and to godliness, mutual affection; and to mutual affection, love. — 2 Peter 1:5-7 NIV
- But the fruit of the Spirit is love, joy, peace, forbearance, kindness, goodness, faithfulness, gentleness and self-control. Against such things there is no law. — Galatians 5:22-23 NIV
- Proverbs 16:32, 1 Peter 4:7, Proverbs 29:11

Shame

- I sought the LORD, and he answered me / and delivered me from all my fears. / Those who look to him are radiant, / and their faces shall never be ashamed. — Psalm 34:4-5 ESV
- There is therefore now no condemnation for those who are in Christ Jesus. — Romans 8:1 ESV
- Isaiah 61:7, Isaiah 50:7, Romans 10:11

Sleep

- If you lie down, you will not be afraid; / when you lie down, your sleep will be sweet. — Proverbs 3:24 ESV
- In peace I will both lie down and sleep; / for you alone, O LORD, make me dwell in safety. — Psalm 4:8 ESV
- Psalm 3:5, Ecclesiastes 5:12, Matthew 6:34

Strength

- I can do all things through him who strengthens me. — Philippians 4:13 ESV
- The LORD is my strength and my song, / and he has become my salvation; / this is my God, and I will praise him, / my father's God, and I will exalt him. — Exodus 15:2 ESV
- Deuteronomy 31:6, Ephesians 6:10, 1 Corinthians 16:13

Suffering

- For I consider that the sufferings of this present time are not worth comparing with the glory that is to be revealed to us. — Romans 8:18 ESV
- Count it all joy, my brothers, when you meet trials of various kinds, for you know that the testing of your faith produces steadfastness. And let steadfastness have its full effect, that you may be perfect and complete, lacking in nothing. — James 1:2-4
- Romans 8:28, Romans 5:3-5, John 16:33

Temptation

- "Watch and pray that you may not enter into temptation. The spirit indeed is willing, but the flesh is weak." — Matthew 26:41 ESV
- For because he himself has suffered when tempted, he is able to help those who are being tempted. — Hebrews 2:18 ESV
- Ephesians 6:11, Ephesians 4:27, James 1:12

Thanksgiving

- Giving thanks always and for everything to God the Father in the name of our Lord Jesus Christ. — Ephesians 5:20 ESV
- Give thanks in all circumstances; for this is the will of God in Christ Jesus for you. — 1 Thessalonians 5:18 ESV
- Psalm 103:2, Colossians 3:17, Philippians 4:6

Trust

- Trust in the LORD with all your heart, / and do not lean on your own understanding. — Proverbs 3:5 ESV
- When I am afraid, / I put my trust in you. / In God, whose word I praise, / in God I trust; I shall not be afraid. / What can flesh do to me? — Psalm 56:3-4 ESV
- Psalm 37:5, Psalm 13:5, Isaiah 26:3-4

Waiting

- But they who wait for the LORD shall renew their strength; / they shall mount up with wings like eagles; / they shall run and not be weary; / they shall walk and not faint. — Isaiah 40:31 ESV
- Wait for the LORD; / be strong, and let your heart take courage; / wait for the LORD! — Psalm 27:14 ESV
- Lamentations 3:25, Psalm 37:7, Micah 7:7

Wisdom

- If any of you lacks wisdom, let him ask God, who gives generously to all without reproach, and it will be given him. — James 1:5 ESV
- But the wisdom from above is first pure, then peaceable, gentle, open to reason, full of mercy and good fruits, impartial and sincere. — James 3:17 ESV
- Proverbs 1:7, Ephesians 5:15-17, Proverbs 19:20

TOOLS FOR GODLY IMAGINATION/MEDITATIONS

Color Psychology

Colors often communicate ideas, moods, and feelings, and they can be especially useful when crafting a visualization or meditation for a client. As you create these activities and tools, you might find it useful to incorporate colors depending on what they will communicate to your clients.

Note that this is a generalized list, and colors can mean different things to each individual. They may also mean different things across different cultures. Each person may use different words to describe what color means to them. Colors are limitless and come in a variety of shades, and therefore their meaning to each individual is limitless. Consider asking your client about what colors signify to them feelings such as comfort, warmth, cooling, love, energy—whatever is needed for their own personal well-being.

Here are some general guidelines about what colors mean in our American culture.

Red	Excitement, Energy, Passion, Courage, Attention, Encourage, Enthusiasm
Orange	Optimism, Independence, Adventurous, Creativity, Fun
Yellow	Enthusiasm, Opportunity, Spontaneity, Happiness, Positivity, Wisdom, Awake, Awareness, Lightness
Green	Growth, Harmony, Healing, Safety, Kindness, Reliability, Balance, Stability, Relax, Revitalize, Nurture
Blue	Freedom, Self-Expression, Trust, Joy, Spirituality, Honesty, Loyalty, Responsibility, Freedom, Inner Security
Violet	Imagination, Spirituality, Compassion, Sensitivity, Mystery
Pink	Compassion, Love, Kindness, Admiration, Playful
Brown	Reliability, Stability, Honesty, Comfort, Nature
Grey	Neutral, Practical, Conservative, Formal, Quiet
Black	Power, Control, Authority, Discipline, Elegance, Formality

Example of a Secular Vision Statement

Notice that when creating a secular meditation for a client, we simply remove the Christian language while still holding onto what is good and of God. This secular meditation was given for a client and her specific need. You will recognize those needs as you read. Each individual client will have their own personal needs. Additional meditation scripts are available at www.YKIcoaching.com.

Relaxation

(Notice the ellipses. They are purposely placed here to encourage you to pause and speak naturally and slowly, allowing your client to hear and absorb what you say.)

Take this time to relax … This is your time … a time to simply just relax … Inhaling deeply … and exhaling. Breathing in deeply, inhale and exhale. Relax your feet … letting each and every muscle in your feet sink deeply into relaxation … melting … relaxing … thankful that you have feet to carry you each and every day … Breathing in, deeply inhale … taking in the fresh air

... and exhale ... moving up your ankles ... allowing them to relax ... as you breathe in deeply visualize your breath moving up your calves ... relaxing each and every muscle ... Relax your knees ... your thighs ... relax your low back ... like a massage, your breath warms your low back causing it to relax ... Breathing deeply into your abdomen, you relax all relationships ... casting any burden you have ... away from you ... as you continue to inhale ... deeply ... and exhale ... deeply ... you relax your mid back ... moving up to your shoulders and neck ... relaxing each and every muscle ... moving down your arms, relaxing them to your hands ... Moving back up to your shoulders ... your breath moves through your lungs as you inhale deeply, you are becoming ... more and more ... relaxed and more peaceful than you have ever been. You are completely safe and loved ... content and peaceful ... As you continue to breathe this fresh air up through your heart ... visualizing your heart strong ... healed ... and restored. Continue breathing up your throat, to your jaw ... relaxing your jaw, releasing any unspoken word and allowing your jaw to completely relax ... You relax your facial muscles ... Moving your breath to the top of your head ... inhaling deeply and exhaling. Your head relaxes and sinks deeply into the space you have given it ... You take this fresh air up through your mind, cleansing your mind ... allowing your mind to simply just relax ... You are content ... relaxed ... safe, peaceful ... and loved ... As you relax ... You feel calm and centered.

Meditation/Vision Statement

You are connected to others. You are capable and able to relate to your children and to love them. You feel so grateful that you are able to care for others and to provide for them.

You are discerning and wise. You have all the resources you need in order to accomplish your goals. You can lend and give time to other people in need in ways that help them accomplish their goals. You have healthy boundaries and great discernment.

As you are now handling your finances efficiently, you are able to budget, save, and decorate your home in order to create a comfortable and warm environment.

You make wise decisions in order to create the life you dream of. You are loved, safe, and at peace.

You use great discernment and wisdom in all your relationships. Because of this you will recognize the companion that is right for you, the one who loves others … one who has great compassion … understanding and is supportive of you. You feel energized and your passion for life is increasing, as is your purpose.

You are becoming more successful in your career as you continue to put forth the effort needed to succeed. You have great clarity and vision. You are empowered, strong, and victorious.

New possibilities are opening for you … moment by moment.

You are increasing in wisdom in all areas of your life, and you are able to bring truth to others. You are more energized, balanced, creative, and fulfilled.

Post-Relaxation

As you breathe in, deeply inhale and exhale, centering yourself. You are grounded, centered, and at peace. Inhale and exhale. You are refreshed and restored … When you are ready, you may open your eyes.

Sample Godly Meditation (God's Blessing)

Here is a sample of a script I have used to create a godly meditation for a Christian client. I insert it here as an example you can use as you create similar blessings for your clients.

Relaxation

Take this time to relax … This is your time … a time to simply just relax … inviting the Holy Spirit to be with you … Simply just relax … inhaling deeply … and exhaling … Breathing in deeply … inhale and exhale. Relax your feet … letting each and every muscle in your feet sink deeply into relaxation … melting … relaxing … thankful that you have feet to carry you each and every day … breathing in … deeply inhale … taking in the fresh air God has provided for you … and exhale … moving up your ankles … allowing them to relax … As you breathe in deeply, visualize your breath moving up your calves … relaxing each and every muscle … Relax your knees … your thighs … Relax your low back ... Like a massage, your breath warms your low back, causing it to relax ... Breathing deeply into your abdomen, you relax all relationships ... casting any burdens you have away from you ... and ... surrendering them to the Lord ... As you continue to inhale ... deeply ... and exhale ... deeply ... you relax your mid-back ... moving up to your shoulders and neck ... relaxing each and every muscle ... moving down your arms, relaxing them to your hands ... relaxing them all the way to your fingers ... thanking God for those wonderful hands ... that serve you and others every day ... Moving back up to your shoulders ... your breath moves through your lungs ... As you inhale deeply, you are becoming ... more and more ... relaxed and more peaceful than you have ever been. You are completely safe and loved ... content and peaceful ... As you continue to breathe this fresh air up through your heart, you relax further, allowing God to renew your heart and heal any broken area. Continue breathing up your throat, to your jaw ... relaxing your jaw, releasing any unspoken word and allowing your jaw to completely relax ... You relax your facial muscles ... Moving your breath to the top of your head ... inhaling deeply and exhaling. Your head relaxes and sinks deeply into the space you have given it ... You take this fresh air up through your mind, cleansing your mind ... releasing any tension you might have ... allowing your mind to simply just relax. You are content ... relaxed ... safe ... peaceful ... and loved ... As you relax, you feel calm and centered.

Godly Meditation/God's Blessing

Because you depend on God to meet your needs ... you are becoming more trusting ... realizing God will provide for you ... and take care of you. You are connected to God ... you are aware of His presence ... and you know He is always with you ... He provides the people in your life to love and support you ... You are capable ... and able to relate to your children ... and to love them as God loves you ... You feel so blessed and so grateful that you are able to bless others and to provide for them ... as God has provided for you ... Because God is directing you and guiding you with each step in your life ... you continue to follow through with all He has called you to do ... You have all the resources you need in order to accomplish the life God has intended for you ... You are able to lend and give time to other people in need ... As you read God's Word and draw near to Him … you have a heightened awareness of people in need and you are able to help them in a healthy … loving way. As you are now handling your finances God's way … you are able to budget … save and decorate your home in order to create a comfortable and warm environment … As God continues to work within you … your wisdom and discernment increases and you are able to make wise decisions … in order to create the life that God intended for you … You know that He is always there for you … and that He answers your prayers … You are loved … safe … and at peace. As you seek God, He will give you great discernment … and wisdom in all of your relationships … Because of this you will recognize the godly companion God is preparing for you … the one who loves God and others … the one who has great compassion … understanding and support … You are trusting God more each day … With God you feel fully energized and your passion for life is increasing … as is your purpose. Your ministry and career are being blessed … as they are in line with God's will … You have great clarity … and vision … Because of God you are empowered … strong … and victorious. You experience God working in your life … creating new possibilities for you moment by moment … Experiencing a close connection with the Holy Spirit creates an awareness of your unlimited potential … to an abundant life … filled with God's purpose. As you read God's Word, you are increasing in wisdom in all areas of your life … and you are able to bring this truth to others. You are more energized, balanced, creative, and fulfilled.

Post-Relaxation

Becoming more aware of your surroundings and preparing for your time ahead … you are restored … refreshed and prepared … As you breathe in, deeply inhale and exhale, centering yourself in the Lord; inhale and exhale, and when you are ready, you may open your eyes.

Prayers

You have been taught how to use God's words to bless others through godly meditation. Prayers follow the same rules. The only difference is they are not usually set to music and are often much quicker. Prayers are to thank the Lord for all that He has done and to ask for your needs and the needs of others. In our practice, we like to thank God for the provision that we know He will deliver to us, even prior to actually receiving it. We trust and know that God is good and that He desires good things in our lives. We seek to honor and obey Him, and given the opportunity, we teach our clients the same.

If you need a model prayer, we suggest the Lord's Prayer found in Matthew 6:9-13. There is also a prayer book we recommend listed in resources.

Model Prayer for Salvation

Dear Lord Jesus, I come to you humbly and confess that I am a sinner. I believe you died for my sins and rose from the dead so that I could be set free from my sins. Please forgive me. I turn from my sins right now. I believe that you are Lord and Savior, and I am asking you to be mine. Come into my heart and life right now. I want to trust and follow you. Thank you for forgiving me and giving me a new life in you. Amen.

RESOURCES

The Daniel Plan: 40 Days to a Healthier Life
by Daniel Amen, Mark Hyman, and Rick Warren

Prayers
by Richard III Broadbent, Daniel Hedigree, Millie Rheinsmith,
and Gwen Burton

Loved into the Light
by La Vonne Earl

Activating God's Power
by Michelle Leslie

Nourishments
by Deborah Buckingham

Who I Am in Christ
by Neil T. Anderson

The Bondage Breaker
by Neil T. Anderson

Feelings Buried Never Die
by Karol K. Truman

Saying What's Real: 7 Keys to Authentic Communication and Relationship Success
by Susan Campbell

The God-Shaped Brain: How Changing Your View of God Transforms Your Life
by Timothy Jennings

The Power of Being a Woman
by Michelle Hammond

10 Curses that Block the Blessings
by Larry Huch

Boundaries: When to Say Yes, How to Say No to Take Control of Your Life
by Henry Cloud and John Townsend

A More Excellent Way, Be in Health
by Henry W. Wright

Switch on Your Brain: The Key to Peak Happiness, Thinking, and Health
by Dr. Caroline Leaf

CPSIA information can be obtained
at www.ICGtesting.com
Printed in the USA
JSHW030235120221
11847JS00002B/16